AIDS Crossing Borders

AIDS Crossing Borders

The Spread of HIV Among Migrant Latinos

EDITED BY

Shiraz I. Mishra, Ross F. Conner, and J. Raul Magaña

WestviewPress

A Division of HarperCollins*Publishers*

We dedicate this book to migrant workers throughout the U.S. and hope that the research reported here will help to spur action to reduce one of the many risks in their lives, that of HIV.

Copyright © 1996 by Westview Press, A Division of HarperCollins Publishers, Inc.

Published in 1996 in the United States of America by Westview Press, 5500 Central Avenue, Boulder, Colorado 80301-2877, and in the United Kingdom by Westview Press, 12 Hid's Copse Road, Cumnor Hill, Oxford OX2 9JJ

A CIP catalog record for this book is available from the Library of Congress.
ISBN 0-8133-8988-7 (hc)

The paper used in this publication meets the requirements of the American National Standard for Permanence of Paper for Printed Library Materials Z39.48-1984.

10   9   8   7   6   5   4   3   2   1

Contents

PART THREE
CONCLUSIONS

Preface

AIDS has crossed every international border and affects all populations throughout the world, including migrant workers. In the U.S., migrant workers are a hidden and sometimes maligned population with limited access to needed health and welfare services, including HIV prevention. Little, however, is known about the impact of the HIV/AIDS epidemic on Latino farmworkers. This absence of systematic research was the impetus for the preparation of this book.

This book is the first collection of research studies focusing specifically on migrant Latino farmworkers. The book brings together seven research studies to provide a profile of the HIV prevention, surveillance and treatment needs of migrant workers. The editors combine their own work with that of nationally and internationally recognized experts to provide a comprehensive analysis of different aspects of the HIV epidemic among migrant Latino workers. They examine issues such as the HIV prevention needs of Latino farmworking women and their children, the sexual beliefs and behaviors of Latino migrant workers, the effects of migration on changes in sexuality and sexual practices, the risk for HIV through use of sex workers, knowledge about the HIV/AIDS epidemic, the effectiveness of prevention programs, and policies and programs that may stem the spread of HIV among this population. The book is notable for including, in addition to researchers' views, the perspectives of migrant workers and policymakers on HIV prevention policies and programs.

This book is the first step in filling the information void on the HIV-related needs among Latino farmworkers. The book attempts to provide the reader with a comprehensive analysis of the impact of the HIV/AIDS epidemic among the Latino farmworking population.

Shiraz I. Mishra
Ross F. Conner
J. Raul Magaña

Acknowledgments

There are many people we want to thank for their part in the completion of this project. First, we are grateful to the migrant workers who participated in the focus groups for their suggestions, comments and encouragement. Second, we want to thank the twelve policymakers in California, Florida and Washington who took part in interviews about the feasibility of the recommendations presented here. Because we guaranteed them anonymity, we cannot list them by name, but they know who they are. We also want to thank the seven sets of researchers who contributed to this book. We appreciate their hard work in preparing their research for presentation here, and we are grateful for their cooperation and good humor in the face of our repeated demands for information, for yet another small change in their manuscript, and the like. Christine Maher was invaluable in assisting with manuscript preparation details. At Westview Press, we are grateful to Michelle Baxter and Jennifer Chen for their helpful assistance and understanding attitude at all stages in the preparation of the book manuscript. Last but not the least, we want to thank our funding agencies, the American Foundation for AIDS Research and the California Policy Seminar, for their support of this project.

S.I.M.
R.F.C.
J.R.M.

About the Contributors

Jaime L. Amsel is a researcher affiliated with the College of Medicine at the University of California, Irvine.

Armida Ayala is a doctoral student in anthropology at the University of Southern California and a member of the State Office of AIDS Community Planning Working Group.

Sandra Benavides-Vaello is the immunization coordinator for the Texas Association of Community Health Centers, Inc. and a member of the Midwest Migrant Stream Advisory Committee.

Mario Bronfman is director of Health Policy and Planning, Center for Research in Health Systems, National Institute for Public Health, Mexico City, and the director of research for Mexico's National Council for the Control and Prevention of AIDS (CONASIDA). He is the chairman of the steering committee for Social and Behavioral Research for the World Health Organization's Global Program on AIDS.

Joseph Carrier is a research consultant at the Orange County Health Care Agency in California.

Ross F. Conner is associate professor, Urban and Regional Planning Department (School of Social Ecology) and Department of Medicine (School of Medicine) at the University of California, Irvine. He is former president of the American Evaluation Association. He is also research director for the evaluation of the Colorado Healthy Communities Initiative.

Olivia de la Rocha is co-founder and principal consultant for *Research Support Services*, a research consulting firm. She is also adjunct professor of research methods and statistics in the School of Nursing, College of Health and Human Services, California State University, Long Beach.

Katherine Fennelly is dean and director of the Minnesota Extension Service, University of Minnesota.

João B. Ferreira-Pinto is assistant professor of behavior sciences at the University of Texas at Houston, School of Public Health.

J. Raul Magaña is associate professor at the University of California, Irvine, College of Medicine.

Shiraz I. Mishra is assistant professor of medicine and social ecology and faculty associate at the Center for Health Policy and Research at the University of California, Irvine.

Sergio López Moreno is a physician specializing in community and family health at the Polytechnic National Institute, Mexico City.

Miguel A. Pérez is assistant professor of kinesiology, health promotion and recreation at the University of North Texas.

Rebeca L. Ramos is the executive director of Compañeros, a HIV/AIDS and heroin treatment program. She is principal investigator of the Centers for Disease Control and Prevention HIV/STD Training and Technical Assistance grant for the U.S.-Mexico Border Region.

Michele Shedlin is president of Sociomedical Resources Associates, Inc., Westport, CT and is an adjunct faculty at Columbia University, the University of Connecticut, and the University of Houston.

Kristi Skjerdal is a public health educator for the San Mateo County Health Services Agency in San Mateo, California. She belongs to the National Society of Public Health Educators and serves on the Board of Directors for the Society's Northern California Chapter.

PART ONE

Introduction

1

Migrant Workers in the United States: A Profile From the Fields

Shiraz I. Mishra, Ross F. Conner and J. Raul Magaña

Introduction

Migrant farmworkers are an invaluable part of the multi-billion dollar U.S. agricultural industry. Without farm labor, the production of many crops would not be possible. Despite the valuable fruits of their labor, farmworkers are marginalized from society and frequently experience prejudice and hostility in the communities in which they live and work. They live often in poverty and work in hazardous environments. Despite their contributions to society, there is little information about their health, especially in regard to HIV and AIDS. In this chapter, we profile farmworkers in terms of their sociodemographics including their migratory patterns and living conditions. Next, we discuss their health status and health care access, followed by a review of the prevalence of HIV and HIV-related cofactors such as tuberculosis (TB) and sexually transmitted diseases (STDs).

A Sociodemographic Profile of Farmworkers

Population Estimates

It is difficult to obtain an estimate of the farmworking population. There is no universally accepted definition of a *farmworker*. According to the Office of Migrant Health's definition, farmworkers are persons who identify agriculture as their primary employment. The definition further classifies farmworkers as either *migrant* or *seasonal* based on their housing characteristics. Migrant farmworkers are persons who utilize temporary housing due to their employment-related migratory patterns. Seasonal farmworkers are those who do not migrate and do not utilize temporary housing [1]. According to the U.S. Department of Agriculture's definition, migrant farmworkers are persons who temporarily cross state or county boundaries and stay overnight to do hired farm work, or those who have no usual place of residence and work in two or more counties during the year [2]. The U.S. Department of Education defines migrant farmworkers as persons who cross school district lines to engage in agricultural or agri-related industry. According to the U.S. Department of Health and Human Services' definition, the inclusion or exclusion of seasonal farmworkers and their dependents in population estimates is based on the number of migrant farmworkers in a county. In counties with few migrant workers (less than approximately 4,000), seasonal farmworkers are not included in the population estimates, thus biasing the enumeration [3]. There are important distinctions in these definitions, such as use or non-use of temporary housing units, different boundaries that define migrant status (school districts, county or state borders), and primary industry of employment. These differences in definitions preclude an accurate enumeration of farmworkers in general, and migrant and seasonal farmworkers in particular.

Although there is a distinction in definition between migrant and seasonal farmworkers, in practice the distinction is often blurred. Depending on factors such as economic conditions, employment opportunities, family responsibilities and health status, it is not uncommon for agricultural workers to alternate between migrant and seasonal roles. Moreover, the uncertainties surrounding these factors also determine in part the transitions between agriculture and other service-related employment. Furthermore, economic conditions and employment opportunities also determine the migratory patterns of farmworkers and the frequency of their migration in terms of the points of destination, length of stay at different labor sites, and the transitions between non-farm-working and seasonal farmworking jobs.

There is a subset of farmworkers who by definition could be classified as both migrant and seasonal. During the agricultural season, some farmworkers "migrate" from their places of residence (mainly in Mexico) and possibly from non-agricultural employment to places of destination that provide agricultural employment. These "migrant" farm-workers find primary employment in agriculture and occupy non-temporary housing such as apartments and trailer homes, thus meeting the requirements for classification as "seasonal" farmworkers.

Besides the lack of a standard definition, other factors that prevent an accurate enumeration of farmworkers include citizenship or work documentation status and family participation in agricultural labor. Farmworkers without authorization to work in the U.S. are hesitant to be included in any type of enumeration or study, thus biasing the population estimates. Family participation is another factor that makes an accurate enumeration difficult to accomplish. Women with young children may leave the agricultural workforce only to rejoin it at a later date. The number of children actively participating in the agricultural workforce also varies based on factors such as their age and health status.

These factors, coupled with the lack of an appropriate data enumeration mechanism, have hampered an accurate assessment of the size of the farmworking population. According to the U.S. Department of Labor's National Agricultural Workers Survey (NAWS) conducted between 1989 and 1990, the migrant and seasonal farmworker population in the U.S. was estimated between 2.7 and 4 million, and approximately 2.8 million of the farmworkers were Latinos [2]. The five states with the largest estimated numbers of farmworkers were California, Texas, Florida, Washington and North Carolina [1].

Demographic Characteristics

Farmworkers in the U.S. present a mosaic of ethnic, linguistic and cultural diversity. According to the 1990 NAWS, nearly two-thirds (62 percent) of the farmworkers were foreign-born. Among the foreign-born farmworkers, the majority (92 percent) were from Mexico and the remaining were from other Latin American countries (4 percent), Asia (3 percent) and the Caribbean (1 percent). Eighty one percent of the foreign-born farmworkers, including the Latinos, were legally authorized to work in the U.S. Moreover, about 27 percent of the foreign-born farmworkers were either legal permanent residents (25 percent) or naturalized citizens (2 percent). In terms of ethnic identification, more than one-half (57 percent) were Mexican and about one-third (29 percent) were non-Hispanic; the rest were Mexican-Americans (Chicanos; 9 percent), Puerto Rican (3 percent) and other Hispanics (2 percent) [2].

Among the 38 percent of U.S.-born farmworkers, the majority were non-Hispanic Whites (60 percent); followed by Hispanics (34 percent), African-Americans (5 percent) and "others" (1 percent).

In 1990, the farmworking population comprised of relatively young, male immigrants of Hispanic origin with limited levels of education [2]. Compared to the national average, farmworkers were a younger population group with a smaller proportion of older adults than the general U.S. population [4]. The median age for farmworkers was 31 years, whereas for non-Mexican-born Hispanics, the median age was 24 years. The life expectancy of a farmworker was about two-thirds that of the national average, 49 years compared with 75 years [5]. Although substantially more men comprised the farmworking population, the number of women (especially Mexican and/or Latin American) joining the ranks as farmworkers has increased in recent years. More than one-half of the Latin American farmworkers joining the migrant streams in the U.S. are women [6]. According to the NAWS [2], a large proportion (70 percent) of farmworkers reportedly were married, however, nearly one-third (30 percent) of those who were married and/or had children lived away from their families. Nearly one-half of the male farmworkers (46 percent) lived without their families at the work sites; 47 percent of foreign-born farmworkers also lived without their families. U.S.-born farmworkers (65 percent) were more likely to be accompanied by their families during their migration compared with Mexican-born (47 percent) and Central American-born (28 percent) farmworkers.

Farmworkers have very limited education. Among those surveyed by the NAWS [2], less than one-half (47 percent) had completed eight or more years of formal schooling. Furthermore, most farmworkers had limited proficiency in English, due to the substantial proportion of Latino immigrants who had limited access to education. As a consequence, many Latino farmworkers were functionally pre-literate in English as well as in Spanish.

The average income for an agricultural worker is below the federal poverty level. Despite the presence of multiple wage earners in the family, nearly one-half of farmworkers have incomes below the federal poverty level [7]. Single farmworkers and those with children are more likely than married farmworkers without children to live in poverty. By some estimates, employment of a second family member in agricultural work can contribute approximately an additional $2,700 to the household [8]. Many families join the migration streams once they have enough children aged 10 and older who are able to work in the fields or in nearby packing sheds [9]. Child labor is a general problem in agriculture. This is especially true among the migrant farmworkers because their relative poverty makes them more dependent on the income generated by their children. It is estimated that about 25 percent of all farm labor in the U.S. is performed by children [10].

There are wide discrepancies in wage earnings of authorized and unauthorized farmworkers. The median family income for authorized farmworkers is between $7,500 and $10,000, and between $2,500 to $5,000 for unauthorized farmworkers. Furthermore, foreign-born farmworkers (who comprise two-third of the farmworking population) compared with U.S.-born farmworkers were twice as likely to live in poverty (62 versus 31 percent). Despite the low wages and the high proportion of farmworkers below the poverty level, fewer than one-fifth (18 percent) receive needs-based social services such as Medicaid and Food Stamps. In addition, after a lifetime of work, many farmworkers are unable to prove their claim for Social Security benefits [11].

Migrant Streams

There are three predominant migratory streams or routes: the West Coast, the Midwest and the East Coast streams [1, 7]. The patterns of migration are not completely rigid and have evolved depending on weather patterns, economic conditions and employment opportunities. The migration cycle begins at a *homebase* area which is usually located in southern Florida, Texas and California. From their homebase areas, farmworkers usually migrate northwards, or to *upstream* sites, to harvest seasonal crops. Upstream sites are also referred to as *non-homebase* areas.

Over the years, the migrant streams and the population composition of the streams have evolved [1]. The West Coast stream originates in California (the homebase) and extends to upstream sites in the states of Arizona, Idaho, Oregon and Washington. California serves as the homebase and has the largest number of farmworkers in the U.S. [12]. The stream is composed predominantly of Latinos of Mexican origin (about 90 percent), and fewer American Indians and Southeast Asians [13]. Until recently, the West Coast stream was comprised predominantly of single, male farmworkers or married farmworkers migrating without their wives. This demographic profile, however, is changing with more families and single females joining the migratory stream. The East Coast stream originates in Florida (the homebase) and migrates along the Atlantic coast to New York state. This stream is the

most ethnically diverse and consists of African-Americans (proportion-
ally the largest ethnic group), Mexican-Americans, Mexicans, Puerto
Ricans, Haitians, and Jamaicans. The Midwest stream originates in
Texas (the homebase) and migrates upstream to states such as Michigan
and Iowa. In addition, farmworkers from Texas migrate to Florida and
California. The Midwest stream consists primarily of Latinos (approximately 90 percent), with small numbers of African-Americans and
Anglos. The demographic profile of the Midwest stream consists primarily of families who migrate together as an unit.

A Farmworker's Living Conditions
in the United States

The pervasive poverty, tenuous employment opportunities and seasonal migration contribute toward substandard living conditions for the
majority of farmworkers. Typically, housing structures range from temporary, make-shift encampments or camp-sites to rental housing in the
general market such as apartment complexes, trailers, mobile homes,
and single family housing units.

There are striking differences in the living conditions of farmworkers between the three migrant streams. In the East Coast stream, the
farmworkers are less likely to live in temporary, make-shift encampments. This is especially noticeable in south Florida where the farmworkers' union, concerned farm owners, and local health departments
and other government agencies have worked together to ensure that
farmworkers live in housing units (apartment complexes, mobile or
trailer homes, or single family homes) that provide some basic amenities and security. In addition, most of the housing units are legal, registered structures and, therefore, have to comply with local and state
zoning codes and health and safety regulations [14].

In the West Coast stream, the farmworkers generally live in very
different conditions. The disparity in the living conditions is especially noticeable in southern California, where there are between
20,000 to 30,000 migrant and seasonal farmworkers during the growing
season. Most farmworkers live in unregistered, temporary, make-shift
encampments. The few registered housing units comprise primarily of
rental housing in the general market or housing sheds provided by
growers that border the agricultural fields. It is not uncommon for six or
more single farmworkers to crowd into an apartment [14].

There is mounting concern among some of the farm owners in southern California about the lack of adequate housing for the farmworkers. Due to vocal resistance from the local communities and the general apathy of the local governments the farm owners, however, are hampered in their efforts to provide grower-sponsored housing to the farmworkers. Misconceptions and fear on the part of the local communities about the loss of their property values, the potential for murder and rape, and the introduction of anti-social activities such as gangs, prostitution and drugs in their backyard have prevented county and other local government officials from moving the farmworkers onto public land and residential zones [15].

The unregistered encampments in southern California are similar to the slums found in Third World countries [14, 16]. Many of the farmworker encampments can be found on hillsides, canyons, river beds, groves, and agricultural fields. The camp-sites consist of a variety of housing structures such as those made of plywood covered with tar paper; corrugated plastic units; old mattresses pulled together as walls and covered with plastic or cardboard sheets; and platforms suspended from trees. In a few camp-sites, some farmworkers clear spaces or dig holes in the ground under thick bushes just large enough for sleeping [16]. These holes, called *spider holes*, are just large enough for a person to crawl in and sleep.

The advantage of sleeping in spider holes is the likelihood of remaining unseen by agents of the Immigration and Naturalization Service (INS) and the Border Patrol, who frequently raid the unregistered encampments [16]. Most unregistered encampments, although difficult to locate from a distance as they are invariably nestled in trees or bushes, are easily detected when in close proximity. A spider hole, on the other hand, has a greater chance of remaining undetected since it is discreetly hidden under bushes.

There are numerous disadvantages of living in unregistered, make-shift shelters. Farmworkers sleeping in the bushes are plagued by rats, fleas, and snakes [16]. Furthermore, the make-shift shelters have no insulation and offer little or no protection against the elements; as a consequence, they are either too hot or too cold and during a storm they invariable get flooded or washed away. Since the encampments are isolated from main thoroughfares and residential areas, the farmworkers have no opportunity to obtain proper nutrition and the basic necessities of life. To accommodate their needs, a person (called *fayuquero*) drives a meal van from encampment to encampment selling meals, toiletry items, and any other goods needed by the farmworkers.

The make-shift shelters are clearly illegal and essentially unsafe and are regularly abated and razed for zoning, health and safety code violations [15]. Few if any of the encampments have potable water, gas, electricity, or waste disposal systems. The lack of basic sanitation and hygiene facilities serves as a breeding ground for the spread of diseases. Some common symptoms presented by farmworkers include stomach aches and diarrhea--symptoms attributable to the lack of clean drinking water, toilets, and waste disposal systems. Old pesticide containers are at times used as storage containers for water. In addition, farmworkers have been known to drink water from the irrigation system, which also supplies fertilizers for the crops [16].

Low-wages, coupled with high rental payments for apartments and the need to save some money, forces many farmworkers to live in make-shift shelters. According to one farmworker living in a metal shed:

> If we paid rent there would be virtually nothing left. There is barely enough to live on now. But by living here, we can exist more or less. Apart from what we spend to live [for food], we have a little left over. I send money to my mother because she is old and lives alone. She can no longer work. ...I had imagined the United States very different. I thought it was one big city. I never imagined it was the same as there [Oaxaca]. In Oaxaca, we live in a small village and we live the same as here. In our house there is no electricity, no water. We must haul water to the house the same as here. We use candles instead of electricity the same as here. There is no stove. We had to haul wood from the mountain just as we do here. Our house is wood like these. It is the same. The same living there as it is here [16, p. 78].

Health Profile of Farmworkers

In this section, we review information about farmworkers' health status and well-being, including occupational factors that negatively impact their health. In addition, we examine the barriers encountered by farmworkers in accessing health care services.

Health Status

Little is known about the health status of farmworkers [17, 18]. Similar to other Americans, they suffer from the same leading causes of death such as heart diseases, cancer and strokes. There is, however, very little information about the prevalence, incidence and risk factors of these and other commonly encountered diseases among the farmworkers. Compared with the general population, they are more likely to experience: poorer health [4, 19]; multiple and complex health problems [4]; bacterial, viral, and parasitic infectious diseases; respiratory disorders and infections; digestive diseases [20]; vaccine preventable illnesses such as Hepatitis B; urinary tract infections; no prenatal care during the first trimester of pregnancy [4]; diabetes mellitus; anemia; dermatitis; trauma; and mental disorders, primarily depression and anxiety [17]. Data from migrant health clinics suggest differences in the frequency of diagnoses of certain illnesses between non-homebase and homebase clinics [17]. For instance, non-homebase clinics compared with homebase clinics report higher frequencies of diagnosis of skin disorders and parasitic infection. The differences in the frequencies of diagnosis may be attributable to the hazardous working and living conditions encountered along the migratory routes.

A recent review of the literature on the health status of migrant farmworkers identified several areas where there are serious gaps in the data on basic health status indicators [18]. Some of the notable areas where data are deficient are: mortality and survival data; perinatal outcome data including birthweight, congenital anomalies, and maternal morbidity and mortality; prevalence of chronic diseases; incidence of cancers; controllable medical risk factors for cardiovascular disorders such as hypertension, diabetes, hyperlipidemia, and smoking; pesticide exposure and poisoning; accidental injuries; malnutrition; tobacco and alcohol use; risk factors for HIV; suicide, homicides, domestic violence; immunization status; and accessibility to health care.

Occupational Health

Agriculture is one of the nation's most hazardous occupations [21-23]. Agricultural workers make up less than three percent of the total work force in all industries, however, accidental deaths in this group account for 15 percent of all occupational fatalities. More than one-half (55 percent) of these farm-related deaths are a result of traumatic machine-related accidents. Furthermore, it is estimated that nearly one-half of all survivors of serious farming-related trauma are permanently impaired, amounting to approximately 120,000 disabling farm injuries each year [20].

Latino farmworkers are exposed to toxic chemicals in fertilizers and pesticides, the perils of which they may not understand due to their inability to read labels [3]. Farmworkers are probably at greater risk than others of both acute and chronic pesticide poisoning. They are exposed to the pesticides in several ways. These include direct spraying, drift from spraying, contact with plants and crops, eating with contaminated hands, wearing contaminated clothings, drinking and eating from contaminated utensils, and using contaminated water for bathing and laundry [17]. In addition, living close to the fields exposes them to pesticides during and after working hours.

Several studies have reported extensive pesticide exposure among farmworkers. A Florida Rural Legal Service survey of 469 farmworkers reported that nearly one-half of the respondents had been sprayed directly with agricultural chemicals at least once while they were working. Moreover, more than one-half experienced one or more symptoms attributable to acute pesticide poising [24]. Barger and Reza [25] found similar results based on a survey of 3,000 Mexican farmworkers in the Midwest. The farmworkers reported having been sprayed or otherwise exposed to pesticides on an average of seven times per year, with more than one-fifth (21 percent) reporting 10 or more exposures. A California Department of Public Health survey [26] of 1,100 farmworker and non-agricultural households reported a 15-fold increase in potentially pesticide-related symptoms among farmworker households compared with matched non-agricultural households.

The complexity of health problems experienced by farmworkers is compounded by the severely disabling medical conditions due to exposure to toxic chemicals. There is evidence documenting higher rates of dermatitis, some types of cancers, respiratory illnesses, and allergies among farmworkers [20]. Exposure to agricultural chemicals has also been shown to have adverse effects on the female reproductive system. During pregnancy, many chemicals used in agriculture can cross the placenta, thus affecting the fetus by inducing stillbirth, miscarriage or congenital deformities [20, 22]. Slesinger and Okada [27] in a study among Latina farmworkers reported a higher number of both pregnancies and fetal loss than the national average.

Other occupational health hazards faced by farmworkers include heat- and musculoskeletal-related illnesses [20]. Farm labor is the primary occupation in which workers seek compensation for heat disorders. In addition, the physically strenuous labor associated with farm work leads to crippling and often chronic musculo-skeletal disorders such as arthritis, nerve compression, degenerative intervertebral discs,

and back pain. Factors leading to these problems arise from many sources including constant bending, kneeling, lifting of heavy objects, working in cold and damp conditions, and using the short hoe (*el cortito*).

Health Care Access

Access to health care for farmworkers is severely limited due to
economic, structural, and linguistic and cultural barriers. Economic barriers seem to be the most pervasive in impeding appropriate access to
and utilization of needed medical and preventive health care services.
Economic barriers include a lack of or inadequate health insurance coverage and high out-of-pocket expenses such as deductibles and copay-
ments. Few farmworkers have health insurance provided by their employers. Moreover, anecdotal evidence suggests that farmworkers are
less likely to seek needs-based medical coverage under the Medicaid
program and apply for workers' compensation. The nature of their occupation, including the intermittent employment and fluctuation of wages
based on the piece rate system of payment, acts as a strong economic
disincentive for farmworkers to seek needed health care [17]. Under
the piece rate system of payment, every minute lost from work translates into a loss of income. A typical clinic visit can take several hours
when counting the travel and waiting time, and the time for the actual
doctor-patient encounter, thus becoming a financial disaster for farmworkers.

The intermittent employment coupled with a sense of vulnerability
and helplessness makes farmworkers reluctant to seek needed health
care. They fear losing their jobs or being deported, if found to lack
authorization to work in the U.S. [16, 17]. One farmworker interviewed
by Chavez typified this reluctance to seek needed health care. A
trailer fell on the farmworker's wife and some of her co-workers but a t
the time neither his wife nor the other workers mentioned the accident
to the foreman:

> ...because of fear of losing their jobs. Soon she began to
> complain that she couldn't move her arm or leg, but she never
> liked to go to a doctor in the United States. When she couldn't
> take the pain any longer she went to Tijuana to stay with her
> mother, and there she died [16, p. 75].

Another farmworker recalled how he was deported when he was injured on the job:

> One time I was working very hard. We had to lift some heavy equipment and I was trying to please my *patrón* [boss]. I pulled so hard I hurt my back. For two day I could barely move. Then my patrón took me in his truck and I thought he was taking me to a doctor. But imagine my surprise when we arrived at the border and he told me to get out and go back to Mexico or he'd call the Border Patrol [16, p. 74].

The lack of concern on the part of some health care providers is another factor that makes farmworkers hesitant to access needed health care. One farmworker interviewed by Chavez exemplified the callous attitude of a doctor:

> The doctor said he could do nothing for me even though I had little strength left in my right hand. It didn't seem to me that he had my interest at heart. When I asked him a question he would shrug his shoulders and say he couldn't help me. When I asked him what would happen to my hand if I went back to harvesting oranges, he said I could work until I hurt it worse and then take a few days off to rest it and then return to work until I hurt it again. A good doctor doesn't say this to someone, they try to cure the problem [16, p. 74].

Structural factors limiting farmworkers' health care access involve a lack and maldistribution of appropriate health delivery infrastructure. There are not enough primary health care and migrant health care clinics to serve the farmworking population adequately, and community health centers cannot fill all the gaps [28]. In 1990, migrant and community health centers provided access to only about 12 percent of the farmworking population [29]. Moreover, the farmworkers are faced with inconvenient operating hours of the clinics and have difficulties reaching the clinics due to a lack of personal or public transportation.

The remote location of many of the temporary, make-shift encampments, coupled with the lack of adequate public or private transportation available to farmworkers, severely limit their access to needed health care. One of the authors (SIM) interviewed and shared the grief of a young Mixtec Indian couple from Oaxaca who lived in a makeshift encampment in southern California. The couple's 42-day old firstborn son succumbed to an unexplained, acute illness. According to the grief-stricken parents, during the days preceding the tragic event, the child appeared healthy except for some influenza-like symptoms and a slight fever. One evening, however, the child's condition suddenly deteriorated. The parents attempted to medicate and comfort the child with Tylenol but to no avail; the child died the next day of acute fever of unknown origin. The lack of transportation or access to a telephone (which are rarely found in temporary encampments) prevented the parents from either rushing the child to an emergency clinic or calling for help. The child's tragic death could have been prevented if the encampment had not been isolated and remote or if the parents had had access to transport or communication facilities.

Those fortunate enough to access health care services may encounter linguistic and cultural barriers such as the lack of translation services and special programs for women's health. Language and culture are important determinants in seeking health care [17]. The majority of Latino farmworkers speak only Spanish or are much more fluent in Spanish than in English. Language and cultural differences between farmworkers and the surrounding culture create barriers to seeking health care and receiving appropriate information. Moreover, the cultural and linguistic differences enhance the social and physical isolation experienced by the farmworkers and increase their likelihood of utilizing non-traditional forms of care such as *curanderos* (healers). Due in part to these differences and the high cost of care in the U.S., many farmworkers either postpone seeking needed health care until they can return to Mexico or self-administer their medications.

HIV/AIDS and Farmworkers

HIV Prevalence Among Farmworkers

Data on HIV prevalence among farmworkers are very difficult to obtain. Farmworkers with an undocumented immigration status are resistant to be part of medical studies and reluctant to use health facilities, even when seriously ill, because they fear detection and deportation. Further complicating the situation is the tendency of workers who become sick, whether with HIV/AIDS or any other illness, to return home to Mexico.

The few local seroprevalence studies conducted among this population have reported seroprevalence rates as low as 0.5 percent to as high as 13 percent [30, 31]. A 1987 study among migrant and seasonal farmworkers in North Carolina reported a seroprevalence rate of 2.6 percent, 11 of the 426 farmworkers tested were HIV-antibody positive. All the seropositve farmworkers were African-American [30]. A 1992 study among migrant farmworkers in Immokalee, Florida reported a 5 percent seroprevalence rate; 15 of the 310 farmworkers tested were HIV-antibody positive. Farmworkers in this study were predominantly male (80 percent) and generally they were Latino (53 percent) or African-American (42 percent). U.S.-born farmworkers compared with foreign-born farmworkers were more likely to have tested positive for HIV. Among this group of farmworkers, other risk factors for HIV antibody seropositivity included having more than two sexual partners during the prior six months, a prior history of syphilis and having had sexual intercourse with sex workers. The seropositive rate of 5 percent in the Immokalee, Florida study was slightly higher than the 3.5 percent seropositive rate found among farmworkers in Belle Glade, Florida [32]. A 1990 study among migrant farmworkers in rural South Carolina [33] reported a seroprevalence rate of 13 percent, 25 out of 198 migrant farmworkers tested HIV-antibody positive. The majority (24 out of the 25 farmworkers) of the seropositive farmworkers were African-Americans and one was Latino. All these seroprevalence studies focused on farmworkers in the East Coast stream, which are more heterogeneous in their ethnic diversity and have specific HIV-related risk behaviors.

The seroprevalence rates in the West Coast stream, which contains predominately Latino farmworkers, are comparable with those reported among Latinos in the East Coast stream. A 1991 study in San Diego County found a seroprevalence rate of 0.8 percent; 3 of the 368 farmworkers tested were HIV-antibody positive [34]. A follow-up study in 1992 found no seropositive cases among the 147 farmworkers tested. The zero seroprevalence rate may be misleading because the study had a large proportion (30 percent) of farmworkers who refused to be tested. There is some evidence to suggest that persons who refuse to be tested are more likely to be seropositive [35].

An indirect method to estimate both the potential of HIV transmission and prevalence among farmworkers is to measure the seroprevalence among sex workers. Guerena-Burgueno and others [36] reported a seroprevalence rate of 0.5 percent among registered sex workers in Tijuana. The low seroprevalence rate reported among the registered sex workers in Tijuana may be a true finding or may underestimate the HIV prevalence for a several reasons. The registered sex workers in Tijuana have to undergo periodic health and serologic assessments. Anecdotal evidence suggests that when the registered sex workers suspect that they are infected, they move into the unorganized, unregistered sector of the business, where sex workers undergo serologic assessments only when they are apprehended for selling sex. There are no estimates of the seroprevalence rate among the unregistered sex workers in Tijuana. There are twice as many unregistered as registered sex workers in Tijuana.

Prevalence of Cofactors

Many infectious diseases including tuberculosis and sexually transmitted diseases may act as cofactors for HIV infection. Given the barriers encountered in estimating the prevalence of HIV among migrant and seasonal farmworkers, these infectious diseases can be used as useful markers for estimating the potential prevalence of and risk for HIV. Poor nutrition, crowded living conditions, having unprotected sexual intercourse with sex workers, coupled with a lack of awareness regarding prevention, provide fertile grounds for the spread of diseases among migrant and seasonal farmworkers, and may facilitate the transmission and/or progression of HIV and AIDS. Furthermore, the transient nature of a farmworker's occupation, the duration of treatment for these infectious diseases, and a lack of appropriate patient tracking systems pose serious barriers to health care providers to assure patient compliance with prophylactic and chemotherapeutic protocols for these infectious diseases.

Tuberculosis. Due in part to the HIV epidemic, there has been an alarming resurgence of TB in the United States. Between 1985 and 1990, the greatest increase in TB morbidity occurred among some minority populations such as Latinos (by 24 percent) and African-Americans (by 22 percent), whereas, a decrease in TB morbidity occurred among American Indians/Alaska Native (by 24 percent), Asians/Pacific Islanders (by 10 percent) and non-Hispanic Whites (by 7 percent) [7, 37]. The largest increase in TB morbidity occurred in children (under age 15) and young adults (between ages 22 and 45). Approximately 4 percent of persons with AIDS have TB. Furthermore, HIV seroprevalence surveys of selected tuberculosis patients have shown positive HIV rates ranging from about 1 to 46 percent.

Although the magnitude of TB among farmworkers is not known, different studies have detected high prevalence of asymptomatic infection and clinical TB among this population. The risk for TB among farmworkers is estimated as six times greater than the total U.S. population. Between 1985-1989, farmworkers accounted for five percent of the TB cases in 29 states [38]. Poverty, malnutrition, crowded living quarters, and the high prevalence of TB in the farmworkers' countries of origin have contributed in part towards the relatively higher prevalence of TB morbidity among farmworkers in the U.S.

A few studies among farmworkers in the East Coast migrant stream provide some insights into the extent of TB morbidity among the migrant and seasonal farmworkers. Jacobssen et al. [39], based on a study among 842 migrant farmworkers in the Delmarva Peninsula, found that 37 percent of migrant farmworkers tested had significant skin test reactions of 10 mm or more. The reaction rates were highest for Haitians (55 percent), followed by Mexican-born Latinos (36 percent), Blacks (29 percent) and U.S.-born Latinos (20 percent). The Centers for Disease Control [40] reported similar rates of infection based on studies conducted in 1984 and 1985 among 1,129 farmworkers in Virginia. Approximately 39 percent of farmworkers tested in 1984 and 48 percent of farmworkers tested in 1985 had significant skin test reactions. Nearly one-fourth of the Latino farmworkers tested in 1984 (25 out of 101) and 1985 (29 out of 113) had significant skin test reaction. There were 12 verified cases of tuberculosis among the farmworkers which represented a prevalence rate of 202/100,000 population for 1984 and 133/100,000 population for 1985; these prevalence rates were about 10 to 20 times greater than the national incidence rate of 9.4/100,000 for 1985. Other screening studies have reported significant skin test rates ranging from 31 percent [41] to 44 percent [32].

Tuberculosis among farmworkers poses a special challenge to both the farmworkers and the health care providers. The disease requires long-term therapy. The high mobility of the migrant farmworkers frequently results in partial or no treatment which increase the risk for the transmission of the infection and the development of drug-resistant strains of tuberculosis. A lack of understanding about the disease also impedes appropriate treatment. Some farmworkers who tested positive for TB but did not have symptoms (i.e., coughing) did not believe that a positive skin test indicated TB [32]. In addition, common signs and symptoms of TB such as weight loss, fatigue and coughing are often attributed to conditions such as bronchitis or common colds and not TB, thus delaying seeking appropriate health care [42].

Sexually Transmitted Diseases. The incidence and prevalence of STDs among farmworkers are difficult to establish because the population at risk is constantly changing and there is no mechanism for the collection of epidemiologic data on STDs among farmworkers. Anecdotal evidence and a few localized studies suggest a prevalence primarily of syphilis and gonorrhea and to a lesser extent granuloma inguinale, lymphogranuloma venerum and chancroid among farmworkers.

A Centers for Disease Control [30] screening study in North Carolina reported reactive serologic tests for syphilis in nearly 13 percent (54 out of 426) of farmworkers tested by the rapid plasma reagin and fluorescent treponemal antibody absorption methods. In another Centers for Disease Control [32] screening study conducted in Florida, eight percent (26 out of 325) of farmworkers had reactive serologic tests for syphilis. Of the 26 farmworkers who had a reactive serologic test for syphilis, one person had primary syphilis; six had secondary syphilis; four had early latent syphilis; and five had late latent syphilis. Five farmworkers had been previously treated for syphilis and five were unavailable for examination. Farmworkers born in the U.S. were more likely than those who were foreign-born to have reactive serologic tests for syphilis. A study of migrant farmworkers in rural South Carolina reported reactive serologic tests for syphilis among 13 percent (32 out of 198) farmworkers [33]. Moreover, more than one-half (52 percent) of the farmworkers had previous histories of STDs.

There is some evidence to suggest that Latino farmworkers lack an awareness about STDs. Smith [43] found serious gaps in knowledge among the Latino farmworkers when compared with African-American farmworkers. Latino farmworkers had lower overall mean knowledge scores on indicators of STD-related (syphilis and gonorrhea) transmission, symptom, treatment, and complications (50 percent of Latino, compared with 72 percent of African-American farmworkers, correctly answered the knowledge items). Moreover, Latino farmworkers compared with their counterparts were more likely to indicate that STDs could be prevented by avoiding sex with multiple sexual partners or checking partners prior to sexual intercourse, and that STDs were caused by supernatural events. Furthermore, Latino farmworkers were less likely to: recognize the asymptomatic period of STDs; know the primary signs of gonorrhea and syphilis; and, indicate that penicillin was the best treatment for gonorrhea or syphilis.

Impact of HIV on Farmworkers

Little is known about the impact of the HIV/AIDS epidemic on farmworkers. This absence of systematic research was the impetus for the preparation of this book. Chapters Two through Eight represent the first collection of research studies focusing specifically on migrant Latino farmworkers. These chapters examine different aspects of farmworker HIV/AIDS risk such as men having sex with sex workers, injection drug use, men having sex with other men, effects of migration on sexual practices. They also discuss levels of HIV/AIDS-related knowledge and attitudes regarding personal susceptibility, transmission, and prevention. Chapter Nine discusses policy and programmatic implications for HIV prevention among farmworkers.

Chapter Two explores issues of HIV among Latino farmworking women and their children. The chapter sheds lights on the providers' perspective on the availability of services (educational, treatment, screening, financial and social support) for farmworkers and the barriers to prevention efforts among farmworkers. In addition, the chapter described the impact of community attitudes on provision of HIV and other health-related services to farmworkers, the response of farmworkers to the diagnosis of HIV/AIDS, and the effects of cultural and linguistic variations on service provision for farmworkers.

Chapters Three and Four describe sexual beliefs and behaviors of Latino migrant workers. Chapter Three provides a comparative analysis of the changes that occur in the sexuality of migrant workers as they migrate between Mexico and the U.S. Comparisons of sexuality are made between migrant and non-migrant workers in both Gomez Farias (Mexico) and Watsonville (United States). In addition, the chapter describes the sexual beliefs and behaviors prevalent among non-migrants and the changes in beliefs, behaviors, and sexual attitudes and expectations among the migrant workers. Chapter Four examines sexual beliefs and behaviors of male migrant workers with female sex workers and with other men.

Chapters Five and Six focus on an important source of HIV infection among Latino men and women, the use of sex workers. Chapter Five describes the lives of Latinas who work in cantinas as bar maids and as sex workers. The cantinas provide a social outlet to migrant and non-migrant Latinos. The chapter describes the women's sexual relations with their customers, their self-perceived risk for HIV/AIDS, and their use of drugs and alcohol. Chapter Six focuses on sex workers at the U.S.-Mexico border, with special attention to the segment of the border in El Paso, Texas and Juarez, Mexico. The sex workers describe their customers' sexual practices, attitudes towards condom use, and barriers to condom use. In addition, the sex workers discuss their drug use habits, factors that affect drug use by them and their customers, and drug-related practices which could increase the spread of HIV.

Chapter Seven describes knowledge about STDs and HIV/AIDS, sexual practices such as same gender sex and use of sex workers, and needle use among Latino migrant workers employed in the mushroom industry in southeast Pennsylvania.

Chapter Eight describes an HIV prevention program developed by and for migrant Latino farmworkers. The program, which used an innovative educational format, was shown to be effective in enhancing knowledge, positively effecting attitudinal changes, and most importantly, changing behaviors (i.e., use of condoms during sexual intercourse with a sex worker) to reduce the spread of HIV.

Chapter Nine discusses policy and programmatic recommendations that are specific for HIV prevention among farmworkers. The chapter synthesizes the policy and programmatic recommendations made by the contributing authors with reactions from state and federal-level policy and program officials and the farmworkers themselves. The contributing authors of Chapter Two through Eight, based on their research, identified specific policy and programmatic recommendations for HIV prevention among farmworkers. The state and federal-level policy and program officials reacted to the policy and programmatic recommendations made by the researchers in terms of whether they were feasible or not feasible. In addition, they identified significant impediments to implementing the policy and programmatic recommendations. The farmworkers also reacted to several of the HIV prevention policy and programmatic recommendations suggested by the researchers. The assessment of the farmworkers' reactions provided them with the opportunity to participate in the process of formulating policies and programs that directly affect them.

References

1. Benavides-Vaello S: *The Health Status of Migrant and Seasonal Farmworkers.* Unpublished Masters Thesis. Austin, Texas: The University of Texas at Austin, 1994.
2. U.S. Department of Labor: *Findings from the national agricultural workers survey (NAWS), 1990: a demographic and employment profile of perishable crop farmworkers.* Washington, DC: U.S. Department of Labor 1990; 89:97-98.
3. Wilk VA: The pesticide crisis: occupational exposure. *In: The Pesticide Crisis: A Blueprint for States.* Washington, DC: National Center for Policy Alternatives, 1988.

4. Dever GEA: *Migrant health status: profile of a population with complex health problems.* Migrant Clinicians Network Monograph Series, 1991.
5. U.S. Department of Health and Human Services, Public Health Services: *An Atlas of State Profiles Which Estimate Number of Migrant and Seasonal Farmworkers and Members of Their Families.* U.S. Department of Health and Human Services, Washington, D.C., March, 1990.
6. Guttmacher S: Women migrant workers in the U.S. *Cultural Survival Quart* 1984; 8(2):60-61.
7. De Palomo FB: *Farmworkers and HIV.* National Council of La Raza Center for Health Promotion. Washington, DC: National Council for La Raza, 1993.
8. Guendelman S, Perez-Itriago A: Double lives: the changing role of women in seasonal migration. *Women's Studies* 1987; 13:249-271.
9. Trotter RT: *Orientation to multicultural health care in migrant health programs.* Austin, Texas: National Migrant Resource Program, 1988.
10. Dunbar A, Kravitz L: *Hard Traveling: Migrant Farm Workers in America.* Cambridge, MA: Ballinger Publishing Company, 1976.
11. National Migrant Resource Program: *Facts About America's Migrant Farmworkers.* Austin, Texas: National Migrant Resource Program, Inc., 1994.
12. National Association of Community Health Centers: *Medicaid and Migrant Farmworker Families: Analysis of Barriers and Recommendations for Change.* Washington, DC: National Association of Community Health Centers, July 1991.
13. Wilk VA: *The Occupational Health of Migrant and Seasonal Farmworkers in the United States, 2nd ed.* Washington, DC: Farmworker Justice Fund, 1986.
14. Mishra SI. Conner RF, Magaña JR: *Future HIV Policy and Practice for Latino Farmworkers.* Final Report to the American Foundation for AIDS Research (grant no. 11116-15-PP), 1996.
15. San Diego Regional Task Force on the Homeless: *Homeless Farmworkers and Day Laborers: Their Conditions and Their Impact on the San Diego Region.* Regional Task Force on the Homeless, San Diego, California, 1991.
16. Chavez LR: *Shadowed Lives: Undocumented Immigrants in American Society.* New York, NY: Harcourt Brace Jovanovich College Publishers, 1992.
17. Meister JS: The health of migrant farm workers. *In:* Cordes DH, Rea DF (eds): *Occupational Medicine: Health Hazards of Farming. Occupational Med: State of the Art Reviews* 1991; 6(3):503-518.
18. Rust GS: Health status of migrant farmworkers: a literature review and commentary. *Am J Public Health* 1990; 80:1213-1217.
19. Goldsmith MF: As farmworkers help keep America healthy, illness may be their harvest. *JAMA* 1989; 261:3207-3213.
20. Friedman-Jiménez G, Ortiz JS: Occupational health. *In:* Molina CW, Aguirre-Molina M (eds), *Latino Health in the U.S.: A Growing Challenge.* Washington, DC: American Public Health Association, 1994.
21. National Safety Council: *Accident Facts: 1993 Edition.* Chicago, Ill: National Safety Council, 1988.

22. Mobed K, Gold EB, Schenker MB: Occupational health problems among migrant and seasonal farm workers. *West J Med* 1992; 157:367-373.

23. Ciesielski S, Hall SP, Sweeney M: Occupational injuries among North Carolina migrant farmworkers. *Am J Public Health* 1991; 81:926-927.

24. Florida Rural Legal Services: *Dangers in the Field: The Myth of Pesticide Safety.* Immokalee, FL: Florida Rural Legal Services Inc., 1980.

25. Barger K, Reza E: *Survey of Midwestern Farm Workers.* Indianapolis, IN: Indiana University Department of Anthropology, 1983.

26. California Department of Industrial Relations: *Occupational Diseases in California, 1979.* San Francisco, CA: California Department of Industrial Relations, Division of Labor Statistics and Research, 1981.

27. Slesinger DP, Okada Y: Fertility patterns of Hispanic migrant farm workers: testing the effects of assimilation. *Rural Sociol* 1984; 49:430-440.

28. National Migrant Resource Program: *Fact Sheet: Basic Health.* Austin, Texas: National Migrant Resource Program, Inc., 1994.

29. Migrant Health Program: *Outreach Health Services to Migrants: The Reality, the Dream.* Rockville, MD: U.S. Department of Health and Human Services, 1990.

30. Centers for Disease Control: HIV seroprevalence in migrant and seasonal farmworkers--North Carolina, 1987. *MMWR* 1988; 37(34):517-519.

31. Castro K, Narkunas J: *Preliminary results: seroprevalence of HIV infection in seasonal and migrant farmworkers.* Migrant Health Newsline. Austin, Texas: National Migrant Resource Program, Inc., 1991.

32. Centers for Disease Control: HIV infection, syphilis, and tuberculosis screening among migrant farm workers--Florida, 1992. *MMWR* 1992; 41(39):723-725.

33. Jones JL, Rion P, Hollis S, Longshore S, Leverette WB, Ziff L: HIV-related characteristics of migrant workers in rural South Carolina. *Southern Med J* 1991; 84(9):1088-1090.

34. Swerdlow DL, Muñoz G, Lobel H, Waterman S: *Health Surveillance in Migrant Camps, San Diego County, July 1991-June 1992.* Report submitted to The Alliance Healthcare Foundation, San Diego, CA, 1992.

35. Hull HF, Bettinger CJ, Gallaher, et al.: Comparison of HIV-antibody prevalence in patients consenting to and declining HIV-antibody screening in an STD clinic. *JAMA* 1988; 260:935-938.

36. Guerena-Burgueno F, Benenson AS, Sepulveda-Amor J: *HIV-1 prevalence in selected Tijuana sub-populations.* Am J Public Health 1991; 81:623-625.

37. Jereb JA: Tuberculosis mortality in the United States: final data 1990. *MMWR* 1990; 40(no. 40 SS-3):23-27.

38. Centers for Disease Control: Prevention and control of tuberculosis in migrant farmworkers: recommendations of the Advisory Council for the Elimination of Tuberculosis. *MMWR* 1992; 41(no. RR-10).

39. Jacobsen ML, Mercer MA, Miller LK, Simpson TW: Tuberculosis risk among migrant farmworkers on the Delmarva Peninsula. *Am J Public Health* 1987; 77:29-32.

24

40. Centers for Disease Control: Tuberculosis among migrant farmworkers--
    Virginia. *MMWR* 1986; 35(29):467-469.
41. Simmons JD, Hull P, Rogers E, Hart R: Tuberculosis control migrant study of
    1988. *NCJM* 1989; 50(6):309-310.
42. Rubel A, Garro LC: Social and cultural factors in the successful control of
    tuberculosis. *Public Health Reports* 1992; 107(6):626-636.
43. Smith LS: Ethnic differences in knowledge of sexually transmitted diseases in
    North American Black and Mexican-American migrant farmworkers. *Res
    Nursing Health* 1988; 11:51-58.

PART TWO

Research Reports

2

A Growing HIV/AIDS Crisis Among Migrant and Seasonal Farmworker Families

Kristi Skjerdal, Shiraz I. Mishra
and Sandra Benavides-Vaello

Introduction

The number of women with the human immunodeficiency virus (HIV) and acquired immunodeficiency syndrome (AIDS) has risen dramatically. HIV/AIDS is now the fifth leading cause of death for women of reproductive age [1]. Disproportionate rates of HIV infection are seen among four groups of women: sex partners of injectable drug users, African-Americans and Latinas, professional sex workers, and adolescents. Seventy-two percent of women with HIV/AIDS are of African-American or Latino background [1, 2]. The most common risk factors for infection among women are sexual contact with an infected man and injectable drug use [2].

One group of women who may be at particular risk for HIV infection is farmworking women. HIV infection among farmworking women of childbearing age can potentially devastate farmworker families, not only because HIV can be transmitted to their children but also because farmworking women are usually the primary caretakers in the family system.

This study assessed the impact of HIV/AIDS on the farmworker (migrant and seasonal) community in general, and farmworking women of childbearing age and their children specifically. The study collected data from representatives of farmworker health and social service organizations (henceforth termed "providers"). We obtained information from these providers on first, how HIV/AIDS had affected three groups: farmworkers infected with HIV, farmworkers in general and farmworking women and their children in particular; and second, on the availability of HIV-related services such as education, screening and treatment.

Farmworking Women and Children

The demographic composition of the agricultural workforce varies by the three major agricultural streams. The East Coast stream predominantly consists of African-Americans, with a large proportion of Haitians, Jamaicans and Puerto Ricans and relatively fewer Mexicans and Central Americans. There are more farmworking families in the East Coast than the Midwest and West Coast streams. The Midwest and West Coast streams consist primarily of Latino farmworkers of Mexican and Central American origin. In the West Coast stream, the number of single females of Central American and Southeast Asian origin is increasing. This demographic shift has resulted in new "female-only" camp.

Information on demographic characteristics and migration patterns of farmworking women and their families is limited due to the transitory nature of farm work and the lack of data collection mechanisms. Available data indicate that the number of women laboring in agriculture is increasing (Mountain K, personal communication). The average age of migrant farmworking women is about 22 years [3] and about 28 percent are of childbearing age [4]. The average level of education for migrant and seasonal farmworking women is sixth grade [4]. As many as 70 percent of farmworking women who are married or live with their partners work in the fields. The majority of seasonal farmworkers is married and/or have children [5]. The decision to migrate is often based on the family size. More family members working in the fields translates into greater family income; an additional family member increases the household income by approximately $2,700 [6]. Many families join the migration streams when they have enough children aged 10 and older able to work the fields or in nearby packing sheds.

Farmworking Women and HIV/AIDS

Little formal research has been conducted on farmworking women and HIV/AIDS. Research on HIV/AIDS among farmworkers, which has predominantly focused on males, has found rates of HIV/AIDS higher than those in the general U.S. population [7, 8]. In addition, this research has reported high rates of HIV-related risk factors such as sexually transmitted disease [9], tuberculosis [10], substance abuse [11], use of needles [12], high-risk sexual practices [13] and limited understanding of HIV prevention measures [14]. By virtue of the fact that farmworking women are the sexual partners of farmworking men, they are at risk. Moreover, infected women can pass the virus to their unborn children. According to estimates, approximately 25 to 30 percent of children born to infected mothers will also be infected [15, 16].

Besides the primary risk of infection through sexual contact with an infected partner, there are several factors that may place farmworking women at a higher risk for HIV/AIDS. Anecdotal evidence suggests that farmworking women lack knowledge of their partners' risks and have a decreased ability to take action to protect themselves from sexually transmitted diseases such as HIV (Mountain K, personal communication). Furthermore, the risk for farmworking women is compounded by their lack of access to preventive services, poorer health status due to occupational exposure to toxins, and sexual practices [17, 18]. Moreover, racism, unemployment and under-employment, poverty, inadequate living conditions, lower levels of education, and limited access to health care and social services may also contribute towards a higher risk of infection for these women [2, 18, 19].

Methods

This study was conducted nationwide through telephone interviews with 60 health and social service organization representatives (the "providers") working with farmworkers. We conducted the interviews in 1993 and assessed both qualitative and quantitative information regarding the providers' perspective of HIV/AIDS among farmworker families. This study was conducted by Skjerdal and Benavides-Vaello.

Study Sites and Participants

In general, the health and social service organizations represented by the providers reflected at least one of the following three attributes. First, the organizations received federal funding through the Migrant Health, Migrant Education, Migrant Head Start and the Job Training Partnership Act programs. Second, they were located in areas anecdotally known to have a high incidence of HIV/AIDS or areas assumed to have a low incidence of HIV/AIDS (Cavenaugh D, personal communication). Third, they were located in one of the three major agricultural streams, which were divided by state in the following manner: (1) West Coast (AZ, NV, CA, OR, WA, ID); (2) East Coast (FL, GA, TN, KT, IN, OH, SC, NC, VA, MD, WV, PA, DE, NJ, NY); and, (3) Midwest (TX, NM, UT, CO, WY, MT, OK, KS, NA, ND, SD, MN, IA, MO, AK, LA, MI, AL, WI, MI). Based on these inclusion criteria, we used network sampling procedures and the Migrant Health Program Directory of Health Centers to identify and select eligible organizations.

The identification and selection of organizations were conducted until we had an approximately even representation of organizations in the three streams. Out of the 52 organizations included in the study, 17 organizations each were in the East Coast and Midwest streams and 18 in the West Coast stream. They included federally funded community/migrant health centers (48 percent, n = 25), community-based organizations/migrant servicing agencies (27 percent, n = 14), State/County Health Departments (15 percent, n = 8), migrant education programs (six percent, n = 3) and pediatric AIDS clinics (four percent, n = 2).

Within the 52 selected organizations, we identified one or more appropriate provider(s) for the interview. The providers gave information that pertained to either one clinic, a group of clinics, or a county or state-wide program. In all, we selected 78 providers from the 52 organizations and sent them the survey instrument. Out of these 78 providers, 60 providers (from 26 states) responded to one or more survey question and provided valid information.

The 60 providers interviewed for the study represented a wide array of health professionals working in health and social services organizations that provided services to migrant and seasonal farmworkers and their families. Among the 60 providers surveyed, 25 percent (n = 15) were outreach workers/health educators, 23 percent (n = 14) were migrant health or education program coordinators, 17 percent (n = 10) were directors of medical (health) or nursing services, 15 percent (n = 9) were directors or executive directors of the selected organizations and 10 percent (n = 6) were AIDS or infectious disease coordinators. The professional designation of 10 percent (n = 6) of the providers was unknown.

Procedures

After selection of the organizations and the identification of appropriate providers, we contacted each provider prior to the actual interview. We informed the providers about the study goals, gave them the survey instrument and scheduled a telephone interview. Each interview lasted approximately 45 minutes and were conducted in English. The unit of analysis for the study was the provider representing an organization that served migrant and seasonal farmworkers.

Measures

We collected quantitative and qualitative data on several topical areas from the providers. The quantitative data included the providers' knowledge about their organizations' HIV/AIDS caseload and the modes of HIV transmission among their infected farmworker clientele. In addition, we inquired about the providers' perceptions of the prevalence of risk factors and the levels of knowledge, attitudes, beliefs and prevalent practices among farmworkers in general and farmworking women specifically. Furthermore, we obtained information on the providers' assessment on the availability and configuration of prevention education, screening and treatment services for farmworkers in general and farmworking women specifically.

We collected qualitative information on issues including attitudes of community members in the providers' area about farmworkers and the impact of these attitudes on the provision of services to farmworkers. In addition, we obtained the providers' perspective on how the farmworkers reacted to a diagnosis of HIV/AIDS, and the cultural and linguistic variations in the provision of services.

There were eight close-ended questions on various aspects of the HIV epidemic such as the organizational caseload; modes of transmission among the infected clientele; risk factors prevalent in the farmworking community; barriers to prevention; knowledge, attitudes and practices prevalent in the farmworking community; and the availability of services and prevention education programs. In addition, three open-ended questions covered the: relation of HIV risk factors to the spread of infection among farmworking women; impact of HIV on farmworking women and their children; and, changes needed at the local, state and national levels to address the needs of farmworkers.

Results

In this section, we present quantitative and qualitative data obtained from the providers. First, we present the quantitative data on the providers' knowledge and perceptions of: their organizations' HIV caseload; the mode of HIV transmission among their infected farmworker clients; the prevalence of HIV risk factors among their farmworker clients; the barriers to HIV prevention among farmworking women; the knowledge, attitudes, beliefs and practices among farmworkers in general and farmworking women specifically; and, the availability and configuration of HIV/AIDS-related services for farmworkers in general and farmworking women specifically. Second, we present qualitative data which has been organized around the following three common themes: (1) the impact of community attitudes on the provision of HIV and other health services to farmworkers; (2) the response of farmworkers to the diagnosis of HIV/AIDS; and, (3) the effects of cultural and linguistic variations on service provision for farmworkers.

Organizational HIV/AIDS Caseload

When asked generally to quantify the HIV/AIDS caseload seen by their organization, the majority (89 percent) of the interviewed providers reported at least one case of HIV/AIDS among their farmworker clientele (Table 2.1). Fifty percent of the providers reported seeing 1 to 5 cases overall in their clinical settings and 11 percent had seen over 35 cases. Among this 11 percent of providers, more providers from the East Coast stream organizations reported HIV/AIDS caseloads of over 35 farmworkers than did those from organizations in the Midwest and West Coast streams. Providers in the Midwest stream reported fewer cases than did those on either coast. Nearly one-third of the providers had seen cases of HIV/AIDS among farmworking women, and two cases of AIDS were mentioned among farmworker children.

Modes of HIV Transmission Among
Infected Farmworkers

In terms of the modes of HIV transmission among their infected clients, the majority (62 percent) of providers cited transmission through heterosexual contact as the most frequent transmission route (Table 2.2). Transmission through heterosexual contact included sex with sex workers (27 percent), multiple sexual partners (21 percent) and other heterosexual contact (14 percent). Fifteen percent of providers reported needle use as a mode of transmission; more than one-half of these providers were from organizations located in the East Coast stream. Other modes of transmission reported included anal intercourse (13 percent) and vertical transmission (four percent), that is, from mother to fetus.

TABLE 2.1. HIV/AIDS Caseload as Reported by Providers Across the Three Migrant Streams (Percentages)

Caseload[a]	West Coast n = 14	East Coast n = 15	Midwest n = 15	Total n = 44 [b]
None	7	7	2	11
1-5	57	27	67	50
6-15	7	27	13	16
16-35	29	7	0	11
Over 35	0	33	0	11

[a] Number of farmworker cases *ever* served by the providers' organizations.

[b] 16 providers interviewed did not provide an estimate of their caseload.

TABLE 2.2. Mode of HIV Transmission Among Infected Farmworkers (Percentages)

Mode of Transmission [a]	West Coast n = 14	East Coast n = 15	Midwest n = 15	Total n = 44 [b]
Anal (male)	22	9	12	13
Needle use	15	20	8	15
Multiple sex partners	26	20	16	21
Sex with sex workers	33	24	24	27
Heterosexual contact	4	13	28	14
Mother to fetus	0	7	4	4
Other	0	7	8	5

[a] Providers could mention more than one possible mode of transmission and, therefore, the percentages add up to more than 100.

[b] 16 providers interviewed did not provide a response to the question.

HIV/AIDS-related Risk Factors

Providers were asked to give their perceptions on the prevalence of HIV/AIDS-related risk factors such as sexually-transmitted diseases, needle drug use, other illicit drug use, tuberculosis, and other factors among farmworking women of childbearing age and farmworkers in general seen at their organization(s). As presented in Table 2.3, the most frequently reported risk factors for HIV infections among farmworking women included sexually transmitted diseases (79), followed by tuberculosis (47 percent) and alcohol abuse (33 percent).

According to the providers, the living conditions of the farmworkers could place them at a higher risk for infection. Most of them lived in close quarters with poor sanitary facilities and limited ventilation. Not only did such living conditions lead to the spread of communicable diseases but they also created a highly stressful environment for the farmworkers. Nearly all the providers interviewed drew an association between the highly stressful living environments, and the high rates of alcohol use and sexual intercourse. They were of the opinion that sex, particularly among single farmworking men, occurred with sex workers and/or multiple sexual partners.

Barriers to HIV Prevention Among
Farmworker Women

Table 2.4 presents potential barriers faced by farmworking women in obtaining HIV prevention education and services. According to the providers, the most common barriers to HIV preventive efforts among farmworking women include cultural patterns in relationships (98 percent), followed by a lack of transportation (87 percent), and a lack of access to health care and health information (78 percent). Other significant barriers reported included low awareness on HIV/AIDS (74 percent) and high mobility (72 percent).

HIV/AIDS Knowledge and Beliefs

Most providers reported that their clientele had a general lack of understanding about HIV/AIDS and had a belief that the disease would not affect them personally (Table 2.5). Nearly three-fourths (72 percent) described their farmworking women clients as holding the belief "I cannot catch AIDS since I am faithful to my husband." Many providers added that a farmworking woman who held this view also

TABLE 2.3. HIV/AIDS Risk Factors Seen Among Male and Female Farmworkers (Percentages)

Risk Factors [a]	West Coast n=14		East Coast n=14		Midwest n=15		Total n=43 [b]	
	All [c]	Women [d]	All	Women	All	Women	All	Women
STDs	86	79	100	86	80	73	88	79
IV drug use	43	14	57	14	20	7	40	12
Other drug use	43	7	29	36	33	7	35	16
Alcohol abuse	79	21	86	29	67	47	77	33
Tuberculosis	71	57	79	43	40	40	63	47
Other	14	21	21	43	13	13	16	26

[a] Providers could mention more than one risk factor and, therefore, the percentages add up to more than 100.

[b] 17 providers interviewed did not provide a response to the question on risk factors.

[c] Denotes farmworkers in general (including farmworking women).

[d] Denotes only farmworking women.

TABLE 2.4. Barriers to HIV Prevention Experienced by Male and Female Farmworkers (Percentages)

Barriers [a]	West Coast n = 15		East Coast n = 15		Midwest n = 16		Total n = 46 [b]	
	All [c]	Women [d]	All	Women	All	Women	All	Women
Language	67	60	67	67	75	67	70	65
Lack of transport	73	87	73	87	81	88	76	87
No health care access	73	73	67	67	94	75	78	78
Cultural patterns in relationships	93	100	100	100	81	94	93	98
Low HIV awareness	87	80	87	87	50	56	74	74
Poor health status	80	73	60	67	75	63	72	67
High mobility	60	53	93	80	88	81	80	72
Limited access to condoms and education	60	67	40	47	56	63	52	59
Other	47	40	53	53	56	50	52	48

[a] Providers could mention more than one barrier and, therefore, the percentages add up to more than 100.
[b] 14 providers interviewed did not provide a response to the question on barriers.
[c] Denotes farmworkers in general (including farmworking women).
[d] Denotes only farmworking women.

TABLE 2.5. Knowledge and Beliefs Regarding HIV Held by Farmworking
Women (Percentages)

Knowledge and Beliefs	West Coast $n = 17$	East Coast $n = 14$	Midwest $n = 15$	Total $n = 46$ [a]
AIDS affects only men	47	36	27	37
AIDS affects only Whites, not Latinos	18	14	7	13
AIDS affects only gay males, not families	59	36	60	52
I can't catch AIDS because I'm faithful to my husband	65	79	73	72
I can tell if my partners are clean	47	64	40	50
People catch AIDS from mosquitoes	41	36	47	41
People catch AIDS when they give blood	41	43	60	48
Other	35	43	20	33

[a] 14 providers interviewed did not provide responses to the knowledge and belief questions.

assumed that her husband was faithful to her. Other beliefs commonly held by the farmworking women included, "AIDS cannot affect families, only gay males" (52 percent), "I can avoid catching AIDS by only being with partners I can tell are clean" (50 percent), and "People catch AIDS by giving blood"(48 percent). Furthermore, a substantial number of providers believed that their farmworking women clientele held erroneous beliefs such as "People catch AIDS from mosquitoes" (41 percent) and "AIDS affects men only" (37 percent).

HIV/AIDS-related Practices

According to the providers, farmworking women sometimes had less opportunity to protect themselves from diseases (or getting pregnant) due to their partners' demands. The providers when asked if the farmworking women they served at their organizations engaged in behaviors that placed them at risk for HIV, they described their farmworking women clients as lacking the ability to negotiate with their partners to protect themselves. Fifty-four percent of providers reported that their farmworking women clients were routinely unaware of their partners' risks (such as sex with multiple partners or drug use habits) and 50 percent of providers reported that their farmworking women clients' male partners did not use condoms. In addition, 43 percent believed that their farmworking women clients engaged in anal intercourse, a practice believed to be common among young females for birth control reasons. Other providers, however, believed that very few of their female clients engaged in this risk behavior because it was not a part of their culture.

Availability and Configuration of HIV/AIDS Services

One of the goals of the study was to learn more about programs to prevent, diagnose and treat HIV infection and AIDS among farmworking men, women and children. Providers were asked to describe all HIV/AIDS-related services available in their areas and the population groups targeted by these services. The services are categorized into four groups: educational, screening (such as risk assessment, counseling and testing), treatment, and financial/social support.

HIV Prevention. Nearly all the providers (98 percent) reported the availability of HIV education programs through their organizations. Furthermore, 80 percent indicated that farmworkers were directly targeted by these educational programs, however, only 28 percent of the programs reportedly targeted farmworking women specifically (Table 2.6).

There was a range of HIV prevention education services available through the providers' organizations (Table 2.7). These services included individual counseling (89 percent); street or camp outreach (81 percent); small group sessions (64 percent); and classes (60 percent). Other avenues for HIV education were the migrant education programs at the local schools and the outreach conducted by some of the local churches. These outreach efforts used innovative methods for bringing HIV edu-

TABLE 2.6. HIV/AIDS Services Available to Farmworkers (Percentages)

Services Available[a]	West Coast n=16	East Coast n=17	Midwest n=17	All[b] n=50[d]	Only women[c] n=50
Educational					
Prevention education	100	100	94	80	28
Screening					
Risk assessment	88	88	76	64	16
Counseling and testing	88	94	88	68	24
Treatment					
HIV medical care	81	76	71	42	14
Financial and Social Support					
Financial support	50	71	71	26	8
Social support	31	53	71	30	10

[a] Providers could mention more than one service and, therefore, the percentages add up to more than 100.

[b] Denotes services that targeted all the farmworkers (males and females).

[c] Denotes services that specifically targeted farmworking women.

[d] 10 providers interviewed did not provide responses to the question on availability of services.

TABLE 2.7. HIV Prevention Education Programs Available Through
the Providers' Organizations (Percentages)

Programs [a]	West Coast n = 17	East Coast n = 14	Midwest n = 15	Total n = 46 [b]
Individual counseling	88	93	88	89
Small group sessions	71	73	56	64
Classes	56	60	63	60
Street/camp outreach	94	80	69	81
Health fairs, other community events	75	53	31	53
Other	56	53	31	47

[a] Providers could mention more than one type of program and, therefore, the percentages add up to more than 100.

[b] 13 providers interviewed did not provide responses to the questions on availability of HIV prevention programs.

cation to farmworkers including public service announcements on radio and television, workshops for Migrant Head Start parents and camp presentations with role playing. The outreach was conducted at STD clinics, homeless shelters, community cultural centers, laundromats, Alcoholics Anonymous meetings, soccer team practices, community movie fests, "smoker's groups," and English as a Second Language classes.

While 60 percent of the providers reported that the main target of their HIV prevention programs were minorities, only 49 percent reported farmworking women as their main target. Nearly all the providers mentioned that the lack of culturally, linguistically, and gender appropriate educational materials for a low-literacy group made it difficult to tailor HIV prevention education sessions to specific target audiences such as farmworkers.

HIV Screening Services. The majority of providers reported the availability at their organizations of HIV screening services including those for risk assessment (84 percent), and counseling and testing (90 percent). Substantially fewer providers, however, noted that these services specifically targeted farmworkers (Table 2.6); about two-thirds reported the availability of risk assessment (64 percent), and counseling and testing (68 percent) that specifically targeted farmworkers in general. Moreover, farmworking women had far fewer specialized services available to them than farmworkers in general. The availability of counseling and testing services specifically designed for farmworking women was reported by about one-fourth (24 percent) of providers and HIV risk assessment services by 16 percent. Furthermore, many of the organizations that did have screening services for farmworkers did not offer these services at times convenient to farmworkers, at places that could be easily accessed by farmworkers, and by bilingual and/or bicultural HIV counselors who were aware of the special needs of farmworkers.

HIV/AIDS Treatment Services. Unlike educational and screening services, few organizations in the study offered HIV/AIDS medical care services. About one-fifth (24 percent) of the providers reported no HIV medical care service available through their organizations (Table 2.6). Furthermore, less than one-half (42 percent) indicated the availability of HIV medical care services that targeted farmworkers, and even fewer providers (14 percent) indicated the availability of medical care services that specifically targeted farmworking women. Due to the absence of HIV/AIDS medical services in their communities, the providers indicated that referrals were often necessary to specialty clinics in metropolitan areas. The distances of these referral clinics, however, prevented the farmworkers from accessing these services when needed since many of the farmworkers lacked appropriate transportation. Many providers described a need for targeted HIV/AIDS medical care training for migrant health providers so that the HIV-positive farmworker clients could be seen longer at the migrant health centers.

HIV/AIDS Financial and Social Support Services. The majority of providers stated that financial (64 percent) and social support (56 percent) services were available to HIV infected people through their organizations. However, substantially fewer providers reported the availability of these services for farmworkers. About one-fourth (26 percent) reported the availability of specifically targeted financial services and 30 percent reported the availability of social support services (Table 2.6). Compared to farmworkers in general, the availability of financial and social support services specifically for farmworking women was severely limited. Fewer than one-tenth (8 percent) of the providers reported the availability of financial services and 10 percent reported the availability of social support services specifically for farmworking women. Many providers described the difficulties encountered in enrolling HIV-positive farmworkers in the Medicaid or other medical assistance programs, particularly if they were undocumented. Other support programs such as housing, food services and pharmacy were even more difficult to access; thus leaving HIV-positive farmworkers without any form of assistance to meet the extreme challenges presented by HIV disease.

Qualitative Data: Three Common Themes

Three overall themes were noted throughout the interviews with the providers: (1) the impact of the community attitudes on the provision of HIV and other health services to farmworkers; (2) the response of farmworkers to the diagnosis of HIV/AIDS; and, (3) the effects of cultural and linguistic variations on the provision of service to farmworkers.

Local Residents' Attitudes Toward HIV and Farmworkers. The providers interviewed indicated how some of the residents of their local communities believed that farmworkers were necessary to harvest the crops and were a valuable addition to the community. On the other hand, there were other residents who felt threatened by the presence of the farmworkers and by their need for health and social services. This threat from farmworkers was due to the perceptions held by some residents that farmworkers were draining the scare resources available to their communities. In addition, the providers indicated that some residents in their communities resented the constant influx of people. Besides the struggles to adjust to the large numbers of people entering the community, the community residents were frustrated by the inability of the migrants to communicate in English and by the different customs and cultural mores practiced by the migrants. The providers felt that these struggles and frustrations were often expressed through prejudice and discrimination by the community residents.

Finally, the providers believed that some of the residents in their communities had misconceived notions about HIV and its source. These residents believed that "all farmworkers have it" and that all farmworkers represented a threat to the health of the residents' families and communities. The providers described how such fears had a significant impact on the provision of HIV/AIDS services to farmworkers. For example, although all the clinics that received migrant health funding were mandated to provide HIV/AIDS prevention services, many clinics discriminated against farmworkers in the provision of services out of fear of reprisals from the local community. In some instances when clinics offered services to farmworkers against the general sentiment of the local community, these clinics were isolated by other community providers and, consequently, found themselves in a less competitive position to apply for federal AIDS funding.

Farmworkers' Response to a Diagnosis of HIV/AIDS. The second theme pertained to how farmworkers reacted to an HIV/AIDS diagnosis. According to the providers, once farmworkers found out that they were infected with HIV or had AIDS they invariably dropped out of their regular support systems such as their families, work crews, friends circle, and the farm work-force. In addition, many of the infected farmworkers moved to metropolitan areas to gain access to HIV treatment services. Such moves, however, left the infected farmworkers with little choice but to join the ranks of the homeless. Some providers described how they had seen farmworkers return to their countries of origin to seek social support from their families, even though many of these countries offer limited treatment for HIV-infected people. The majority of providers felt that the mobility of the newly diagnosed farmworker was a significant impediment to their HIV/AIDS surveillance and treatment efforts. According to the providers, the infected farmworkers often fell through the cracks because they either left the migrant stream or continued their migration. They indicated that this challenge could be lessened with the creation of an interstate record transfer system and/or a cross-border information exchange system.

Effects of Cultural and Linguistic Variations on Service Provision. The third overall theme concerned the special needs of an extremely diverse farmworker population. The providers remarked on the ethnic, linguistic and cultural diversity of their farmworking community. This was especially true for farmworkers who were brought to this country through special labor programs such as the H-2 worker program and for those who had crossed the borders in search of employment opportunities. Farmworkers without legal documentation had difficulties with the language, held divergent beliefs on health and illness, and had varying approaches to medical practices and healing. To effectively address the HIV prevention needs of these less acculturated farmworkers, the providers indicated the importance of taking into account the mosaic of linguistic and cultural patterns, and the familiarity with the U.S. health and social service systems.

Discussion

This is one of the first studies to shed some light on the risk for HIV experienced by farmworking women and the challenges they face in accessing much needed preventive services. While the providers interviewed for the study represented organizations that differed in size and location, common patterns emerged concerning HIV awareness, risk factors, barriers to HIV prevention and the availability of services. The study supported and expanded on previous HIV/AIDS research conducted among farmworkers.

The results indicate that farmworkers find themselves at a relatively high risk for HIV infection. The primary mode of transmission was unprotected heterosexual contact; either through sexual intercourse with a sex worker, sex with multiple partners, or anal sexual intercourse. Furthermore, the study results suggest that farmworking women may find themselves at a higher risk for HIV infection due to a higher prevalence among them and/or their sexual partners of HIV-related cofactors such as sexually transmitted diseases, tuberculosis and injectable drug use. Moreover, the farmworking women strongly believed that they were not at risk for HIV infection if they remained faithful to their husbands. Due to this erroneous belief, they engaged in sexual practices such as anal intercourse and unprotected sexual intercourse without knowing their partners' risks.

The study identified several factors that may preclude farmworkers' access to HIV-related preventive, medical and social services. On the part of the farmworkers, these factors include cultural barriers including language difficulties, misconceptions about their risk for HIV, misconceptions about the cause and transmission of HIV, lack of transportation, divergent views about health care, lack of awareness about the availability of services, and, in some instances, discrimination by the providers or community residents. On the part of the providers, these factors include lack of resources, lack of bicultural and/or bilingual personnel, negative attitudes in the community, and lack of appropriately targeted services for farmworkers and their families.

According to the study findings, farmworking women faced greater barriers in accessing preventive, medical and social services. For the most part, these barriers were due to the unavailability of services that especially targeted farmworking women. In addition, the farmworking women lived in more severe social and economic conditions, were more likely to be isolated and were invariably dependent on their partners. Furthermore, although many organizations in the study had services for farmworkers, there were only a few organizations that had services catering to the special needs of farmworking women.

Some caveats must be kept in mind when interpreting the findings. First, we gathered the data through interviews with providers from organizations that served farmworkers. There could be a bias since the data were not gathered directly from the farmworkers. On the other hand, it is important to document the perceptions of providers since they make the decisions regarding the provision of services and programs. Second, the network sampling methods used to identify organizations may introduce a selection bias. We did attempt to match organizations across the three migrant streams to reduce the possibility of a potential selection bias. Third, the results do not control for the size and location of the providers, factors which may skew them in favor of larger organizations based in or near metropolitan areas.

Implications

The paucity of data on the HIV experience of farmworkers provides numerous opportunities for future research. Furthermore, the data have implications in the design of effective prevention strategies that target farmworkers in general and farmworking women specifically.

First, there is a need for further research in the gender roles and behaviors practiced by the farmworkers. This is especially important since the understanding of the gender roles and behaviors will facilitate the design of effective prevention programs. According to the providers interviewed for the study, roles and behaviors that may serve to hold together the social fabric of the community in a country from which a farmworker comes may not be adaptive in the United States, particularly considering the increased risk of exposure to HIV that may be encountered here. For example, there were many variations in the cultural and gender groups to which the farmworkers sought affiliation. Furthermore, these affiliations defined the degree of acceptance of various sexual practices such as sexual intercourse outside of marriage or committed relationships. Understanding these group dynamics may help in the development of targeted intervention programs.

Second, there was some evidence that cultural definitions of patterns of relationships may heighten the risk for HIV as experienced by the farmworking community and pose significant barriers to effective HIV prevention efforts. To better understand the cultural definitions of relationships, researchers need to examine the realities of gender roles and sexual equality. This issue becomes especially important during the negotiations for use of condom during sexual intercourse. The context within which this negotiation occurs has a strong undercurrent of culturally defined gender roles, which reinforce male dominance and female submissiveness. A lack of understanding of the patterns of relationships and their cultural implications may help explain the ineffectiveness of most prevention efforts that have promoted the use of condoms. A better understanding of the patterns of relationships may help us design strategies that empower women and make them more effective when negotiating safer-sex practices.

Third, the results highlight the need for culturally and linguistically appropriate prevention efforts. The organizations included in the study are mandated by law to have HIV prevention efforts for their community. However, due to several factors noted in the study, many of these organizations have not implemented programs that target their community in a manner that is culturally and linguistically appropriate. Given that farmworking communities in the catchment areas of these organizations are predominantly pre-literate, from Mexico and Central America, and harbor divergent views about health and illness, there is a pressing need to develop innovative programs that cater to this diverse population.

Lastly, the farmworkers' response to a diagnosis of HIV/AIDS discussed earlier provide some insight into the challenges faced in our public health efforts. To reiterate, many farmworkers who receive a diagnosis of HIV or AIDS drop through the cracks by either returning to their country of origin, moving to an urban center, or continuing on in their migratory pattern. In the light of this finding, there is a need to develop appropriate cross-border information exchange systems and interstate record transfer systems that can provide continuity of surveillance and treatment of the infected farmworkers.

In conclusion, there is a large potential for HIV/AIDS to devastate the farmworker family. The need for programs to counter the growing crisis among farmworkers is critical. All too often in the United States, decision-makers and others in the position to affect change fail to act until forced to do so by a problem reaching crisis proportions. If this scenario occurs in the case of HIV/AIDS among farmworker families, it may be too late for effective action.

Acknowledgments

The study was supported by a grant from the American Foundation for AIDS Research (AmFAR) to the National Commission to Prevent Infant Mortality. The contents of the manuscript are solely the responsibility of the authors and do not necessarily represent the views of the funding agency.

References

1. Schuman P, Sobel JD: Women and AIDS. *Australian New Zealand J Obst Gynec* 1993; 33(4):341-350.

2. Ickovics JR, Rodin J: Women and AIDS in the United States: epidemiology, natural history and mediating mechanisms. *Health Psych* 1992; 11(1):1-16.
3. Horton D: Considerations for a Migrant Health Information System. *Migrant Health Newsline* 1989; 6(2):40-43.
4. National Association of Community Health Centers: *Medicaid and Migrant Farmworker Families: Analysis of Barriers and Recommendations for Change.* National Association of Community Health Centers, Washington, DC, 1991.
5. US Department of Labor: Findings from the national agricultural workers survey (NAWS), 1990: a demographic and employment profile of perishable crop farmworkers. Washington, DC: US Department of Labor, July, 1991.
6. Guendelman S, Perez-Itriago A: Double lives: the changing role of the women in seasonal migration. *Women's Studies* 1987; 13:249-271.
7. Centers for Disease Control: HIV infection, syphilis, and tuberculosis screening among migrant farmworkers--Florida, 1992. *MMWR* 1992; 41(39):723-725.
8. Centers for Disease Control: HIV seroprevalence in migrant and seasonal farmworkers--North Carolina, 1987. *MMWR* 1988; 37:517-519.
9. Schoonover Smith L: Ethnic differences in knowledge of sexually transmitted diseases in North American Black and Mexican-American migrant farmworkers. *Res Nurs Health* 1988; 11:51-58.
10. Simmons JD, Hull P, Rodgers E, Hart R: Tuberculosis control migrant study of 1988. *North Carolina Med J* 1989; 50:309-310.
11. Black SA, Markides KS: Acculturation and alcohol consumption in Puerto Rican, Cuban-American, and Mexican-American women in the United States. *Am J Public Health* 1990; 83(6):890-893.
12. Lafferty J: Self-injection and needle sharing among migrant farmworkers. *Am J Public Health* 1991; 81:221.
13. Magaña JR: Sex, drugs and HIV: an ethnographic approach. *Soc Sci Med* 1991; 33:5-9.
14. Bletzer KV: Knowledge of AIDS/HIV infection among migrant farmworkers. *AIDS & Public Policy J* 1990; 5:173-179.
15. Chin J: Epidemiology: current and future dimensions of the HIV/AIDS pandemic in women and children. *Lancet* 1990; 336:221-224.
16. Working Group on HIV Testing of Pregnant Women and Newborns. HIV infection, pregnant women, and newborns: a policy proposal for information and testing. *JAMA* 1990; 264:2416-2420.
17. Wilk V: *The Occupational Health of Migrant and Seasonal Farmworkers in the United States: Progress Report.* Farmworker Justice Fund, Inc. (Washington, DC), 1988.
18. de Bruyen M: Women & AIDS in developing countries. *Soc Sci Med* 1992; 34(3):249-262.
19. Sakala C: Migrant and seasonal farmworkers in the United States: a review of health hazards, status, and policy. *Int Migration Rev* 1987; 21(3):659-687.

3

Perspectives on HIV/AIDS Prevention Among Immigrants on the U.S.-Mexico Border

Mario Bronfman and Sergio López Moreno

Introduction

Ten years after the appearance of the Acquired Immune Deficiency Syndrome (AIDS), there is no doubt that we are dealing with one of the most extended pandemics of the present century. The World Health Organization (WHO) has reported cases in all regions of the world, in every age group, in all social classes and in every life-style. Things being this way, everything seems to indicate that, while no universal mechanisms for its prevention exist, we should use all the knowledge, imagination and creativity a human being is capable of to develop ways to stop the spread of this illness. A study of the sexual relations, life conditions and the social environment can allow, without doubt, the rapid achievement of the desired control of the pandemic.

In Mexico's case, for many reasons, it is of fundamental importance to reinforce this type of research among the population migrating to the United States. First, this phenomenon is of considerable magnitude and complexity. Second, Mexican migrants transit from areas with relatively lower rates of HIV/AIDS infection to areas with higher rates of infection. Third, Mexico does not have enough information, based on reliable research, on the sexuality of its population and, in the case of migrants, there is no information at all. These characteristics make it necessary to analyze the relationship between migration and the risk of HIV infection from a different perspective, one which evaluates the potential impact of migration among migrants and the residents of both the places of origin and destination.

Mexican Labor Force Migration to the United States

Even though the migrating flow from Mexico to the U.S. has been significant since the end of the last century, the characteristics of this phenomenon has been gradually modified. New regions of origin and destination are added, while the old regions move to a second level. Over time, the qualifications of migrant workers have improved, and women are now included in the migratory patterns. In addition, the labor insertions occur in sectors of the economy different from the traditional sectors and displacement of workers has increased. The continuous migration of Mexicans to the U.S. fundamentally responds to the demands of certain sectors of the economy, sectors where jobs are rejected by the local residents due to both low wages and greater on-the-job physical demands.

The majority of the migrant workers are from rural areas in Mexico. Many have lower levels of education, are pre-literate, and with practically no knowledge of the English language [1]. Furthermore, very few have the necessary documentation that permits them to work abroad, making them "illegal" or "undocumented" persons in the U.S. The great majority of these migrants stay only temporarily in the U.S. because they are deported or expelled, because they finish their work, or because they return home to spend some time every year in their place of origin.

The predominant demographic profile of the migrating flow is that of young men who travel alone. Of the total migrating flow, 89.1 percent are male; 84.3 percent are between 15 and 34 years of age, with an average age of 26.2 years [1]. In addition, 58.3 percent are single and of those who are married, the majority travel without their wives.

Migration and HIV/AIDS

From the point of view of risk of infection with HIV, it is noteworthy that the demographic profile (in terms of age and sex) of the migrating flow is very similar to that of the AIDS cases registered in Mexico[1] [2]. Although this coincidence does not by itself prove a causal relationship between the two phenomena, other characteristics among the migrants can be linked to the risk of HIV infection. These characteristics include the facts that the majority of migrants are in an age group with the highest levels of sexual activity and that more than one-half are single. Furthermore, the migrants transit to a society with more "open" sexual customs than their own. In addition, the migrants have lower receptiveness to the HIV prevention campaigns due to their living conditions, low educational levels and their lack of knowledge of English. Based on these characteristics, one can infer that this group will very probably maintain risk practices.[2]

The destinations in the U.S. of the migrating flow have a higher rate of HIV/AIDS incidence than the places of the migrants' origin. By January 1993, WHO registered a rate of 990 cases per million in the U.S.; while in Mexico, the rate was 136 [3]. Within the U.S., the most affected states are New York, California, Florida, Texas, New Jersey and Illinois [4]. Within these states, the concentration of Mexican migrants is 72.2 percent [5]. Furthermore, approximately 30 percent of the AIDS cases in the U.S. are located in the southern states [4], the main areas with Mexican migrant populations.

As for the regions in Mexico contributing to the migrating flow, in 1984, 75 percent of the migrants originated from Chihuahua, Michoacán, Baja California, Jalisco, Guanajuato, Zacataecas, Durango and San Luis Potosi [6]. In 1992, one-half of the AIDS cases in Mexico were identified in regions that exported 75 percent of the total migrating flow but were home to only 35 percent of the national population [2]. Furthermore, 10 percent of the AIDS cases in Mexico had resided in the U.S., and their demographic profile was very similar to that considered as typical among the AIDS cases in North America.

These data support the hypothesis of the relationship between migration and the risk of getting AIDS. To explain this relationship, it is necessary to understand the different processes through which migration affects the risk practices of a social group, specifically their sexual habits, as sexual contacts constitute the most important way of getting infected with HIV.

Methods

An outside observer enjoys the privileges and inconveniences of distance. By not being involved directly in the events under study, the researcher can have a wider perspective and appreciate a complete panorama, although not in great depth and vividness. On the other hand, a researcher with close contact with the events under study (although he remains at the margin) can produce particularly rich observations of events. The research described below is of the later type.

This chapter is based on an ethnographic study among migrant workers and their families residing in two towns, one in Mexico and the other in North America [7]. The Mexican town of Gomez Farias was the point of origin and the North American town of Watsonville was the point of destination. The study examines in-depth the information on the dynamic changes in the sexuality of the migrant population, the characteristics of the migration context, and the relationship between the two. In addition, the study examines migrant sexuality, linking it to the characteristics of transmission of HIV and the possibilities for prevention. The study was conducted by researchers of the "El Colegio de Mexico."

The technique chosen to gather information was a detailed interview conducted with "common" and "key" informants. A guide was developed to conduct the interviews and it also specified the topics to be covered. The information gathered was processed using the computer package *Ethnograph*. This paper summarizes the research.

Description of the Participants

Gomez Farias and Watsonville Population. The state of Michoacan has one of the highest rates of migration in Mexico. Participants for interviews in the population of origin were selected from Gomez Farias, a town in Michoacan with 3,000 inhabitants. On average, two men from each family in Gomez Farias are part of the migrant labor force. In this migrating population, 62 percent of the heads of households do not own any land and work on a remunerative basis. Most of them are between 17 and 41 years of age and have no possibilities of obtaining land.

In Gomez Farias, 75 percent of the economically active population work in the primary sector, and 9.4 percent and 12.1 percent in the secondary and tertiary sectors of the economy, respectively. In 1990, 96.6 percent of the households had running water, 94.7 percent had electricity and 87.9 percent had sewage systems. The town has one preschool, two elementary schools and the junior high school courses are broadcast over the television, all a part of the federal government programs. The majority of the population is Catholic. There is no national newspaper in the town. The public health system is integrated with a Rural Medical Unit, run by a doctor and two nursing aids, and a mobile unit donated by the migrants to the U.S. There are two doctors who practice private medicine and two drugstores. The majority of the migratory labor force from Gomez Farias returns home, although an increasing number of families is staying back in the U.S. The majority of the people migrating from Gomez Farias (three out of every four) goes to Watsonville (the point of destination) [7].

Watsonville is located in Santa Cruz County (California, USA) and has a population of 30,000 [8]. The economy of Watsonville has always been linked to agriculture and agro-business. More recently, some high technology industries and a naval spare parts factory have moved into Watsonville. The service sector of the economy also provides an important source of employment. About 60 percent of the population in Watsonville is "Hispanic," with the majority being of Mexican origin.

In terms of HIV/AIDS, 80 percent of the HIV seropositive persons in Watsonville are either homosexual or bisexual men. In 1991, only six female cases had been reported. However, there appears to be a rapid increase in HIV infectivity among heterosexual women as indicated by the increase in the rates of infection among newborns [8].

The Migrant and Non-migrant Study Sample. The data presented here are based on interviews with 60 common informants and 20 key informants. These interviews were conducted at both the points of origin (Gomez Farias) and destination (Watsonville) of the migrant population. In Gomez Farias, we interviewed 33 common informants, 13 men and 20 women. Of the 13 men interviewed, seven lived permanently in Gomez Farias; and six were part of the migrant labor force and were temporarily in Mexico. Of the 20 women interviewed, 13 had never migrated whereas the remaining seven were part of the migrant labor force. In Watsonville, we interviewed 27 common informants, 18 men and 9 women, all of whom were part of the migrating labor force. The interviews focused on six main topics: sexual habits, use of condoms, knowledge about HIV/AIDS, risk practices, credibility of the information received, and impact of migration on all these aspects.

Based on the relative distribution of the risk for HIV among people with different sexual preferences, we selected the informants to reflect a diversity of sexual preferences. Among the 24 migrating men interviewed at the two sites, 16 were heterosexuals, three were bisexuals and five were men who had sex only with other men. All the 29 women interviewed were heterosexual. Since research indicates that the risk of infection through lesbian contact is practically non-existent, no lesbian women were recruited for the study.

The results were categorized and analyzed in four groups based on the sex and migrating experience of the sample. The four groups comprised of migrating men, migrating women, non-migrating men and non-migrating women.

The 20 key informants interviewed consisted of five from Gomez Farias and 15 from Watsonville. The five key informants from Gomez Farias included two nurses, two medical doctors, and a sex worker. The 15 key informants from Watsonville included social scientists (n = 4), self-identified heterosexual migrant workers (n = 3), self-identified Latino or non-Latino gay men (n = 3) and sex workers (n = 2). The three remaining key informants included a medical doctor, a health worker, and a priest. The focus of the interviews with the key informants was similar to that of the common informants. The information obtained from them was categorized into two groups: according to their position as *observers* (that is, the health personnel and social scientists) or *participants* (that is, sex workers and men who had with other men) in activities directly related with the sexual habits of the community.

Results

In this section, we present information collected from the key and common informants. The key informants provide a panoramic view and general information about the issues under study. These issues include how the migrants and non-migrants conceive of and live their sexuality, habits and practices, disposition to take preventive measures such as using condoms during sexual intercourse, knowledge about AIDS, and the credibility of the sources of information. The real panorama, however, contains multiple and varied specific experiences. The interviews with common informants provide a more complete picture of the way in which they perceive and interpret their reality, thus getting closer to the phenomenon from the new perspective of the actors. We first present information collected from the key informants, followed by a reconstruction of the experiences of the common informants.

Migration Characteristics

The migration from Gomez Farias to Watsonville follows different models. Some men either travel alone or travel in groups of men. More frequently migrants travel with their wives and children or parents and brothers. Some of the migrants interviewed were visiting the U.S. for the first time, while others reported multiple visits. The purpose of the migrants' travel also differed. For some, the travel was to earn and save money for a home or to establish a business. Some others traveled to Mexico during vacations so as not to interrupt their children's school in the U.S. The majority of the migrants earned all their income in the U.S. and returned to Mexico for their holidays.

The migration of women is a recent phenomenon. Women who were interviewed had a pattern that differed from that seen among the men. The women never traveled alone or as a personal option. All of them traveled with their husbands or, prior to their marriage, with their parents. Furthermore, among the women interviewed, there was no expectancy of independence. Neither adventure nor experience were reasons given by women for their migration. All the women mentioned only economic reasons.

Interviews Conducted in Mexico

Sexuality of the Non-migrants. In general, the non-migrant Mexican population in Gomez Farias gave scarce and superficial information regarding sexual practices. They had little disposition to mention them and preferred to refer to them indirectly. However, all the informants agreed in mentioning the importance of the migrating phenomenon on the sexual life of the community. Regarding this impacts, it was confirmed that when it took place: "(men) who stay behind are either too young or too old, they almost do not have sexual life."

All the non-migrants interviewed agreed that their sexual practices were *normal*, that is heterosexual and vaginal. The strength with which this affirmation was repeated allows us to suppose that the population in Gomez Farias had a clear definition between what was normal or not normal in sexuality, where normal was a quality positively valued and was subject to strong social control. Some of the strong social rules included the prohibition to talk about sexuality and the confinement of sexuality to an exclusively private level. This sentiment was reflected in a typical response, "[O]ne is not aware of the sexual habits of other people, but apparently there are no deviations. It is normal..."

In the case of women, *normal* also meant to have sexual relations only with their partners, "You never hear from women sleeping around, and if it is known, they are repudiated and even expelled from town." According to the female informants, the concern of men to satisfy or give pleasure to women was practically exceptional: "when a man finishes making love, he just stands up and leaves." Sexual behavior of women was normative and social rules were accepted and rigorously obeyed.

The information obtained from men was a little more detailed, probably because the sexual practices were less restricted among them. The men also preferred the *normal* sexual act, but among them, the norm included sex with sex workers. Alcohol seemed to play an important role among the men, since men in Gomez Farias "search [for] women when they are drunk. They do not say 'let's go for whores' but rather they go for drinks and it is understood that they will look for whores. If they are not drunk, they do not go with them [sex workers]."

The use of condom was not very common. For the sex workers, in general, even when they carried condoms with them, they were hesitant to insist on the use of condoms because their clients did not approve of their use. In the particular case of the sex worker interviewed (one of the key informants), she demanded the use of a condom when she did not know the client. However, she stopped demanding the use of condom after two or three dates with the same client. According to the informant, knowing the client created an element of trust which eliminated the need to take care. This created a paradoxical situation. The perceived risk of infection was in sexual relations with strangers, and she took precautions only with them but not with frequent, stable and close clients. The latter scenario, due to the lack of preventive behavior, converted the relationship into one of high risk.

From the interviews with the female informants we can infer that the same mechanism occurred among married women. Among these women, the use of a condom was not required in everyday situations but was requested when "confidence" was lost, that is for example, when their partner goes North (to the U.S.) or when they suspected that their husbands were with other women. Once again, when the relationship at the personal level was intimate, there was a greater risk for HIV infection since the intimacy of the relationship resulted in contradictory behavior, the non-use of precautions with someone you knew well and loved.

For men, there were several factors which may have acted as barriers to the use of condoms. There was the shame felt by men in obtaining a condom. The loss of sexual sensitivity was another reason mentioned by the men. In addition, the probable association between the use of condoms and homosexual practices may have precluded their use.

In terms of sexual behaviors, homosexual and bisexual relations were rarely mentioned by the informants. Health personnel (key informants), however, indicated being aware of the existence of one homosexual case in Gomez Farias. The sex worker key informant offered more insights into these sexual behaviors. She mentioned that AIDS was a homosexual disease and because of it, she did not work with men who had homosexual practices. This belief held by the sex worker offers some insights into the definition of sexual behaviors. First, the belief indicates that the concept of homosexuality was exclusively applied to men who took a passive role in a relationship [9-11]. Second, even though bisexuality was never overtly mentioned, bisexual behavior was an available option in the sexual life of men.

With the exception of a reference made by the sex worker key informant, AIDS was not mentioned in the interviews conducted in Gomez Farias. In interviews with other key informants such as health personnel, the doctors mentioned a few cases of sexually transmitted diseases, mostly among men; however, they did not elaborate on the subject.

Sexuality of the Migrants who Returned to Gomez Farias. The general opinion of the informants in Mexico was that there were minimal or non-existent changes in the sexual habits of the population as a result of migration: "I do not believe they change their sexual habits. Those who migrate learn different positions, but this is in a low percentage." It is possible, however, that the social control did not allow the migrants to openly express changes in their sexual conduct. As a consequence, those who do not migrate could not be aware of such changes. It was also possible that the sexual practices allowed for the migrants in the U.S. were not allowed (at least not in the same way) when they were back home in Mexico. Furthermore, on their return, the migrants might also have re-established their previous lifestyle, following the same codes of conduct prior to their migration.

A high proportion of migrants consumed drugs such as marijuana, cocaine or barbiturates. The use of intravenous drugs, however, was not reported. This may be primarily due to the fear of the needle, fear of the inability to quit and the high cost of the drugs.

Interviews Conducted in the United States

Sexuality in the North. The information gathered through interviews with the informants in the U.S. was more detailed than that obtained in Mexico. The information focused more directly on HIV/AIDS and the risk practices associated with it. According to the informants, the majority of the male migrants were heterosexual who maintained their sexual relations with their partners in Mexico or with sex workers [12].

As in Mexico, the information on feminine sexuality was limited. The sexuality of women continued to be as controlled as in their place of origin in Mexico. Mexican women in the U.S. had little power of decision over sexual practices. Women had intercourse when their partner decided to be intimate and usually did not talk about sex with them. Furthermore, women were ignored, and at times, beaten when they requested the use of condoms. They had little information on contraceptive, condoms and sexuality and followed the ideas of the Catholic church on these issues. They rarely inquired about AIDS or sought medical services. The subordinate relationship with men placed them at a high risk for infection since preventive measures were out of their control. The increase in the AIDS cases observed among women, which was comparatively higher than that registered for men [13], could be a result of this subordinated, submissive role of the women.

There were some differences in the sexuality and sexual practices of migrant men. In the U.S., although the heterosexual men preferred vaginal sex, they practiced different positions for this type of sex and also practiced anal intercourse with women, the later being especially requested from sex workers. Other sexual practices requested from sex workers besides vaginal sex included oral sex, masturbation and anal sex. According to the sex workers interviewed, the first experience these men had had with anal sex was with them.

The frequency of condom use was higher among those men who had spent more time in the U.S. According to the sex workers, Mexican men changed their customs in the U.S. as sex workers usually demanded the use of condoms. Other informants, however, reported that the majority of migrants did not use condoms in part because they were not used to them.

The use of drugs seems to be gaining importance among the migrants. Some of them began using and dealing in drugs as early as the age of 12. In Watsonville, it was easy to get into the business and the use of drugs since the town was an open door for the transit of drugs from the South to the North of the country.

The migrants received HIV/AIDS information from a multitude of sources including Spanish language television, radio and personal contacts. In terms of the credibility of the sources, the migrants believed that the most reliable sources were those who were seropositive, and the sick and their families. These sources of information were frequently shown on the television and were most credible since the infected persons and their families described their own experiences. Similar evidence has been documented by other studies conducted among the Mexican community in the U.S. [14, 15].

In terms of homosexuality, two beliefs were detected among the migrant men with respect to men who had sexual relations with other men. The first belief considered as a homosexual any man involved in sexual relations with another man, a belief in agreement with the conceptualization of homosexuality in the U.S. The second belief considered a man who has sexual relations with another man a heterosexual provided the latter was the one who was the penetrator, a belief similar to that seen among the residents of Gomez Farias [9, 10, 16].

Due to these beliefs about homosexuality, bisexual men who considered themselves as heterosexuals sometimes practiced anal intercourse and played the active role. In the work fields, for example, sex with passive homosexuals occurred frequently. Besides anal intercourse, oral sex was also commonly practiced. Bisexual men who considered themselves as heterosexuals generally received oral sex from their partners but, when the roles were reversed, they never received semen in their mouth. Mexicans preferred this division of roles since it defined their sexual preferences. North Americans who considered themselves homosexuals, on the other hand, usually alternated the active and passive roles with their partners. In addition, even if the North American homosexuals had a role preference, they could eventually assume the alternate position. It is clear that among the majority of migrants there was no social stigma for the one playing the insertive role [9], because penetration (in men or women) was seen as a source of masculine attributes, including virility [10].

According to some informants, homosexual practices were intimately linked to alcohol consumption, due in part to the belief that what happened under the influence of alcohol did not count. Alcohol facilitated the homosexual contacts. Alcohol consumption constituted another effective mechanism to protect masculinity and reinforced the separation of roles. An informant offered a hypothesis that, under the influence of alcohol, even the passive role was accepted. Not all those who were interviewed agreed with this theory which related homosexuality to alcohol consumption. Some of those interviewed considered alcohol consumption and homosexuality to be independent acts and that the relationship between them could not be generalized.

Some of the informants interviewed admitted to having sexual relations with other men for money. Among young male migrants there appeared to be the occurrence of traditional commercial sex. These young migrant males offered their services (generally as passive partners) to older men. These commercial sex practices occurred when the young male migrants were unemployed or needed money. This practice placed them in the group with high risk practices.

The informants' interviews suggested that homosexuals used condoms sparingly. The main reasons offered for not using condoms were: a lack of knowledge on how to use them; shame involved in purchasing them; the supposed loss of sensation; the belief that they had no risk when they assumed the active role; and a certain ideology that risk and/or "putting your life on the line" strengthened the masculine image. Many of these reasons were similar to those expressed by the heterosexuals. Unfortunately, only some of these misconceptions about condom use can be eradicated with information campaigns since most of these reasons had their origins in the ignorance of the subject. Other reasons and misconceptions for not using a condom had their basis in cultural norms which were deeply rooted in the population and, consequently, their modification would be extremely difficult and complex.

From the interviews with the U.S. informants, it can be concluded that migration has both a negative and positive effect in terms of HIV risk. On the negative side, migration may increase the risk for HIV infection because of factors such as higher prevalence of sex with sex workers, learning about and adoption of higher risk sexual practices (i.e., anal sex), and increased sex among men either due to more tolerance of these practices or the lack of women. On the positive side, migration may reduce the risk of HIV infection due to factors such as an increase in knowledge about HIV and an apparent increase in the use of condoms.

Comparing the positive and negative effects of migration on HIV infection, it is evident that migration resulted in a higher likelihood of acquiring risk practices for HIV infection than of acquiring practices that may prevent or reduce the risk. The characteristics of risk practices, as previously described, are complex and difficult to modify.

Reconstruction of the Experiences

As mentioned earlier, interviews with the key informants provided a general overview of the issues under study. The real panorama, however, contains multiple and varied specific experiences. We now attempt to provide, after reconstruction of the interviews with the common informants, a closer vision of how the common informants perceive and interpret their reality, thus getting closer to the phenomenon from the perspective of the actor.

Initiation of Sexuality Among Migrants and Non-migrants

In general terms, the common informants (men and women, migrants and non-migrants) had an early initiation to sexual activity. The majority of the common informants started sexual activity in their adolescent years, when they were between 13 and 18 years of age. Migration did not affect the characteristics of this first experience since the majority of the informants had their first sexual experience in Mexico. An analysis of the initiation of sexual activity by sex revealed marked differences, especially in the case of the sexual preferences of men.

Heterosexual and bisexual men recalled their initiation of sexual activity as the time when they experienced intercourse with a woman. Many also mentioned previous experiences with female animals such as calves and donkeys. Masturbation and erotic games were practically omitted from their recollections, suggesting that for these men the initiation of sexual activity implied, in some way, the act of penetration. Among the heterosexual and bisexual men, the first sexual experience was frequently with a sex worker, but it could have also been with cousins, friends, or older women. Almost all the heterosexual and bisexual men found their initiation to sexual activity to be agreeable.

The majority of men who had had sex with other men had their first sexual intercourse when they were penetrated by another man. Of the five men who had had sex with other men interviewed, two related their first experience as violations by older family members which occurred at an early age (when they were 8 and 12 years old, respectively). For two others, their sexual initiation was not violent although only one described it as pleasant. The first man interviewed indicated that his sexual initiation was a heterosexual experience that was not satisfactory. The correlation between sexual preference and the partner of the first sexual experience (even though the partner may not have been chosen voluntarily) is very interesting and allows us to hypothesize that, in this context, the first relation has an influence over the choice of erotic interest.

Women provided a consistent response as to the partner with whom they had initiated their sexual activity. For the majority of women, the partner with whom they initiated sexual activity was their husband. For a few of the women, the partner was a boyfriend and for, two of the women interviewed, the partner was a person with whom they had no affective relationship--one of these women was the victim of rape. None of the women mentioned experiences with other women or with animals.

The women expressed divergent experiences of their sexual initiation. Some expressed that they were pleasant and satisfactory. Among these women, the majority indicated that emotional reasons were the principal source of their satisfaction, "It was very pleasant for me because I am very much in love with my husband." Besides an expression of satisfaction, almost all these women mentioned a feeling of embarrassment. These two emotions of satisfaction and embarrassment combined produced opposite sensations, "I felt fine except for a little shame." For an important proportion of women, their initiation to sex was an unpleasant experience due to the pain, violence, discomfort, lack of information and the negative consequences of the intercourse such as a vaginal infection (experienced by one informant): "Well, I didn't like it because it was very painful, [and] that is why I did not like it."

Present Sexual Practices

In the case of present practices, migration along with gender plays a preponderant role on the conformation of the experiences. There are interesting differences between men and women, and between migrants and non-migrants.

Present Sexual Practices Among Non-migrants. The single non-migrant men who were sexually active identified friends or sex workers as their sexual partners. The married non-migrant men indicated that they maintained a sexual relationship only with their wives although some did mention having had sex with other women. The frequency of sexual activity varied from two or three times a week among those with a steady partner to once every three months among those without a steady partner. As for the sexual positions, the majority of the men indicated that they had vaginal sex in the *missionary* position (the man on top and the woman underneath). A few men described variations in their sexual positions but these always included vaginal penetration. Some men expressed their dislike of variations in positions because, according to them, the practice was abnormal, "...I believe that changing positions is as if we were some kind of little animals playing around, and that makes me feel dirty."

There was total rejection of oral sex and anal intercourse among the non-migrants. These practices were rejected based on certain widely believed prejudices. According to these prejudices, indulging in these practices brought about diseases. As one non-migrant observed, "I do not think it is correct to put it inside the mouth; that is something I believe causes some kind of diseases." This sentiment was echoed by another non-migrant who stated: "There are some women (sex workers) who like to be fucked from the back, but I do not have that preference; you can get a disease, don't you?"

For the non-migrants, the source of information on the various sexual positions and practices was their fellow countrymen returning from the U.S. As one of the informants said, "I once saw a magazine that someone brought from the North; they also bring films, that is how I found out it can be done in other ways." Another informant indicated, "we just fool around talking among friends. Because they are involved with girls of the U.S.A, they believe they know too much." Upon their return to Mexico, the migrants share with friends changes in their sexual experiences. The non-migrants are apparently opposed to this new information. Although the only purpose of sharing is to widen the universe of possible practices, we should not rule out the possibility that the information and experiences will slowly impact the sexual practices of those who stay back in Mexico.

The non-migrants (all heterosexual) interviewed expressed a strong rejection of homosexual practices. As one non-migrant indicated, "I only like women. By no means would I fuck a *queer*!" This statement confirms the impressions of the key informants that in sexual practices among men, only one of them was considered homosexual. The *queer* was the one being penetrated; whereas, the other "who could have sex with him" was not considered homosexual. Nevertheless, the report of the first homosexual relation allows us to infer that first penetration of a man by other men was a more frequent practice than generally admitted. Second, due to the social stigma encountered by the man accepting that he was once penetrated, we cannot disregard that, in the relations described where a man penetrates another man (who is *homosexual*, the *queer*), the roles are never reversed.

Interviews with non-migrant women shed some light on their current sexual practices. Based on the interviews, it was clear that there was a complete disregard among men of the perspectives of the women. Sexual acts were something that men did to women, not with them.

There was no dialogue between men and women regarding sexual practices; and consequently, it was difficult to imagine the adoption of preventive measures by women with their partners.

The lack of importance given to the pleasure of women was reiterated during many interviews. One of the informants mentioned, for example, "It has been a long time since I do not use other woman than my own." The symptomatic word is *used*. Some of those interviewed condemned this attitude expressed by others and spoke of themselves as an exception, "The majority still say *women are for that*. They know that if his woman also *comes* when they have sexual relations, he feels as if she is turning into a whore and would hit her."

As expected, non-migrant women only have sexual relations with their husbands. Sexual relations usually took place in the conjugal bed and there was practically no modifications throughout their married lives. The majority of the women exclusively had vaginal sex, generally in the same position, "only through the *cola*, where the babies are born, well, where else? We only do it through there, my husband has never asked that we do it any other way." A few indicated having had anal intercourse. Oral sex evoked mistrust, especially when the women suspected or knew that their husbands had other partners. Although men practiced infidelity, infidelity by women was a crime of high importance, "Here to have sex with other people is not the custom. A husband would kill his wife if she had sex with another man."

During the interviews, the sexuality of women was expressed in passive terms. Sexual propositions by women were unthinkable. Many of the women interviewed had never had an orgasm. One woman noted, "since I got married I do not know what coming means, I just wait for my husband to finish and that is all." A second woman had similar experiences, "I have never known what coming means, I hear that men finish but I have never finished. I am ashamed to ask the doctor." The absence of sexual gratification coupled with knowing that the man was the only one who benefited by the sexual relation reinforced among women their lack of desire.

This sexual dynamic between husbands and wives is a constant source of humiliation for the women. They had no sexual desire because there was no sexual gratification. Furthermore, there was no gratification because their husbands did not sexually acknowledge them. This sexual tension between husbands and wives forces the women to turn to other women for advice, "Almost all my friends say that men just want to be satisfied, even if their wives do not come, that is why we talk about sex among us; trying to improve our sexual relations and avoid that our marriage is broken, to learn why our husbands look for other even uglier women, what they see in them or what they do that they enjoy so much."

Present Sexual Practices Among Migrants. Similar to their non-migrant countrymen, almost all the heterosexual migrants stated a remarkable preference for vaginal sex in the *normal* position. Several of the migrant men had never experienced different sexual practices and rejected anything different, "As it should be, the way you should fuck a woman, she is underneath and you on top. Always the same" or "only the natural, the others who do it are maniacs."

It cannot, however, be denied that contacts with another culture has had an impact, in varying degrees, in the modification of schemes, rules and customs. For example, the majority of the migrants interviewed agreed that, due to migration, their sexual practices had changed. A higher proportion of the migrants than the non-migrants indicated that they had had multiple sexual partners, especially with sex workers. In terms of new sexual practices, the migrants mentioned variations in sexual positions for vaginal intercourse. In addition, compared with the non-migrants, a higher proportion of migrants admitted to having oral sex and, sometimes, anal intercourse with women. These changes in sexual practices were reflected in the comments made by the interviewees. One migrant commented: "They are different here, I met *gabachas* (North American women) that enjoy to do it in different ways. In Mexico I only knew how to do it from the front and I never had oral sex with a girl, but I do it over here and I like them to do it to me." Another migrant indicated, "I learned better ways to do it: on my knees, mutual oral, she on top, standing up and sometimes anal." A third migrant reflected, "I have changed, other things are known over there, and when I come back, well, I feel free to do it with my wife."

Despite changes in sexual practices, migration does not necessarily provide a better learning or an opening for sexual opportunities. For some of the migrants, their situation of loneliness and isolation was reflected in their sexual lives, "Sex was better in Mexico because I knew the people with whom I did it with, there was a relationship between us; here sexual encounters are simply a need." Though the magnitude of the affective loneliness cannot be evaluated, it is clear that it contributed in important ways to the modification of sexual habits, although these new relations did not produce complete sexual or emotional satisfaction.

Migrants, like their non-migrants counterparts, held similar conceptions about homosexuality. For instance, bisexuals did not consider themselves as homosexuals since they did not allow penetration. For some, sex with another man was an infrequent occurrence where apparently money played an important role, "Sexual relations no, but twice a guy sucked me and gave me money. He worked with me. I do not know if I would do it again, I do not know..." For others, sex with another man was more frequent, "I haven't had sex with men, but sometimes on the beach some men have given me a blow job or masturbated me." For one of the migrants interviewed, sex with other men was a way for him to stay faithful to his wife. As one man noted:

> I cannot do strange things with my wife, she only does the regular things. She is a Protestant and I respect her, because I love her. But sometimes I would like to do things, many times I go all the way to Seaside to watch sex videos. When I go to the videos there is always someone who wants to suck you, and one gets hot, and sometimes I allow them to suck me.

Some of the homosexual migrants interviewed preferred to have a relationship with Americans. Other homosexual migrants interviewed preferred to have Mexican partners. This ethnic choice of partners was based on the belief that AIDS was exclusively a *gabacha* (from North America) disease. As one migrant indicated, "Here I have learned to take care of myself. I almost do not fuck with *gabachos*, not because I do not like them, but I am afraid that they have AIDS."

Contrary to the experiences of the migrant heterosexuals, there was more sexual activity among migrant homosexuals who had no steady partner. Furthermore, homosexuals without a steady partner had varied sexual preferences with some penetrating and others being penetrated. As indicated by some of their comments, the majority of them indulged in a variety of behaviors with their sexual partners. One man commented, "...about everything, I masturbate them, I suck them and they penetrate me, they like me to play the role of a woman." Another indicated, "well, about everything, depending on the guy, if they want to penetrate they do not allow to be penetrated; sometimes I masturbate them, some only like to fuck, some only suck." Regardless of whether or not the informants had homosexual relations in Mexico, all the homosexuals indicated that the diversity of sexual practices was learned during migration.

There were some differences in the present sexual practices of migrant women as compared with their non-migrant counterparts. Similar to the non-migrant women in Mexico, the migrant women indicated that they had sexual relations only with their husbands and preferably practiced vaginal intercourse. However, as seen among migrant men, the majority of the migrant women mentioned having learned new sexual positions. As one woman indicated, "I learned new things, to better move and different styles." Another woman echoed a similar experience, "...fried chick position, on the knees, with the tongue, these things are new here." Another very significant change, besides learning new positions, expressed by the migrant women was the consideration shown for feminine pleasure. As one migrant woman noted, "Sex is better here, because here men are sweeter and they take longer to finish." This sentiment was also expressed by another woman, "sexual relations are different here, they are more pleasant."

These new experiences of women seem to be linked to the cultural differences in sexuality between the North Americans and Mexicans. Not all the migrant women, however, had similar positive experiences through contact with the North American society. Some of them felt sexually alienated, in some ways, more so than the non-migrant women in Gomez Farias. This sense of alienation was reflected in the remarks of one migrant woman:

> Well through the *cola*, from where children are born. I do not know what oral or anal sex is, until now that I hear these words from you, if you do not explain it to me, I would never have known that a husband could do it through there. Look, when I had my first baby, I did not know through where he would come out..."

Despite the sense of sexual alienation they experienced, the migrant women, by and large, felt they had greater access to alternatives in the United States. In reference to their lack of sexual education, the informants noted, "that is why I am going to educate my children, so this will not happen to them."

A first general evaluation of this information indicates that migration brought about a richer sexual experience for both sexes. Migration, however, did not modify certain sexual practices. These practices continued to operate on an unequal frame between the sexes with strong moral imperatives and a silent dialogue regulating relationships. The new sexual experiences were integrated into the social and cultural reference frame of the migrants. This is the context within which it is necessary to evaluate the risk for HIV infection in this population.

Knowledge about AIDS, Use of Condoms, and Sources of Information

Knowledge about AIDS. The migrants and non-migrants on both sides of the border had some exposure to information regarding the disease, although there were diverse levels of assimilation among the people in Mexico and the U.S.

Different levels of knowledge about AIDS were found among the non-migrant women. The lack of information was especially noticeable among the most alienated women who had no means of communication and very few sources of information. As one of these women expressed, "I have not heard anyone say that word AIDS, not even when I go to the clinic do they talk about AIDS." The main source of information for women with some, albeit low, levels of information were their social relationships. However, these sources were not sufficiently authoritative and many doubts were raised about the information imparted by these source. As one of the women interviewed indicated, "I heard some people talking about AIDS, that is all, but I did not pay any attention because people are untruthful, that is why I do not believe them." Another woman mentioned, "My husband does not believe in the existence of that disease, he says it was invented to avoid that they have sex with other women." Furthermore, disbelief about the information on AIDS seemed to be based on the lack of concrete references related to the disease. One woman expressed, "Up to now in Gomez we have never heard of someone who has died of that disease." In addition, non-migrant women who had greater access to means of communications such as radio or television were well informed about AIDS. These women correctly mentioned the main characteristics of AIDS.

All the non-migrant men interviewed knew about AIDS and had levels of knowledge superior to that found among the non-migrant women. Some misconceptions, however, were also found among the non-migrant men. For example, some of the non-migrant believed that HIV was transmitted through clothes. Furthermore, due to the lack of sufficient knowledge, there was stigmatization of the *risk groups* (men who had sex with other men and sex workers) who were most likely to get the disease.

Migrants had greater levels of AIDS-related knowledge than the non-migrants. In addition, knowledge about AIDS among migrant women seemed to be slightly more precise. All the migrant women interviewed mentioned at least two mechanisms of transmission and referred to the use of condoms during sexual contact as a preventive measure.

Among the migrant women, with the exception of one woman, all added "watch out with who you have sex." Compared to the non-migrants, the migrants did not express any prejudice or stigmatization against the *risk groups*.

Use of Condoms. Among the migrants and non-migrants, the levels of condom use was much below that considered as an effective preventive practice. Among the non-migrant men interviewed only two had used condoms regularly--one as a birth control method and the other as a precaution against disease. The remaining men used a condom only occasionally or not at all. Those who did not use a condom during sex argued that its use was uncomfortable and that there was no need to use it since they had sex only with their wives or, in some instances, with women they knew and considered them without risk. As one non-migrant man indicated, "No, I never use condoms. Well, because I only have safe relations and I do it with women I know well and I do not sleep around with many. Besides, doing it with a condom is more difficult than doing it naturally."

The testimonies of the non-migrant women agreed with and provided a counterpoint to those provided by the non-migrant men. The majority of the non-migrant women did not use a condom during sex and the main reason given was the refusal of use by their husbands. Almost all the women interviewed were afraid of their husbands' reaction if they requesting the use of a condom during sex. These reactions ranged from a threat of seeing other women to abandoning them (i.e., their wives). Other reasons provided by the non-migrant women for them not using condoms were more mechanical in nature. For example, some women mentioned the difficulty in putting on a condom, and the lack of knowledge on how to use it, "he says it can be left inside me." Another woman mentioned that since the couple shared a room with other adults, she and her husband did not want to make a noise.

Among the migrant men and women, there was a total disagreement between knowledge about condom use and the practice of use. In the case of the women, even though 15 of the 16 women interviewed identified the use of condoms during sexual relations as a preventive measure against AIDS, none of them used a condom on a regular basis. As observed among the non-migrant women, a high percentage did not use a condom because of the refusal of their husbands, "the boss does not like it" or because they trusted him, "we talk about the AIDS problem and he tells me he does not sleep with other women. I could ask him to use it, but I believe there is no need to ask, because we trust each other."

The reasons for the use of condoms were not associated with the risk of infection with HIV. The efforts of the information campaigns to associate condoms with the prevention of AIDS have not replaced the age old message of the condom as a contraceptive.

It was difficult to find a consistent response about condom use among the men who had sex with other men. Some of those interviewed mentioned using a condom at all times. For instance, one of them mentioned, "I like to take care of myself, I do not allow them to penetrate me if they do not have a condom. They get pissed, but I tell them that if they do not use a condom, they will have nothing." Another man said, "Generally yes (use them), even though I do not like them. It took me a lot to get used to them, but I believe it is the best protection against the disease at the moment."

The reasons given by the homosexuals for not using a condom varied. Some of these reasons included a lack of sensitivity and the discomfort of the partner, "I almost never use them. I do not like to, you do not feel the same. With my friends, with the other gays who know me, they say I should use a condom, but the majority of my friends (sexual partners) dislike it. It is very difficult that a farmer use it." Other reasons given were associated with perceptions of what is a risk practice. Among the migrant homosexuals, anal intercourse but not oral sex was recognized as a risk practice and, consequently, a condom was used (if at all) only during anal intercourse.

The majority of the heterosexual men did not use a condom during sexual relations. Some of the reasons given by them included the loss of sensitivity, the discomfort caused due to the use, having sexual relations with only their wives or with partners they knew, or simply not thinking about using a condom, "I have never used them, and I do not know why." However, despite the lack of condom use by the majority of migrant men, the number of migrant men who are using a condom is increasing. Some of the migrant men indicated that they used a condom as a preventive measure. We feel that migration appears to have a positive effect on the use of condoms.

Credibility of the Information. Both the groups interviewed, the migrants and non-migrants, mentioned that the television was the most credible source of information. Furthermore, they gave special consideration to programs which provided live interviews on various topics, including AIDS. The fact that sick people were actually *seen* gave the television and these programs the credibility. As one of the person's interviewed indicated, "I believe in television that presents real cases of persons with the disease." Another person mentioned, "Well, the television transmits programs and very important news and, there you are, actually seeing what is happening; on the radio, you just listen without seeing. One has to see to believe things."

The non-migrants expressed diverse views about the credibility of information source. Non-migrant women, especially those who did not possess a television or those who did not watch it, indicated that they did not believe in anyone. This meant that besides the means of mass communications, there were no other reliable sources of information for these women. Non-migrant men, on the other hand, trusted doctors because, "they are the ones that make the television programs." Priests, however, have low credibility with respect to information on sexuality because, "what can they know?"

Social sources of information seemed to be sufficient to transmit general knowledge to the population. The great majority of the migrants and non-migrants received some information about the disease through these social sources. The information provided by the social source, however, was not sufficient to modify risk practices. For instance, the use of condom had not been generalized and the majority of those interviewed did not consider themselves at risk of contracting the disease.

Discussion

Data collected through interviews with the key and common informants in Gomez Farias, on the Mexican side, allow us to appreciate the challenges faced in AIDS prevention. The most important obstacle in the design of AIDS prevention campaigns, especially those emphasizing the use of condoms, is the place that sexuality holds in terms of social relations among the inhabitants of Gomez Farias. The taboos around sexuality, the confinement of sexuality to an exclusively private matter, the lack of communication between the sexes and their differences in the exercise of power regarding sexuality are major obstacles in the modification of risk practices. It is difficult to imagine an effective information campaign which is capable of establishing communication with the target population, having an effect on their behavior and, at the same time, not being offensive or imposing to their conception of sexuality.

The results of this study are not very different from those observed by others. A study conducted by the *Consejo Nacional Para la Prevención y Control del SIDA (CONASIDA)* concluded:

It has been reiterated that in the absence of drugs or effective vaccines, the only resource we have at hand is education. This concept has created, due to its repetition, the illusion that information is sufficient to modify the conduct of people. Experience, although in certain aspects encouraging, does not seem to support it overwhelmingly. ... Spreading information on AIDS is necessary, but not enough, because myths, fears and discrimination must be combated. A constant and repetitive presence of clear and explicit educational messages on all media is required, with the purpose of not allowing the existence of this disease to be forgotten, thus, putting down our defenses. Other more specific and delimited strategies are also required for certain groups and sectors, as these have demonstrated more efficiency in promoting the passage from knowledge to changes in behavior [17].

Implications and Recommendations

Results from this study constitute the first approach to the information needed in the design of specific educational strategies for migrants. Massive campaigns cannot carry specific messages to certain groups in the population. Consequently, in practice it is necessary to implement special programs which satisfy the migrants' unique needs. The findings from this study provide insights into the details of campaigns for migrants in terms of their implementation, audience specificity and message contents.

In terms of the implementation of campaigns, television and radio meet the prerequisites necessary for general information, offering a real referent to the illness through personal testimonies of infected individuals. Due to its ability to portray realistic experiences of infected people and their families, television continues to be an important medium with major credibility.

Other modes of implementation include magazines and pornographic videos, sources of information about sexuality commonly relied upon by men. Magazines and pornographic videos have been labeled consistently as the place where there is discovery of new practices and generation of intense interchange of information. These media could include information regarding risk prevention using the same images as the original material. In this way, at the time that migrants learn new sexual options, they will also learn to prevent contagious risk. Furthermore, condom use would be integrated as a natural topic of dialogue with friends. This idea would be a challenge to implement but could affect actual human behavior.

A mode of implementation that is more on the traditional side would be to include AIDS within the realm of difficulties to be solved by migrants. A strategy would be the regional and local creation of Mexican homes where the migrants (men and women) could meet together without the risk of being turned down or persecuted. These homes could be located in an area with a high density of migrants. To encourage participation in such meetings, these homes should offer general problem-solving information in the areas of banking, legal counseling, job listing, shopping, as well as AIDS. Whatever the composition, this AIDS information should be added to the efforts that are being conducted by diverse groups, especially the non-governmental organizations (NGOs), and benefit from their existing resources. The specific campaigns, in addition to being implemented in places where migrants live such as work camps, should find other optimal places for the transmission of information for this population.

The message content of the educational campaigns needs special considerations. For the development of a campaign specifically addressing the migrant population, by virtue of their low levels of sex education, the messages should be much more explicit from those developed for other populations. It is not sufficient merely to recommend condom use as the method to prevent sexually transmitted disease; it is also necessary to explain how to use it, where to obtain it, the functions of lubricants, etc. Likewise, the expression "sexual relation" possibly evokes only vaginal coitus; it should be defined in the message to include other risky practices such as oral and anal sex.

Another aspect of which the message content that needs special attention is the differentiation between the seropositive and the ill. It is imperative to emphasize that the lack of external symptoms is not a necessary condition to distinguish a healthy person from one who is infected with HIV.

The study findings also suggest that there are certain messages which should be exclusively for each gender, and there should also be distinctions according to age. In the case of men, their is the potential that a man may have sex with another man. Therefore, circumstances demand that information be given to all the populations, irrespective of their sexual orientation, since it is difficult to specify the population of "bisexuals." The message should contain information on prevention and high risk behaviors. In the case of women, it would be important that messages detach condoms from the lack of trust in the couple, with the end result that its use is not interpreted as evidence of infidelity, nor that it means a contradiction with feelings of affection and love.

Furthermore, there should be an identification, for each group, of spokespersons who could facilitate and legitimize the dialogue about the use of condoms and the risk of AIDS. Of those, the ones that stand out are the teacher for the under-aged, the leader in teens' groups, the priest in the religious. All of these potential spokespersons should be furnished with relevant AIDS prevention information to make them more effective. These trusted spokespersons could be invaluable for the improvement in the results of AIDS prevention campaigns.

Any health campaign directed at migrant workers should disassociate AIDS from groups with high risk behaviors such as sex workers and men who have sex with other men. The message should also disassociate AIDS from the condition of being "from the United States" or being a *gringo*; instead emphasizing that we are all susceptible to illness. The main intent is to convey that each person has the possibility and obligation of self-care, thus combating the idea that infection is associated only with certain groups or is out of the individual's control.

The implications and recommendations that have been presented are valid with and generalizable to similar situations to the ones that are described here: Migration from rural condition to areas where employment in agriculture is near small cities which offer resources and urban benefits. We cannot generalize to different contexts, although there is the possibility of generating hypotheses that can be tested in other contexts.

This study constitutes an initial approach to AIDS educational campaign. The development of new projects with the application of new techniques would enhance, without doubt, our understanding of the relationship between sexuality, immigration, and risk of getting AIDS. To count with quantitative data about the magnitude of the identified tendencies could provide us with elements, including, to redefine the problem more precisely. It is important that these new programs include rigorous research so that we can better define and understand the AIDS problems. Every health prevention methodology should be paired with a complementary method of investigation.

An initial application of the results from this study was the production of a Mexican television program thanks, to the combined efforts of CONASIDA and the private enterprise, Television International Syndicators, Inc. The format chosen was a soap opera because it allowed the information to be presented in a colloquial and socially accepted way. The soap opera was called *La vida de todos los dias o Si fueramos angeles* (The every day life or If we were angels) and was shown in more than 40 cities in the United States with a high concentration of migrants and in more than 90 cities in Mexico with a high number of migrating people. The estimated audience was more than the six million television viewers. The number of calls to Spanish AIDS hotlines increased, and the Mexican consulates in the U.S. reported that viewers were very interested in the program and suggested that it should be replicated and more widely disseminated.

The program described here is only one example of how information about sexual behaviors could be utilized to design specific information campaigns for different social groups. The development of more thorough educational campaigns would require the work of interdisciplinary groups, where professionals, migrants and patients collaborate in the achievement of an effective educational campaign.

Much has been accomplished with the prevention of AIDS campaigns but there is still more to be done. The AIDS problem is composed of an interwoven web of specific problems that each population subgroup has to address. This suggests the necessity of designing specific campaigns for each population subgroup that recognizes the particular dynamic of their problem with AIDS. The implications and recommendations discussed above address specific aspects of prevention campaigns. It would be naive to assume that a campaign of information dissemination alone will impact all groups in all their behaviors.

In conclusion, our work has confirmed the relationship between migration and AIDS as a priority for both countries, Mexico and the United States. The information presented should be used and revisited in future actions. Migrants constitute a population exposed to many dangers: illegality, insecurity, eradication, racism, and now, AIDS. Unlike the other dangers, AIDS has the advantage that perhaps it could be prevented. It is necessary to guide all our efforts and offer the necessary elements for that opportunity not to be wasted.

Notes

1. Unless noted to the contrary, all data on AIDS in Mexico referenced in this chapter reflect the situation of the suffering in the country until May 31, 1992, a date coinciding with the end of field work reported in the chapter.

2. *Risk practices* is the term used to describe activities and practices which increase the possibilities of contracting an illness. These include, some sexual practices like anal or vaginal intercourse with multiple sexual partners without using a condom, or the sharing of needles for intravenous drug use.

References

1. National Information Center and Job Statistics (Centro Nacional de Información y Estadísticas de Trabajo (CENIET)): *Encuesta Nacional de Emigración a la Frontera Norte del País y a los Estados Unidos.* Mexico, 1979.
2. Consejo Nacional Para la Prevención y Control del SIDA (CONASIDA): *Monthly Bulletin SIDA/ETS.* CONASIDA, Mexico 6(6):June, 1992.
3. World Health Organization: *Weekly Epidemiological Record.* World Health Organization, Geneva 68(3): January 15, 1993.
4. Centers for Disease Control: *HIV/AIDS Surveillance Report (July 1990-June 1992).* Centers for Disease Control July, 1992.
5. Warren R, Passel J: A count of the uncountable: estimates of undocumented aliens counted in the 1980 U.S. census. *Demography* 1987; 24(3).
6. Consejo Nacional de Población (CoNAPo): *Survey in the North Border with Undocumented Workers Deported by the United States Authorities (ETIDEU).* Consejo Nacional de Población (CoNAPo), 1984.
7. Bronfman M, Minello N: *Sexual Habits of Temporary Mexican Migrants to the U.S.A: Risk Practices for HIV Infection.* Centro de Estudios Sociológicos, El Colegio de Mexico, Mexico, D.F., 1993.
8. Erwood L, Manov W: *Santa Cruz County Master Plan Needs Assessment (Final Report).* Health Service Agency, Santa Cruz, CA, 1991.
9. Carrier J: Mexican male bisexuality. *In:* Kelin and Wolf (ed): *Bisexualities: Theory and Research,* 1985.
10. Alonso A, Coreck T: Silences: "Hispanic", AIDS and sexual practices. *Differences* 1989; 1(1):101-124.
11. Magaña JR, Carrier JM: Mexican and Mexican American male sexual behavior and spread of AIDS in California. *J Sex Res* 1991; 28(3):425-441.
12. Magaña JR: Sex, drugs and HIV: an ethnographic approach. *Soc Sci Med* 1991; 32(9):1-5.
13. Valdespino J, García LM, del Rio Zolezzi S, Sepúlveda A: Mujer y SIDA: epidemiología. *In: Mujer y SIDA.* Interdisciplinary Study Program on Women. El Colegio de México, México, 1992.
14. Hu DJ, Fleming D: Communicating AIDS information to Hispanics: the importance of language and media preference. *Am J Preven Med* 1989; 5(4).
15. Marín G, Marin BV: Perceived credibility of channels and sources of AIDS information among Hispanics. *AIDS Educ Quart* 1990; 2(2).
16. Carrier JM, Magaña JR: Use of ethnosexual data on men of Mexican origin for HIV/AIDS prevention programs. *J Sex Res* 1991; 28(2), 189-202.
17. Consejo Nacional Para la Prevención y Control del SIDA (CONASIDA): *Una Responsabilidad Communitaria. Día Mundial de Lucha Contra el SIDA.* CONASIDA, Mexico, 1993.

4

Sexual History and Behavior of Mexican Migrant Workers in Orange County, California

J. Raul Magaña, Olivia de la Rocha and Jaime L. Amsel

Introduction

Epidemiologists have long been aware of the relationship between lifestyle, behavior and disease, and they have sometimes successfully exploited these relationships to the benefit of disease victims. What makes the pursuit difficult, however, is the fact that each new occurrence of a disease-behavior relationship requires many studies to uncover the opportunities for prevention and cure that deeper understanding may afford.

This chapter presents results from an ongoing investigation of the relationship between drugs, sex and the spread of HIV among female sex workers and Latino migrant workers in Orange County, California. Its primary objective is to present data from a structured interview of 54 Mexican migrant workers that illustrate the connection between sexual beliefs and behaviors and the increased risks of HIV transmission. Its secondary objective has two parts: (1) to demonstrate that differences in patient and allopathic models of disease have important implications for the successful education of patients; and (2) to again suggest that investigations of the relationship between behavior and disease have much to gain from utilization of a value-neutral ethnographic methodology and health education pedagogy in which teachers themselves become learners.

Background

In 1987, one of us [1] began an ethnographic study of the sociological relationship between two high-risk populations, intravenous drug using female sex workers and Mexican migrant workers in Orange County, California. The investigation focused on the link between heroin addiction, prostitution and the sex lives of Mexican migrant workers living apart from their families and routinely availing themselves of the services of female sex workers. The earlier work described the sex workers' lifestyles as they intersected with those of the migrant workers, but treated the lifestyles of migrant workers only incidentally. In this chapter, we balances the picture. This chapter describes the sexual beliefs and behaviors underlying the migrant workers' utilization of female sex workers and other males, and as a consequence, the mechanisms underlying their enhanced risk for HIV and other sexually transmitted disease (STD) infections. Consistent with the recommendations made by Miller, Turner and Moses [2], these studies served as pilot and baseline for a larger survey of behavior now in preparation.

Sexual Beliefs Among Mexican Males

At the time the study began, a major goal of the investigation was to design an educational intervention that would successfully communicate the relationship between sexual practice and the increased risk of exposure to HIV [3]. The ethnographic approach to the investigation was motivated by the belief that an intervention's effectiveness is directly related to the beliefs and practices of the people for whom it is intended. If it does not suggest viable alternatives to current practice or ignores medical models and beliefs, it has little hope of success. Therefore, an understanding of sexual practices and models for the etiology and cure of STDs was crucial to the design of a successful intervention for these two populations.

There is probably no culture in which a single sexual belief system applies to all individuals. However, there remains a basic set of beliefs that constitutes a theme around which individual variation occurs. We will briefly describe here the dominant belief system for Mexican males, but they are described in more detail elsewhere [4-6] and apply in large part only to recent immigrants.

As is the case in many cultures, sexual gratification plays an important role in a man's identity as a person. In Mexican culture this implies a relatively high tolerance for sex outside marriage, as well as beliefs that govern which acts, when performed, constitute "good sex," i.e., a complete sexual encounter.

Among Mexican males, and no doubt among men of other cultures as well, penetration plays a primary role in a complete sexual encounter. The acts of foreplay, while not omitted, do not in themselves constitute a completed sexual encounter, as they can elsewhere. Instead, penetration is the earmark of manly sex, and a man who experiences an ejaculation without penetration is not fulfilled.

There is little ambiguity about the role of penetration or the manliness of the act when the sexual partner is female. However, when the sexual partner is male (not necessarily that rare an event, especially when men are living away from their families), clear sex roles emerge that become essential in distinguishing homosexual from heterosexual sex.

In the Mexican belief system, behavioral expectations for sex partners who are both male are patterned after heterosexual transactions insofar as there are distinct male and female roles. The male who penetrates has assumed the male role and the male who is penetrated the female role. The male role is consistent from heterosexual to same-sex encounters. Therefore, so long as a male achieves penetration and is not himself penetrated, the gender of the partner is irrelevant.

The manliness and sexual orientation of a male is only questioned if he is penetrated. In this system, a male who is penetrated undergoes a form of social "feminization" which may or may not be accompanied by his acceptance of the role or the manifestation of so-called effeminate behaviors. Taken together, this set of beliefs leads to a definition of homosexuality that differs markedly from European-American beliefs. That is, only those males who are penetrated are, by definition, engaging in homosexual encounters; their male partners are not [1, 4, 7].

This sexual definition manifests itself in several variations, two of which are of special interest. Specifically, this study focused on sex with paid female sex workers (where it is often the case that several men share the same female partner) and sex with other males [1].

An Outbreak of Syphilis and Chancroid

Between 1981 and 1983 an outbreak of chancroid (*Haemophilus ducreyi*) that was the largest ever recorded in U.S. history occurred in Orange County [8], and a short time later (between 1983 and 1986) a sharp increase in the number of syphilis cases was also observed [9]. Both the chancroid and syphilis outbreaks were observed to effect inordinate numbers of Latino males and female sex workers, who were the second distinct group identified as victims of syphilis and chancroid. Since other investigators [10-12] had also begun to suggest that these two genital ulcerative diseases facilitate the heterosexual transmission of HIV, health workers in the county were alarmed.

To complicate matters for the worse, at least 19 confirmed cases of congenital syphilis were also observed among newborn Latino children during the same period. Therefore, it was now apparent that syphilis was going untreated to the extent that some wives and children were being infected as well. Clearly an educational intervention was called for, but without a deeper understanding of the situation, the kind of intervention that would be effective was unclear.

Methods

Setting for the Study

Like other regions of California, cultural life in Orange County was shaped over a two-hundred year period by the mingling of Asian, Mexican, European and indigenous peoples. Today the descendants of these groups remain engaged with one another and with the various economic enterprises of the county, one of which is agriculture.

Although it is unclear just how long Mexico has been an important source of labor for U.S. agriculture, the direct importation of Mexican citizens as agricultural laborers began officially in 1943 with the *bracero* program [13]. Under this program, laborers gained temporary legal residence to work in the United States for a short period of time and carried identification cards ("greencards") which confirmed their legal status. Although the program was eventually terminated, the tradition of hiring temporary residents or "sojourners" [14] who returned to Mexico after completing their seasonal work has continued. The distinction between immigrants who take up residence in the U.S. and sojourners who routinely travel back and forth is important because of the fact that sojourners usually travel without their families [14], a circumstance having important implications for the men's sex lives.

The area of Orange County in which the study took place is an unusual mixture of high-rise industrial parks, affluent suburban villages and large vacant fields dedicated to agriculture. Data for the study were collected in one of the agricultural areas on the grounds of an industrial nursery where the sojourning migrant workers reside during their time in the U.S. While they do no work for the nursery, the nursery maintains their living quarters which consist of a group of dormitories, eating facilities and a small chapel, clustered in a village-like arrangement. For some time, the nursery owners have contracted with a well-known agri-business operation in the county to house employees at this site. However, the cost of living in the dorms is borne by the individual laborers who pay a monthly rent for sleeping space. They can also opt to pay for their board, and many of them do. Although the facilities are quite old, they are clean and well-kept.

During the observation period, the daily routine of the workers began around 4:00 a.m. and lasted until the late afternoon. After work, the men tended to gather together on the grounds of the village to converse in small groups and make plans for the evening. The congregation of 200 or 300 laborers in the village center at sunset bore a strong resemblance to village life in Mexico, with the important exception that females were conspicuously absent.

Prior to the amnesty program of the 1980s, most of the men residing in the nursery dorms were reluctant to leave the compound during the evening, presumably because many were at that time undocumented, and spent weekday evenings in the dorms with 75 to 100 of their roommates. Sex played an important role in their evening diversions.

As reported elsewhere [1], it was not uncommon for female sex workers to bring their services directly to the nursery village during the evening. Sometimes they would drive a camper onto the grounds and use its facilities to provide services. At other times individual sex workers would spend the evening in the dorm itself. On these occasions a sex worker might commandeer the bed of a single migrant worker. His reward for lending his bed in this way could be that the lady might spend the remainder of the night there. The cost, of course, was that the bed had been used by everyone.

Regardless of the locale, it was also not uncommon for several men to pool their resources and share the sex worker's services. This practice, which led the migrant workers to refer to themselves as *milk brothers*, is described in greater detail elsewhere [1].

The openness of these exchanges was a consequence of the nursery's high tolerance and "look the other way" attitude toward the practice. Ostensibly, the women had no official access to the nursery's "gated" community, but they carefully monitored the paydays of the residents and when paychecks arrived, they traveled to the compound and encountered no obstacles to their entry.

At the time of the study, there was a man in one of the dorms who frequently engaged in sexual relations with the other men. He formed "relationships" with several individuals, performing small favors such as doing their laundry, in addition to having sex with them.

Study Subjects

As part of an ongoing health education program in the county and in response to the health alerts resulting from the outbreaks of syphilis and chancroid, health fairs were presented on the nursery grounds and at other sites throughout the county. The fair consisted of different card-table like stations at which fair participants could avail themselves of information about the dangers of high cholesterol, receive blood pressure checks and nutritional advice and participate in a variety of other educational activities aimed at prevention. The fair attracted considerable attention among the migrant workers. It provided a break for them, and they enjoyed receiving the variety of fair handouts such as sample glucose urine tests, condoms and other printed materials. Their attendance was encouraged by their employers who, in lieu of health insurance, were eager to head off medical problems through prevention.

The village chapel, with statuary appropriately draped, was set aside as a special STD clinic and was the only fair location at which any testing was conducted. A phlebotomist drew blood to screen for both HIV and syphilis. Follow-up HIV counseling was also included, although the tests indicated there were no positive HIV results [15].

It was at the follow-up counseling visits that volunteers for the structured interview were recruited. Each migrant worker who reported for follow-up counseling was invited to participate in the longer interview, and 54 consented. This number represented approximately 25 percent of those who were asked. The majority of those who declined said they had no time because they had to return to work. A small number reported they were too embarrassed to respond to the type of questions contained in the interview. Thus those who did participate did so because they had the time and were not embarrassed. These limitations should be born in mind when interpreting the results.

Results

The interview itself dealt with issues in four areas: The subjects' demographic background, sexual history, current sexual practice and beliefs about STDs, their etiologies, preventions and cures.

Demographic Background

Table 4.1 summarizes the demographic backgrounds of the 54 men

TABLE 4.1. Demographic Characteristics

Characteristics	n	Percent	Mean	SD	Min	Max
Age groups, yrs						
Under 20	9	17				
20-29	23	43				
30-39	10	19				
40-49	9	16				
50 and over	3	5	29.5	10.6	18	56
Years of education						
0-6	34	64				
7-12	19	36	5.7	1.9	3	12
Literacy [a]	53	98				
Marital status						
Single	28	52				
Married	26	48				
Years married						
Less than 10	10	37				
10 or more	17	63	13.4	8.4	2	30
Number of children						
1-2	9	33				
3-5	14	52				
6-10	4	15	5.9	2.4	1	10
Years in the U.S.						
1-5	42	78				
6-10	6	11				
> 10	6	11	4.9	6.5	1	30
Number of address changes in pervious year						
none	4	7				
1-2	21	39				
3-4	23	43				
> 5	6	11	2.7	1.6	0	7
Occupation						
Field hand	24	50				
Construction	8	17				
Other	16	33				

[a] The percentages denote respondents who answered "yes" to the questions.

who completed the structured interview. The group was not particularly youthful with a mean age of nearly 30 and a standard deviation just over 10 years. The youngest respondent was 18 while the oldest was 56. The largest segment was men in their twenties but a nearly equal number ranged into their thirties and forties. The educational level was generally quite low, with well over one-half having six years of education or less. The average number of years in school was just under six with a standard deviation of approximately two years. All but one respondent reported they were literate.

The interviewees were nearly evenly split in their marital status, with 48 percent reporting they were married and 52 percent reporting they were single. Among married men (n = 26), a small majority had been married 10 years or more. The average length of marriage for this group was just over 13 years. All of the married respondents had children, with the average number being about six. Just over one-half (52 percent) reported having three to five children and 15 percent reported seven to ten children.

Most of the interviewees (78 percent) had been in the U.S. for five years or less and a notable segment (43 percent) were quite mobile with three to four address changes in the previous year. Only a few (7 percent) had no address changes at all. Exactly one-half of the men were migrant workers or field hands before coming to the U.S.; 17 percent reported they had previously worked in construction and 33 percent reported other jobs.

Sexual History

The men were queried in some detail about their sexual history, and their responses are tabulated in Table 4.2. On average, the men had their first sexual encounter at about age 17 with a standard deviation of nearly two years. One respondent reported a first encounter at age 10, while the latest age reported was 22.

Every man interviewed had had contact with a female sex worker. Over the past year the number of contacts varied from a minimum of 1 to a maximum of 60. There was considerable variation in the frequency of contact as suggested by the large standard deviation, but just over one-half (52 percent) reported one to five contacts in the last year, while 29 percent reported 6 to 10 and 12 percent reported 11 to 20. Only four men reported contacts in excess of 20. Only one respondent reported regular use of condoms in these encounters. And although 48 percent reported they sometimes used a condom, fully one-half reported they never did.

TABLE 4.2: Sexual History

Characteristics	n	Percent
Age of first sexual experience [a]		
Under 15	5	9
15-16	12	23
17-18	29	55
19-22	7	13
Sexual contact with sex worker in the U.S. [b]	54	100
Frequency of contact with sex worker in the last year [c]		
1-5	27	52
6-10	15	29
11-20	6	12
Over 20	4	7
Condom Use		
Always	1	2
Sometimes	26	48
Never	27	50
Sexual contact with men [b]	12	23
Frequency of contact with other men		
None	41	76
Once	6	11
More often	6	11
Know where to get treatment for STDs [b]	35	65
Treated for STDs outside U.S. [b]	14	28
Easier to have sex in U.S. [b]	40	95

[a] Mean = 16.9, Standard Deviation = 1.9, Range = 10 to 22.

[b] The percentages denote respondents who answered "yes" to the questions.

[c] Mean = 8.8, Standard Deviation = 9.6, Range = 1 to 60.

Twelve respondents, or 23 percent, reported that they had had sexual contact with other men. About one-half of the men who responded "yes" reported having sex with another man only once, while the other one-half said they had such contact more often.

Nearly two-thirds of the men reportedly knew where to seek treatment for STDs and just over one-quarter reported they were treated for STDs prior to visiting the U.S. A large majority reported it was easier to have sex in the U.S.

Sexual Practice

The sexual behaviors reported by the interviewees are summarized in Table 4.3. The first four behaviors described refer to sexual encounters with female workers. The last item refers to sex with other men.

The first item describes the frequency with which specific sex acts are performed. The tabulated responses demonstrate the preference for penetration. No respondent reported engaging only in fellatio. All respondents reported vaginal penetration, the difference being whether or not it was only vaginal penetration (65 percent) or penetration with fellatio (35 percent). When the sex partner is female, men in this sample reported no anal penetration. Again emphasizing the importance of penetration over foreplay, very few men reported that they performed cunnilingus with the sex workers.

When asked whether, when sharing a female partner, order was important, a large majority (87 percent) responded it was not. Just over one-half the interviewees reported paying $20 or less for the sex workers' services, while the remainder paid over $20. When engaging in sex with other men, all the interviewees reported taking the active, male role. A few (n = 5) also reported receiving fellatio and being masturbated (n = 2).

Knowledge and Beliefs about HIV and Other STDs

The subjects' responses to items on knowledge and beliefs about HIV and other STDs are summarized in Table 4.4. A large majority (91 percent) reported they knew at least something about AIDS. A somewhat smaller majority (81 percent) reported they knew how AIDS is spread. Of those 44 respondents, 35 percent responded that it was spread by sexual contact, 18 percent responded it was spread by blood and 28 percent reported that AIDS was spread by homosexual contact. Most of the in-

TABLE 4.3. Sexual Behaviors

Sexual Partners	n	Percent
Female Sex Workers (n = 54)		
Type of Sex Practice		
Fellatio	--	--
Vaginal Penetration Only	35	65
Vaginal and Fellatio	19	35
Anal penetration	--	--
Perform Cunnilingus [a]	4	7
Is Order Important Among		
"Milk Brothers" [a]	7	13
Amount Paid		
$20 or less	30	56
Over $20	24	44
Other Males (n = 12)		
Type of Sex Practice		
Anal Active	12	100
Anal Passive	--	--
Fellatio (Receive)	5	9
Masturbation	2	4

[a] The percentages denote respondents who answered "yes" to the questions.

terviewees (83 percent) also reported learning about AIDS while in the U.S., and 75 percent responded that they had known about the disease for three years or more.

When asked if there was a vaccine or cure for AIDS, nearly one-half (46 percent) replied in the affirmative. A sizable majority also reported they were aware that an infected person can infect a sex partner but only 10 percent (n = 5) said they knew how children were infected. One-fifth of the men said they could tell if a sex worker injected

TABLE 4.4. Knowledge and Beliefs About HIV and Other STDs

Knowledge and Beliefs	n	Percent
Do you know anything about AIDS? [a]	49	91
Do you know how AIDS is spread? [a]	44	81
Mode of spread? [b]		
Sexual contact	19	35
Blood	10	18
Homosexual contact	15	28
Where were you when you heard about AIDS for the first time?		
USA	39	83
Mexico	8	17
How long have you known about AIDS?		
1-2 years	12	25
3-5 years	24	50
6-8 years	12	25
Is there a cure or vaccine? [a]	25	46
Are there foods that improve sex?		
Yes, seafood	25	46
No, none	29	54
Are there foods that prevent STDs?		
Yes, seafood	2	4
Yes, fruits and vegetables	2	4
No, none	50	92

[a] The percentages denote respondents who answered "yes" to the questions.

[b] The percentages denote respondents (n = 44) who answered "yes" to the question, "Do you know how AIDS is spread?"

drugs; however, a large number (83 percent) said they did not know that a person could appear healthy and still be HIV positive.

With respect to other STDs, the majority (75 percent) responded in the affirmative when asked if they knew how gonorrhea and syphilis were spread. Just a little over one-half (57 percent), however, knew that condoms can prevent their spread. A sizable majority (70 percent) also believed that STDs can be cured with lemon juice or alcohol. Almost one-half the interviewees (46 percent) also reported that some seafoods improved sex, but only a few (n = 4) responded that seafood, fruits or vegetables could prevent STDs.

Discussion

The chapter had two objectives. The first was to present ethnographic and survey data that would illustrate how sexual beliefs and practices are leading to increased risk of HIV transmission among migrant farmworkers. The second objective had two parts: first, to demonstrate that differences in patient and allopathic models of disease can have important implications for the successful education of patients; and second, to suggest the usefulness of a value-neutral ethnographic method and health education pedagogy in which the teachers themselves become learners.

The data have met the first objective, perhaps to an alarming degree. They suggest, as have the results of earlier investigations [7, 16-19], that the risk of HIV and other STD transmission is heightened by the sexual practices of the migrant workers. Not only did all of the interviewees report having contact with female sex workers, many of whom were intravenous drug users, but they also often shared the services of a single sex worker, thus enabling a new mechanism of male-to-male transmission among *milk brothers* (several males who have had intercourse with a single female [1]). The migrant workers also reported, almost to a man, that they used condoms only some of the time or not at all.

Some of the workers were also having sex with other men, although the number in this sample was relatively small. Since it was, no doubt, sometimes the same man with whom other men were having sex, the likelihood of heightened risk was again present, if the partner happened to be HIV positive.

While it continues to be important that we note the enhanced risk associated with male-to-male anal intercourse [20], it is easy to overlook a secondary consideration that emerges as a consequence of the ethnography. The definition of homosexual encounter can vary from belief system to belief system or from culture to culture. For example, Mexican men hold the belief that only the male who is penetrated is engaging in a homosexual act. Failure to take this into account can lead to the construction of educational interventions that miss the mark. If we teach that homosexual encounters are high-risk, tacitly assuming the European-American definition of homosexual encounter (any sexual act between two males), the Mexican migrant worker may easily take away from the intervention the false belief that he is safe because he himself has engaged in no homosexual acts, at least not by his definition.

A better understanding of these practices may also lead to different appraisals of the frequency of certain types of sexual activity and the consequent risk that may exist at an international level [21]. Moreover, the beliefs among Mexican men described here may also be common to other cultures [22, 23] and to other migrant labor populations in Europe and the Middle East, as well as in Latin America. Consequently, the need to design interventions that are sensitive to these sexual practices and the risks associated with them is not limited to the southwestern United States.

These data exhibit not only a difference in the definition of what constitutes a homosexual encounter, but also, perhaps more subtly, what differentiates a patient's model of a disease from the one held by physicians, other health care providers or health educators [24]. For example, 70 percent of the migrant workers reportedly believed STDs, or more specifically, the genital ulcers resulting from syphilis could be cured with lemon juice or alcohol. If we compare the patients' model to the model represented in medical descriptions of primary, secondary and tertiary syphilis, the patients' ideas about effective cures present a dangerous and erroneous view.

From the point of view of the migrant workers, however, and any number of other people we might ask, an ulcer or abrasion that responds to the application of alcohol or other acidic treatment with a stinging pain is being *cleansed*, an important precondition of healing without infection. Who of us does not think back with discomfort at the remembrance of a skinned knee and the highly predictable appearance of the school nurse's Mercurochrome bottle? These are the memories out of which such medical models are made in the minds of patients.

We might well ask, then, how does such a model persist as a disease like syphilis progresses? Why, at the emergence of a rash on the palms, do they not seek treatment? For the migrant workers there is a simple answer. Since the men work with pesticides and other noxious agents on a daily basis, rashes are a common occurrence [25, 26]. Thus there is an explanation for almost any rash that might arise, and persons who are made only mildly uncomfortable by a rash do not seek new diagnoses for something they have already explained, however incorrectly. Only education--and a special form of education at that--can be used to successfully address problems of this type.

What will be a common finding in all health-related ethnographies, what is in fact the most important implication of enthnographic investigation, is that health education must be bi-directional [27-34]. Physicians, health care providers and health educators have no mandate just to teach the public; they must learn from them as well. An educator cannot educate unless he or she is willing to engage in the process as a learner also. It is the willingness to learn and be educated as part of the education process that consigns the problem of prevention to the patient and provides him with the psychological wherewithal to assume responsibility for it [35-38].

References

1. Magaña JR: Sex, drugs and HIV: an ethnographic approach. *Soc Sci Med* 1991; 33:5-9.
2. Miller HG, Turner CF, Moses LE (eds): *AIDS: The Second Decade*. Washington, DC: National Academy Press, 1990.
3. Conner RF: *AIDS prevention with Hispanic farm workers: a formative evaluation*. Final Report to the California Community Foundation, Los Angeles, CA, 1990.
4. Carrier J: Sexual behavior and spread of AIDS in Mexico. *Med Anthropol* 1989; 10:129-142.
5. Carrier JM, Magaña JR: Use of ethnosexual data on men of Mexican origin for HIV/AIDS prevention programs. *J Sex Res* 1990; 28:189-202.
6. Magaña JR, Carrier JM: Mexican and Mexican American male sexual behavior and spread of AIDS in California. *J Sex Res* 1991; 28:425-441.
7. Parker R: Sexual culture and AIDS education in urban Brazil. *In:* Kulstad R (ed). *AIDS 1988: AAAS Symposia Papers*. Washington, DC: American Association for the Advancement of Science, pp. 169-173, 1988.
8. Blackmore CA, Limpakarnjanarat K, Rigsu-Perez JG, Albritton W, Greenwood JR: An outbreak of chancroid in Orange County, California: Descriptive epidemiology and desert measures. *J Infect Dis* 1985; 151:840-844.
9. Lawrence MA, Duque A, Foster LM, Greenwood JR: *Prevention and control of early and congenital syphilis in Orange County*. Unpublished manuscript.
10. Cameron C, Plummer F, Simonsen J, Ndinya-Achola J, D'Costa L, Piot P: *Female to male heterosexual transmission of HIV infection in Nairobi*. Abstracts Volume III, International Conference on AIDS. 1987; 25.
11. Schmid GP, Sanders LL, Blount JH, Alexander ER: Chancroid in the United States: Reestablishment of an old disease. *JAMA* 1987; 258:3265-3268.
12. Solomon MZ, DeJong W: Recent sexually transmitted disease prevention efforts and their implications for AIDS health education. Health Educ Quart 1986; 13:301-316.
13. Los Angeles Times: *Celebrate! Orange County's first 100 years*. Los Angeles

Times, Orange County Edition, p. 64, May 22, 1988.

14. Chavez, L: Settlers and sojourners: The case of Mexicans in the United States. *Hum Org* 1988; 47:95-108.

15. Magaña JR, Greenwood R, Carrier J: *Seroprevalence and behavioral study of farm workers in the state of California.* 1st International Symposium on Education and Information about AIDS, Ixtapa, Mexico, 1988.

16. Nelkin, D: Aids and the social sciences: Review of useful knowledge and research needs. *Rev Infect Dis* 1987; 9:980-986.

17. Martin JL, Vance CS: Behavioral and psychosocial factors in AIDS: Methodological and substantive issues. *Am Psychol* 1984; 39:1303-1307.

18. Velimirovic B: AIDS as a social phenomenon. *Soc Sci Med* 1987; 25:541-552.

19. Carballo-Diéguez A: Hispanic culture, gay male culture and AIDS: counseling implications. *J Couns Devel* 1989; 68:26-30.

20. Padian N, Marquis L, Francis DP, Anderson RE, Rutherford GW, O'Malley PM, Winkelstin W: Male to female transmission of human immunodeficiency virus. *JAMA* 1987; 258:788-790.

21. Trichopoulos D, Sparos L, Petridou E: Homosexual role separation and spread of AIDS. *Lancet* 1988; 2:965-966.

22. Nsanze H, Fast MV, D'Costa LJ, Rukei P, Curran J, Ronald A: Genital ulcers in Kenya. *Br J Ven Dis* 1981; 57:378-381.

23. Hunt CW: Migrant labor and sexually transmitted disease: AIDS in Africa. *J Health Soc Beh* 1989; 30:353-373.

24. Martinez C, Martin HW: Folk diseases among urban Mexican-Americans: Etiology, symptoms, and treatment. *JAMA* 1966; 196:147-150.

25. Goldsmith MF: As farmworkers help keep American healthy illness may be their harvest. *JAMA* 1989; 261:3207-3213.

26. Mobed K, Gold EB, Schenker MB: Occupational health problems among migrant and seasonal farm workers. *In:* Cross-cultural Medicine--A Decade Later [special issue]. *West J Med* 1992; 157367-373.

27. Freire P: Education as cultural action: An introduction. *In:* Colonnese L M (ed): *Conscientization for Liberation.* Washington, DC: Division for Latin American, United States Catholic Conference, pp. 109-122, 1971.

28. Freire P: *Education for Critical Consciousness.* New York: Seabury Press, 1973.

29. Freire P: *Pedagogy of the Oppressed.* New York: Seabury Press, 1970.

30. Freire P: *¿Extensión o comunicación? La concientización en el medio rural.* Mexico: Siglo Veintiuno Editores, SA, 1973.

31. Wallerstein N: *Language and Culture in Conflict: Problem-posing in the ESL Classroom.* Reading, MA: Addison-Wesley, 1983.

32. Magaña JR, Ferreira-Pinto JB, Blair M, Mata A: Una pedagogia de conscientizacion para la prevencion del VIH/SIDA. *Rev Latinoamericana Psicol* 1992; 24:97-108.

33. Bracho de Carpio A, Carpio-Cedraro F, Anderson L: Hispanic families learning and teaching about AIDS: A participatory approach at the community level. *Hisp J Beh Sci* 1990; 12:165-176.

34. Torres RE: Health status assessment of Latinos in the midwest. *Latino Stud J* 1991; 2:53-70.

35. Bandura A, Adams N, Beyer J: Cognitive process mediating behavioral change. *J Personality Soc Psych* 1997; 35:125-139.
36. Bandura A: Self-Efficacy: Toward a unifying theory of behavioral change. *Psychol Rev* 1977; 84:191-211.
37. Bandura A: Self-Efficacy Mechanism in human agency. *Amer Psychol* 1982; 37:122-145.
38. Bandura A: Perceived self-efficacy in the exercise of control over AIDS infection. *Eval Program Plan* 1990; 13:9-17.

5

The Underground World of Latina Sex Workers in Cantinas

Armida Ayala, Joseph Carrier and J. Raul Magaña

Introduction

A sizable number of Latino migrant women work in the sex industry in Southern California and in doing so may put themselves at risk for HIV infection. While the exact number is unknown, those familiar with the situation believe that many migrant women are involved. Since the sex industry in California is illegal, these women also put themselves at risk for arrest by law authorities. This means that they must operate in an underground world which adds to the difficulty of providing them with good public health programs for the prevention of sexually transmitted diseases.

Latino female sex workers in southern California carry out their underground activities in many different circumstances and locations and with different motivations. They may, for example, operate clandestinely out of motels in urban areas and serve a specific clientele [1], as streetwalkers on certain streets and boulevards, and in drinking establishments located in high density Latino neighborhoods that cater mainly to migrant men from Mexico and Central America. Their motivations for earning money as sex workers vary according to the situations they find themselves in as migrants, often illegal, with little or no source of income in an alien country. Some of the women have played the role of prostitute prior to leaving their home country. Many, however, as a result of economic conditions or desperation, may be playing the prostitute role for the first time in their lives.

This chapter presents some preliminary information on the sexual behaviors and belief systems of Latino migrant female sex workers who operate out of popular drinking establishments, commonly referred to as *cantinas*, and suggests ways in which the information may be used to help create culturally appropriate educational HIV risk reduction programs for them.

Methods

Few data are available on the behaviors of Latino migrant female sex workers in California, and almost none are available on those migrant women who operate out of cantinas. Recognizing the need for culturally relevant behavioral information on cantina sex workers for HIV prevention programs, the *Harbor Area Ethnographic Study*, as part of a larger study in the area dealing with HIV/AIDS, focused on the drug, alcohol and sexual behaviors of these women in the context of the sociocultural settings in which they occur. The rules and roles the women had to adhere to in basing their prostitute operations in cantinas were also studied in detail.

Procedures

The information was gathered in an ethnographic study carried out by the senior author and her colleagues in the Harbor City area of Los Angeles in the early 1990s. The field research for the ongoing ethnographic study, which began in 1990, comprised of participant observations, structured and open-ended interviews, informal meetings, and focus group sessions with the sex workers. Twenty structured interviews and two focus groups of 10 women each have been completed to date. Throughout the course of the study, participant observations and informal interviews of the 20 women were conducted where they work (in the cantinas) and where they live. The 20 women varied in age from 17 to 41 years; the median age of the group was 29 years. Two-thirds of them were from Mexico (13 of 20), and the rest from Central America. Friends of the women and several owners and managers of cantinas were also been informally interviewed.

We used convenience sampling methods to identify and interview the women. Due to the stigma attached to their profession, most of the women do not identify themselves as sex workers to outsiders. This prevented us using random sampling procedures in the selection of our sample. Consequently, during the participant observation phase of the study, we identified for the informal interviews a convenience sample of 20 women who were willing to reveal this part of their lives. Gaining access to the 20 women was made possible through the social networks of several cantina women who early on in the study understood and approved its objectives. One of the women in particular, an ex-sex worker, became a gatekeeper for the study and helped establish credibility and rapport with the women who agreed to participate.

Participant observations and informal interviews in cantinas and in the respondents' living spaces were carried out monthly for about a two-year period. Interviews and conversations with the women were conducted in Spanish and usually took place when the women were least busy at their profession. The busiest times in cantinas are Friday and Saturday evenings and Saturday and Sunday afternoons.

Study Setting

As one drives along the ocean side area in the city of San Pedro then inland to the cities of Wilmington and north Long Beach, one can see the shift from affluent beach hotels, taxis, and entertainment associated with tourism to the manufacturing companies, run down motels, small businesses, liquor stores, cantinas, and a large number of Latino vendors associated with the lack of employment and extreme poverty. Inhabitants of the harbor area, which includes the cities of Wilmington, Carson, Harbor City, Lomita and north Long Beach live in houses arranged on a north-south axis between Anaheim Boulevard, Pacific Avenue, and Pacific Coast Highway. A significant number of the inhabitants, growing ever larger over time, are Latinos and a large majority of them are of Mexican origin.

Cantinas are usually clustered along the main streets of predominantly Latino neighborhoods in the harbor area. One finds rundown motels, liquor stores, small Mexican and Salvadoran restaurants, lunch wagons and street vendors in their immediate vicinity. Many street vendors sell tropical fruits and home-prepared foods; others sell inexpensive items such as plastic flowers, blankets, and bootlegged cassette tapes of popular Latino music. Migrant families of diverse nationalities live in small shabby apartments located above the cantinas and shops. Bed sheets often cover apartment windows. At the street level, graffiti cover the walls and iron security bars cover the windows of the buildings. Crack houses and shooting galleries may be located in some of the motels and apartment buildings with the resulting sale of drugs and exchange of sex for drugs.

There are several different types of cantinas in the harbor area. Some have only male customers while others have both males and females; some have female workers and others do not. This study focused only on the most popular type of cantina, the ones which are almost exclusively patronized by men who are served by female employees. The men come to cantinas to drink and gossip with their male friends, dance with the female hostesses, and find sex partners. The females work as *cantineras* (barmaids), *ficheras* (dance hostesses), or *taloneras* (exclusive sex workers). These drinking establishments are usually owned and operated by Latino men. A few are restaurants during the day and become cantinas at night or are frequented by Anglos during the day and convert to Latino gatherings at night. Spanish is the main language spoken in cantinas, English is rarely spoken.

An outsider entering a cantina for the first time may be quite intimidated. In an attempt to maintain social order and maximize profits some owners, for example, employ security guards to frisk customers for weapons and alcohol before letting them in. Inside, cantinas are dark and smoky with exceptionally loud music. Drunken fights between men over money and women are not uncommon and there are occasional drug deals and shootings. Generally speaking, cantinas provide a friendly environment for a large majority of their customers who are migrant Latino men wanting to recapture the feelings of being back home. These men know the scene and thus operate agreeably under the same rules and precautions as they did in their home countries.

The cantinas we studied can be divided into two types based on whether or not they had an admission fee. The ones charging an admission fee have younger, more beautiful women, one or two live bands and are usually better maintained. The admission fees vary from three to eight dollars. Some patrons are able to bargain with security guards to pay less if they arrive as a group close to closing time. Those which do not charge an admission fee are smaller, untidy, have only a juke box or a couple of individuals playing live music.

Latino sex workers in cantinas operate in completely different work environments than do the mostly Anglo, African-American and U.S.-born Latino female sex workers hustling for customers from the street. Occasionally, Latino street sex workers may go into a cantina to look for a customer but this is rare; when they do try to operate inside (as will be explained below) they are usually asked to leave.

Women in cantina work in a structured environment and generally must follow a fairly rigid set of rules maintained by owners so that their drinking establishments can survive economically and legally. These rules are usually administered by *cantineros* (bartenders) with whom the women must interact closely. Some of the rules are related to the state alcohol beverage control board and city ordinances which establish the sales hours of beer and liquor, the number of occupants allowed inside the cantina at any one time, and health standards. The other rules are mostly related to the owners' desire to maximize the sale of alcoholic beverages and control the behaviors of cantina women.

The major proprietor rules that cantina women are expected to follow are: (1) they must push the sale of beer and liquor, (2) they can exchange sex for money but the transaction should not take precedence over getting their clients to drink in the cantina, and (3) they cannot get drunk while working. As long as these rules are followed, almost any Latino woman can come in and work without being formally hired. Women who come in from the outside just to exchange sex for money and do not follow these rules are referred to as *putas* (whores). They are usually asked to leave since they take customers away from the cantinas who would otherwise spend their money drinking.

Results

The Cantina Scene

A typical scene in cantinas is composed of male patrons who sit talking together at a long bar on high stools or at tables in small chairs. In addition to socializing with male friends, some men also interact with the women present, the *cantineras*, *ficheras* and *taloneras*. Live musicians or juke boxes provide loud *banda* type songs from northern Mexico, *cumbias* from Colombia, or *salsa* from the Caribbean as background music or for dancing. In some cantinas, pool tables provide additional enjoyment for the male patrons.

Although *cantineras* and *ficheras* may play the role of sex workers, it is not their principal assignment. *Cantineras* wait on tables and get tips in return. They allow men to caress them but usually do not drink or dance with them. Their major task is to push drinks for the cantina. *Ficheras*, on the other hand, approach men to socialize with them either at the long bar or at their tables with the purpose of getting men to both dance and to buy them drinks. Once a man agrees to dance with or buy a drink for a *fichera*, he is encouraged to buy himself a drink. Although not a common practice, in some cantinas the bartenders give her a token (a *ficha* in Spanish) for every drink she sells. These tokens later may be turned in for cash. *Ficheras* mainly dance and drink with a man until he runs out of money and then move on to another potential patron. In return for the drinks and dancing, she allows them to caress her at no extra cost. Most *ficheras* do not like to be kissed by the men on the mouth, therefore, their caressing is mostly limited to stroking and kissing on the neck and shoulders. If the *cantineras* and *ficheras* want to earn some additional money from sex, toward closing time they start negotiations with potential sex partners. The sexual encounters are carried out only after they finish their shift in the cantina.

Taloneras customarily only play the role of sex worker. Most are relatively recent young migrants from small towns in rural Mexico who have limited schooling and no particular job skills. As a rule, they are isolated from other women and have turned to prostitution because they cannot find permanent well-paying jobs to support themselves. Since they do not receive any money from cantina owners their weekly income ordinarily is not as substantial or dependable as that of the *cantineras* and *ficheras*. They are therefore the most marginal Latino women who operate as prostitutes in cantinas.

Background of Cantina Sex Workers

The women studied came from the rural areas of their home countries. A large majority of them had never worked in a structured setting. Most of their previous jobs in the U.S. and in their home countries were limited to working as *domesticas* (domestics). As a rule they had little formal schooling and, therefore, had limited reading and writing skills. Many of the women who had come to the United States undocumented had done so with the help of a *coyote* (a person who charges money to get someone across the border). Crossing the border was very expensive for the women who were later placed in cantinas by the *coyote*. In most cases, the *coyote* obtained his/her charge for getting the women across the border from the cantina owner who had previously made arrangements with the *coyote* to exchange the women for the crossing fee. Many of these women had never even been inside a cantina, let alone worked as sex workers. At the time of the study, many of the women had children and headed their households. Some of the women who were married in their country of origin had left their husbands and their children behind. Others had children in their country of origin but were not married and had left the children with their mothers or members of their extended families. Many of the women felt stigmatized by their work in the sex industry. They said they had little in common with *otras mujeres* (other women who are not prostitutes). Nevertheless, they were very assertive, direct and resourceful, and the study data indicate that, generally, most of them coped well with the difficulties posed by their job.

For the Latino migrant female sex workers in cantinas, prostitution provided the additional income needed to survive. Some of the women, for example, had worked in the informal sector of the economy selling food (like corn and cheese tamales), earrings and factory damaged clothing. Some of them had done piece sewing and cleaning homes. Income from these jobs, however, was not sufficient to support their families so they were forced to seek employment in cantinas where they turned to prostitution. The available information suggests that as much as 75 percent of their income came from prostitution and the rest from vending, waiting on tables and working as domestics.

The Clients

Most of the clients of cantina sex workers are migrant men from Mexico and Central America [2]. As is the case with the sex workers, many of these men had left their loved ones (wives and families) behind in their country of origin. A few U.S.-born Latino men seek prostitutes in cantinas but this is not a very common practice. These U.S.-born Latino men usually went to cantinas to exchange drugs for money with their *border brothers* (non-U.S. born Latino men).

A large majority of the Latino migrant men who frequented cantinas were employed in the formal sector of the labor force, and others worked in the informal sector. As a rule, those employed by the formal sector worked for manufacturing companies as truck drivers, dock workers, and other relatively low-skilled jobs or performed menial type jobs in restaurants, hotels, and auto body shops. Those earning income in the informal sector usually worked as day laborers in construction and gardening or in sidewalk sales of home-prepared food, *paletas* (ice cream), and trinkets made of Plaster of Paris or plastic.

Cruising Patterns

The cruising patterns of both the sex workers and their customers were determined in large part by their fear of being entrapped and arrested by law enforcement officers. Since the highest likelihood of arrest for both parties was on the street, the pursuit of sexual partners in cantinas appeared to offer them the best location to minimize the risk of encountering police. Besides cantinas, migrant Latino men also find sex partners on the street and take them back to their living space. In addition, some street prostitutes operate in apartments that house large numbers of migrant Latino men with whom they have serial sexual intercourse [3-5]. Nevertheless, our findings indicate that both parties understand the value of cantinas as one of the best and safest places for cruising for sex partners. Although we cannot measure the percentage of all Latino migrant male sexual encounters accounted for by female sex workers found in cantinas, our data suggest that they are significant in number in the Harbor area of Los Angeles. Our data also show that cantina sex workers as a rule interact with their customers one at a time and the sexual transaction, usually only vaginal intercourse, is customarily conducted by *cantineras* and *ficheras* after they have completed their work in the cantina.

Interactions Between Sex Workers and Clients

As long as their clients were not too drunk, many of the cantina sex workers generally thought of them as being kind and generous. In response to a question on who her clients were and how she felt about them, one sex worker stated that:

> They are men who are here either away from their wives living in another country and sending money back home or who have *necesidades* (a need for sex) that are not being met by their wives. Many of the men ask me to do things that their wives do not do, like oral sex. Some of the men ask me to let them do it to me from behind but I don't let them...it's not right you know ...God gave you that part of your body for other purposes. They come to me because they know that they can ask for sexual favors that their wives or girlfriends do not do...like oral sex, you know many respectable women don't like doing that. Some come for the companionship...you know...someone to listen to them, get drunk with them.

Another sex worker stated her feelings about clients as follows:

> I think they are lonely. They want to have sex but many of them
> want company too. I think their wives are as much of a prosti-
> tute as I am because they still have to have sex with these men
> even though they don't want to but have to survive. Me ...well
> that's another story. I charge them, get their money...but don't
> have to see them every day, prepare their food, clean their
> clothes, and on top of this *cojermelos* (have sex with them) and
> be blamed for their actions. *Pues, si* (yes)...because if you are
> home as a housewife and you don't have sex with these guys
> right you get blamed. And if you are the *puta* (whore) in the
> cantina you get blamed too for having sex with them. The only
> difference between the poor woman who is married to these
> guys and myself is that I get paid for the sex and they don't.

Most of the sex workers concluded that, when their clients got *too
drunk*, they become quarrelsome and difficult to handle. It was also
quite clear that some of the sex workers had a great deal of anger
towards their clients even when they were relatively sober and did not
ordinarily trust them. In response to the question "Do you feel like you
are being taken advantage of by your clients?" one sex worker replied:

> Sometimes, but I know why I do this...to pay for my kid's food
> and clothes, not because I really like prostituting myself. I do it
> because I have to and I can make quick money and get things for
> me and my children. Once in a while these men can get rude...you
> know...they start fighting with you while they are drunk and
> can get into fights with other men. But usually they are nice. I
> would not say that I enjoy having sex with them...hell, no! Some
> of them are ugly and have no teeth, but most of the time they are
> tolerable. Of course, you have the jerks who try to take it for
> free. I know of this girl who was taken to a client's house and
> she got raped by eight...of his friends who did not pay for it. Yes,
> it can happen in this kind of life.

A large majority of the sexual encounters took place either in cheap
hotels, which were paid for by the clients, or in the womens' apartments. Customarily, sex workers were paid in cash at the time of their
sexual encounters. Many of the women we interviewed said, however,
that their clients did not always pay them in cash but would later take
them shopping for food, clothing for their children, or other things.

Sexual Practices of Cantina Sex Workers

There is some evidence to suggest that vaginal intercourse in the missionary position was preferred and practiced by a large majority of Latino female sex workers in California and Mexico [6, 7]. Oral sex (both fellatio and cunnilingus) and anal intercourse may be carried out by some of the sex workers but they were the exception rather than the rule, and clients customarily paid more for these sex acts which were considered perverted by both the men and women.

Information obtained on the sexual behaviors of the Latino migrant women interviewed for the study supported these findings. Eighteen women stated that they only engaged in vaginal intercourse. Only two women said that they also engaged in oral and anal intercourse; and it was usually done, they said, for extra money or as something special for a good customer or lover. That anal and oral sex were considered different and unusual was illustrated by the terms such as *regular* or *straight* used by the women to describe vaginal intercourse.

HIV Prevention and AIDS

Responses by the 20 sex workers to questions dealing with HIV prevention and AIDS revealed their clear understanding of the link between sexual practices, needle sharing in IV drug use, and HIV infection. They knew, for example, that anal sex between men was the highest risk sex practice. This fact was cited by several women as another reason for not doing anal sex, which they referred to as *homosexual* sex. The sex workers also know that vaginal sex with an HIV positive partner can lead to HIV infection and AIDS. They did not, however, believe it to be as high risk a sexual behavior as *homosexual* sex. None of them expressed any concern about getting themselves infected through *regular* sex. They were more concerned about getting pregnant and earning enough money to survive than they did about AIDS. As a result, they generally downplayed the risk of HIV infection from vaginal sex.

Motivations for Using Condoms

The cantina sex workers' motivations for using condoms were not related to HIV infection at all, but instead were related to more important short-term economic considerations such as getting pregnant or contracting sexually transmitted diseases. The costs associated with being pregnant and then having another mouth to feed were tangible outcomes which motivated them to use condoms. Ironically, their fear of pregnancy may also lead them not to use condoms if they were taking birth control pills. Furthermore, several cantina sex workers noted that they did not have to use condoms because they never allowed their customers to come inside them.

Sexually transmitted diseases other than HIV/AIDS may also motivate some cantina sex workers to use condoms. Many of them knew the downside of these diseases, the symptoms of which, unlike HIV infection, may be visible in short periods of time. Furthermore, once infected with a sexually transmitted disease, the cantina sex workers would get a bad reputation among their clients who would know that they had a disease. Infection with sexually transmitted disease did not, however, provide a strong motivation for condom usage in that most cantina sex workers knew they can be easily cured with available medications.

Reasons Given for Not Using Condoms

Cantina sex workers gave many different reasons as to why they did not use condoms to protect themselves from getting infected with the AIDS virus. Some of the reasons related to mistaken beliefs about how HIV infected persons may be identified; others were related to economic problems they faced in the short run, like having enough income to live on.

A major reason given by cantina sex workers for not using condoms was related to beliefs about cleanliness and disease. They associated being infected with being dirty. For instance, they indicated that they did not have to use a condom with a clean man since he would not likely be infected with the AIDS virus. A good illustration of this belief was provided by an interviewee who in explaining why she did not need to use condoms said: "I carefully screen the *amigos* (guys) I have sex with ...I make sure they are clean." Saying that condom usage was not all that important, another interviewee in referring to her *amigos* noted that "these men are clean." And yet another pointed out: "I make sure the men are clean."

The cantina sex workers' major economic motivation for not using condoms was related to the income they would lose if their customers refused to use them. This fact was most often brought up by them when asked if they would go ahead and have sex with a man when no condoms were available or when he refused to use a condom even though they were available. One woman said she would have sex without a condom if none were available: "because I need the money and sometimes these guys put it in before you know it." Under the same circumstances, another woman said she would "go ahead and have sex because I need the money;" and that her friends would do the same "if the guy pays them good." Still another pointed out that she would "have sex because when you are hot or need the money, you don't care about not using one." And she said her *fichera* friends would do the same because the guys do not like using condoms and "they need to make money."

Cantina Sex Workers and the Law

Cantineras and *ficheras* who also played the role of a prostitute and solicited customers for this purpose needed to ensure at all times that this aspect of their work in cantinas was by and large concealed. According to the State of California Penal Code, Section 647.(b), prostitution is defined as "disorderly conduct and every person who violates this law is guilty of a misdemeanor and subject to arrest, confinement in the county jail, and a fine that may run as high as $1,200." In addition, the judge may order the arrestee to be tested for HIV and attend a one or two hour educational session dealing with HIV/AIDS. If they tested positive and continued to work as sex workers and were re-arrested, the charge would be a felony rather than a misdemeanor.

Fear of arrest further marginalized the sex workers who already suffered a major social stigma associated with their profession. One result was that they could be easily exploited for the financial gain of others. *Cantineros*, for example, may force the women to pay them hush money not to tell cantina owners about their prostitution. Some customers may threaten to do the same thing. Since not all of the women who work as *cantineras* and *ficheras* also play the role of prostitute, many of the sex workers attempt to blend in and thus were very secretive and tried not to reveal the fact that they were soliciting customers for sex. The fact is, however, that all women working in cantinas were usually considered to be *putas* (whores) even if they are not.

Life Histories

The life histories of Alma and Laura provide a brief look into the lives of two cantina sex workers. They give the reader a chance to view these women in the context of their past and present. The names of the women have been changed to protect their anonymity.

Alma

Alma was born in 1975 in a small Mexican border town near Mexicali, Baja California and Calexico, California. When she was very young, Alma and her family crossed the border without proper documentation to work as farmworkers in the fields of the Imperial Valley near El Centro, California. Alma grew up there, moving from camp to camp, and working side by side with her mother and father.

Because her family frequently moved, Alma did not attend school and so she did not learn how to read and write. Her mother and father continued on as farmworkers until her father died when Alma was in her teens. Soon after her father's death, when she was just 18 years old, Alma became pregnant. She then informally married the father of her child and moved to Fresno, California.

Shortly after she gave birth to her first child, Alma's husband was violently murdered in the labor camp where both worked as migrant farm workers. She was never able to find out what led to his murder and decided to move to the Harbor area of Los Angeles where she got her first job in a cantina. Alma spent the next two years working in the cantina and developed a reputation for playing pool skillfully and, as a sex worker, standing up to her clients.

Recently, Alma has been suffering a series of severe bouts of depression and alcoholism while working in the cantina. She assesses her current situation as follows:

> This job will lead you to drinking...it is the hardest thing I have ever done in my life, harder than bending down to pull onions from the fields or working during the day in the desert heat picking grapes. The men...you have to know how to handle them. You never let them know that they can intimidate you because if you do, the amigos won't pay you. It is hard not to drink while you turn tricks. It is the only way that you can get enough courage to do it [sex] for money.

Laura

Laura was born in Sonora, Mexico in the spring of 1951 to parents who owned a small farm where they grew corn, made goat cheese and raised pigs for sale. Located a few miles from Hermosillo, the farm occupied only six acres of land. They lived in a small three-room house situated in the center of the farm. According to Laura, other farms were located quite far away so neighbors only socialized during *bailes* (dancing parties), fiestas, or while selling and trading their crops and animal stock. Women met men at these social gatherings. Some of the men asked the women and their families permission to get married. Weddings were then often arranged. Families in Sonora were still generally over protective of the women and maintained traditional mores. Virginity and in-wedlock children were still the norm and parents continued to supervise much of the women's behavior.

Along with her mother, father, grandparents, and 16 brothers and sisters, Laura lived most of her life in extreme poverty in the farm house where she was delivered by a *curandera* (folk healer). She was not allowed to date men or go out by herself. She often wondered why her brothers were allowed to stay out at night and go dancing by themselves. During her early teens, at one of the community dances, she met what she calls a *pocho* (a Mexican-American man). She left home and ran away with him to the United States. She married him, and they moved into a small house in the Harbor area of Los Angeles where they have lived ever since.

Since she moved to the U.S., Laura's life has been full of pain and despair. The man she married had just returned from Vietnam and was addicted to heroin and other drugs. Unable to support his family, he got Laura a job in a cantina where she started working as a *cantinera*. After a time, she realized that prostitution was profitable and started exchanging sex for money. Her husband welcomed the money to buy his drugs and often battered Laura if she refused to give him part or all of her income from her sex work.

Laura is still a very beautiful, tall, stately looking woman in her early forties. She has maintained a statuesque body and wears heavy makeup to cover the bags under her eyes from crying and insomnia. Most people judge Laura to be much older than she really is. She dresses in flamboyant gold and shiny silver dresses with high heels matching the big bows in her hair. She is still married and lives with her husband. Laura has become accustomed to supporting his heroin addiction.

Laura talks with both humor and bitterness about her work. She gave the following explanation of her work situation and perceived risk for HIV infection:

> Even though I always heard of *mujeres de la calle* (prostitutes), I never thought that I'd become one. I hated to see my kids crying for food and my *pendejo* (stupid) husband suffering from *malillas* (withdrawal symptoms). I may be more of a *pendeja* to you for staying with him and letting him take my money *en el talon* (in prostitution). But you know that I really don't like what I do. I don't worry about AIDS from my tricks because I make them wear a condom or no deal. I worry more about getting AIDS from my old man because I know that he shares needles with his friends and sometimes we don't use condoms.

About her use of drugs or alcohol while conducting sex transactions, Laura relates:

> I try not to get drunk or do *coca* because you can get raped and ripped off. These men can rape you with the help of their friends if you get drunk, and of course you don't make any money like that. I have seen that happen right here by the bathrooms. Yes...sometimes I get drunk and do *coca* with my regular customers.

Reflecting on her sexuality, Laura says that she does not enjoy her sexual encounters with either her husband or her customers. Laura's first sexual encounter, at the age of seven, occurred involuntarily with one of her adult cousins. When she was 15 years old, just before her sweet 16 confession, she told her mother about the incident. Her mother told her never to do it again before marriage. Two years later Laura went into a deep depression over her living circumstances and decided to run away with her husband. Not long after leaving she learned that her mother was very angry and referred to her as a *puta*.

Laura decided that some day she would return home and prove her mother wrong by having her husband and children with her, hoping somehow she would be accepted by all of them. Laura was accepted by her mother but not by her father who was still very angry. Her mother and brothers and sisters eventually came to visit her in the U.S. During her mother's visits, Laura hid the fact that she worked as a prostitute by telling her that she worked at nights in a factory.

Laura now spends her time raising her children and working in cantinas. She supplements her cantina and prostitution income by selling earrings which she buys wholesale in downtown Los Angeles. She also sells cheese brought to her by relatives from Sonora, Mexico. In addition to supporting her family, Laura manages to send money on a regular basis to her relatives still living in Mexico.

Discussion

The preliminary findings presented here provide some important basic insights about the lives, sociocultural settings and sexual behaviors of female sex workers operating out of cantinas in the Harbor area of Los Angeles. Although these findings cannot be generalized to all Latino migrant female sex workers, they can be used to help design educational HIV prevention programs for cantina sex workers in other barrios in California and elsewhere in the U.S.

These findings illustrate how the cantina sex workers' need for income clearly dominated their lives and was one of the primary motivating factors both in their playing the role of prostitute and in their not using condoms when having sex with their *amigos* (customers). They could not afford to lose money by turning down *amigos* who resisted or refused to use condoms on the grounds, mostly, that it took away much of the pleasure of sexual intercourse. In the minds of the women, the benefits of using condoms included preventing pregnancy and sexually transmitted diseases other than HIV/AIDS. These benefits were, however, far outweighed by the need for money to pay rent for housing, and buy food and clothes for themselves and their children. They also knew that pregnancy prevention could be easily accomplished with pills, and sexually transmitted diseases, like syphilis and gonorrhea, could be cured with antibiotics.

The cantina sex workers also appeared to lack a strong motivation for using condoms with their *amigos* because they generally did not see themselves as being at a particularly high risk for HIV infection. Many of them believed that as long as they did not have sex with "IV-drug using men who share needles" or "gay men" they were not at risk for AIDS. Since their *amigos* ordinarily did not fall into either category, the cantina sex workers did not perceive themselves at a particularly high risk for infection. The HIV prevention problem for them, however, was in correctly identifying *amigos* who had shared needles or who had had anal sex with other men. Their greatest difficulty in doing so would probably be related to identifying bisexually behaving masculine *amigos* who might have gotten infected with HIV through anal sex with men. Like most Latino women, cantina sex workers customarily equated male homosexuality with effeminacy.

Implications

The study findings have several implications for education and prevention efforts. The low levels of educational attainment by the these women coupled with their limited mastery of the English language means that health education programs aimed at the general population will not be effective for a majority of the Latina cantina sex workers. This explains why early efforts to educate the general public regarding the prevention of the spread of AIDS may have had little effect on the Latino population and thus may be one factor contributing to the disproportionate number of AIDS cases among Latinos.

The fact that *cantineras* often have very little formal education has profound implications for the design of health education programs aimed at this group. There is evidence that people that have not had extensive experience with formal education lack syllogistic reasoning ability. This means that they may be unable to make inferences based on a general premise. Therefore, messages should be concrete and rooted to a temporal reality. Also, printed materials need to be developed at a low reading level so that they can be easily understood [8]. Preferably those materials should be iconographically presented as much as possible, so that they rely more on symbols than on the written word. All written materials targeted to this population should be in a format and literacy level that matches that of the target population, which usually is lower than the average level of the population.

Approaches to enhance prevention measures among the targeted population should be contextualized and culturally appropriate. The level of acculturation of the women and their clients should be measured and used as input to customize materials and approaches for HIV/AIDS prevention among the target population. Furthermore, materials addressed to this population should also be developed in Spanish and should include the many different regional words for specific terms, in order to be easily accessed by all women, regardless of their level of knowledge in English.

Studies in cross-cultural settings have demonstrated that individuals with low educational attainment absorb new information best when it is presented in a way that relates the new information to their current environment and life circumstances as much as possible [9]. This means that health educators would do well to search for ways to present new information so that it is related to the every day experience of cantina sex workers. This is especially important since women working in cantinas have complex and more immediate problems for survival like violence, poverty, drug addiction, discrimination and court cases over the custody of their children. For this reason these issues have to be addressed in conjunction with HIV/AIDS prevention strategies.

In terms of prevention efforts, community-based agencies should implement active outreach plans and take their services out of their offices and into the places inhabited by the target population. In addition, health agencies and community-based organizations should hire people from the same community. They will know the gatekeepers, community norms, informal leaders and can speak their language.

Finally, condoms should be distributed for free of charge to the women and their clients at the sites and there is a need to provide access to HIV/AIDS prevention materials with referrals to local health agencies directed to the women and their clients.

References

1. Carrier J, Nguyen B, Su S: Vietnamese American sexual behaviors & HIV infection. *J Sex Res* 1992; 29(4):547-560.
2. Chavez L: Settlers and sojourners: the case of Mexicans in the United States. *Hum Organiz* 1988; 47 (2).
3. Magaña JR: Sex, drugs and HIV: an ethnographic approach. *Soc Sci Med* 1991; 32 (9):1-5.
4. Magaña JR, Carrier JM: Mexican and Mexican American male sexual behavior and spreads of AIDS in California. *J Sex Res* 1991; 28 (3):425-441.
5. Carrier JM, Magaña JR: Use of ethnosexual data on men of Mexican origin for HIV/AIDS Prevention Programs. *J Sex Res* 1991; 28 (2):189-202.
6. Bronfman M, Lopez S: Perspectives on AIDS/HIV prevention among rural migrants on the USA-Mexico border. *In:* Mishra SI, Conner RF, Magaña JR (eds): *AIDS Crossing Borders: The Spread of HIV Among Migrant Latinos.* Boulder, CO: Westview Press, 49-76.
7. Roebuck J, McNamara P: Ficheras and free-lancers: prostitution in a Mexican border city. *Arch Sex Behav* 1973; 2(3):231-244.
8. Hochhauser M: Readability of AIDS education materials. Paper presented at the 95th annual convention of the American Psychological Association. New York, December 1987.
9. Laboratory of Comparative Human Cognition: Contributions of cross-cultural research to educational practice. *Am Psychol* 1986; 41:1049-1088.

6

Mexican Men, Female Sex Workers and HIV/AIDS at the U.S.-Mexico Border

*João B. Ferreira-Pinto, Rebeca L. Ramos
and Michele Shedlin*

Introduction

A short walk over a downtown bridge spanning the Rio Grande/ Bravo River brings Mexicans and Americans to the center of El Paso, Texas or Ciudad Juarez, Chihuahua. As in many border cities, there is a large assortment of legal and illegal businesses and entrepreneurs providing the goods and services demanded by both populations. Among the goods and services available are legal and illegal drugs and sex for money. Given the relationship between drugs, sex and HIV transmission, we examined the drug using behavior of female sex workers in both cities, and how these behaviors affected the spread of sexually transmitted diseases (STDs), including HIV, among a specific segment of the Mexican male population, namely, migrant farmworkers.

Although the exchange of sex for money or drugs is common on both sides of the border, there is a differential in the customers and sex workers procurement of sex services and clients. It is more customary for El Paso male residents to avail themselves of sex services in Juarez and, only occasionally for Juarez residents to procure these services in El Paso. On the other hand, it is more common for Juarez sex workers to cross the border in search of better paying customers in El Paso, than for

El Paso sex workers to offer their services in Juarez. Despite the occasional movement of male and female sex workers across the border, Mexican and American female sex workers have different sexual behaviors, drug using patterns and motivations for engaging in the sex trade. Some of these sexual behaviors place them at a higher risk for contracting HIV or other STDs, which impact on their health and the health of their clients, and all who may eventually become sexually involved with their clients.

The purpose of this study was to examine behaviors which place female sex workers in El Paso and Juarez and their clients, among them migrant farmworkers, at risk for HIV infection. We investigated the differences in drug use and sexual behaviors between two cohorts of female sex workers in El Paso and Ciudad Juarez, and the implications of these behaviors for HIV transmission. We discuss the possible risks of HIV exposure for sojourners, who live in Juarez and spend the day working in the fields in the U.S. side, and those for migrant workers who come from the interior of Mexico and stay in the border region only for the time necessary to secure safe transportation to other agricultural zones in the interior of the U.S.

Based on previous research [1] we postulate that there is a low use of protective measures by female sex workers on both sides of the border which places them at a high risk for infection with STDs, including HIV/AIDS. We also postulate that El Paso females sex workers are exposed to a higher risk of infection in comparison with those from Juarez due to their higher degree of use of injectable drugs. Furthermore, female sex workers in Mexico have also a high risk for HIV infection because there is a high possibility that their sexual partners are injectable drug users (IDU) who share infected needles and syringes [2].

The Border Region

The 23 United States counties contiguous to the U.S.-Mexico border are separated by a political boundary but are united by many shared socioeconomic, cultural and environmental characteristics which have profound implications for the public health of the region. These similarities between the two sides of the border make this region different from the hinterland of Mexico or the U.S. We may safely state that Ciudad Juarez resembles more Texas than Mexico City, and El Paso resembles Chihuahua more than it does Washington DC. In all U.S. border counties, except San Diego County in California, at least one-fourth

TABLE 6.1. Total Population in the Ten Largest Counties Contiguous to the U.S.-Mexico Border and Percentage of Latinos, Latinos 14 to 24 Years of Age, and Poor Latino Families in These Counties [a]

Counties	Population	% Latinos	% Latinos 14-24	% Poor Latinos
San Diego (CA)	2,498,016	9.3	13.9	19.8
Pima (AZ)	666,890	24.5	29.9	18.4
El Paso (TX)	591,160	69.6	79.6	26.8
Dona Aña (NM)	135,510	56.1	59.3	20.7
Imperial (CA)	109,303	26.4	26.4	38.2
Yuma (AZ)	106,696	59.4	51.1	19.5
Cochise (AZ)	97,624	70.9	80.9	21.2
Val Verde (TX)	38,721	70.5	70.4	26.4
Santa Cruz (AZ)	29,670	78.2	89.2	na
Luna (NM)	18,110	47.3	65.1	24.9

[a] Source: Pan American Health Organization, El Paso (Texas) Field Office.

of the population is classified as Latino and in 87 percent of these counties, Latinos aged 14 to 24 years constitute over 40 percent of the population.

Table 6.1 presents relevant demographic information about the 10 most populous counties in the region. On an average, almost one-fourth of the Latino families in these counties reportedly live below the poverty line. This is not so surprising, since 40 percent of the 10 poorest metropolitan areas in the United States are located in the U.S.-Mexico border region: Las Cruces, Harlingen, Brownsville and El Paso.

Given this high level of poverty, few studies have examined how the impact of poverty, homelessness and other forms of social displacement affect the decision of Latino women to become sex workers. One study conducted in Los Angeles among Hispanic homeless female sex workers reported that the main reason most of these women entered the sex trade was their need to secure their families' survival. The main

TABLE 6.2. Number of HIV Infections and STD Cases in 10 Selected U.S. Border Counties for 1992 [a]

Counties	HIV	Syphilis	Gonorrhea	Chlamydia
San Diego (CA)	145.4	19.1	74.5	225.8
Pima (AZ)	14.1	10.0	63.9	275.8
El Paso (TX)	34.9	31.1	57.5	274.8
Dona Aña (NM)	17.7	10.3	44.3	na
Imperial (CA)	19.2	16.5	35.7	223.2
Yuma (AZ)	9.3	29.9	54.2	196.4
Cochise (AZ)	4.1	10.2	70.7	195.6
Val Verde (TX)	46.5	23.2	25.8	na
Santa Cruz (AZ)	6.7	3.4	20.2	64.0
Luna (NM)	27.6	na	11.0	na

[a] Source: Pan American Health Organization, El Paso (Texas) Field Office.

reason for the adoption of this line of work was the welfare of the family, and only secondarily the need to finance a drug habit [3]. We present ethnographic evidence which suggest that similar factors are at play among female Latino sex workers in El Paso and Juarez.

HIV Risk Factors

Table 6.2 lists epidemiological data for the same 10 counties on the incidence of STDs for 1992. High levels of STDs are reported for several counties; significantly, El Paso county reported a high rate of incidence of STDs relative to other counties in the border region. Compared with other counties, El Paso county ranks the highest in prevalence of syphilis, the second highest for chlamydia infection, and the third highest for gonorrhea and HIV infection.

At present the incidence of new HIV cases remains relatively low throughout the border region, but with a youthful population entering its most sexually active years and living in areas currently experiencing epidemic levels of syphilis and gonorrhea, there is a high risk for an increase in the rate of HIV infection in the near future, if some preventive measures are not initiated. For example, El Paso has the highest rate of syphilis and also the largest percentage (80 percent) of youth between 14 and 24 years of age.

Reproductive health experts report that Latinos in the border region have their first sexual experience at a younger age than the general population. Moreover, rates of teenage pregnancy are high among Latinos. This indicates that teenagers may lack the knowledge on how to avoid pregnancy or the behavioral skills to so. This lack of knowledge is highly correlated with the lack of knowledge on how to avoid contracting STDs, including HIV. In addition, Latino youth in the border region engage in other behaviors that put them at a higher risk for HIV transmission, including the use and abuse of alcohol, marijuana and inhalants. To further increase the possibility of HIV transmission there is a constant bi-directional flux of people across the border to work, shop, and play--and sex for pay is one of the services sought, bought and sold.

For some time now public health experts on both sides of the border have been concerned about the spread of AIDS into Mexico via contagion of Mexican sex workers by U.S. clients, and American clients of these sex workers. This has prompted several prevention campaigns among sex workers by Mexican health authorities in the border states in recent years. The same concern is voiced by U.S. health authorities. In 1992 the United States Conference of Mayors in a publication entitled "AIDS the Second Wave" stated that "...cities, which are physically linked by bridges over the Rio Grande River, significantly impact each other in many ways with the movement of people...and communicable diseases going in both directions. This same phenomenon applies to HIV/AIDS" [4]. As we have stated before, the urbanized counties along the U.S.-Mexico border region are magnets for migrants in search of work in border towns and in the U.S. hinterland. Also, the movement of border migrants to and from the interior of Mexico is not spread evenly across the U.S.-Mexico border but is concentrated in large Mexican urban centers like Torreon, Coahuila and Juarez [5].

There is a well documented relationship between the patterns of migration from the interior of Mexico to the interior of the U.S. and the AIDS prevalence in certain regions in Mexico. For example, 20 percent of the HIV-positive population in Michoacan has been in the U.S. at one time or another. It is suggested that approximately 10 percent of all HIV-positive individuals identified in Mexico have been in the U.S. some time in the past (Bronfman M, personal communication).

No systematic study has been conducted among HIV-positive men or women who are sojourners, were engaged in seasonal work in the agricultural fields near the border, or were returning to the interior of Mexico after working in the agricultural fields in the U.S. hinterland. This is a very hard population to track and many are not aware of their seropositive status when they return to their home villages. Individuals who work as seasonal migrant workers and who, after being infected with HIV in the U.S., have returned to Mexico, most likely have traveled through one of the main migration corridors for agricultural workers, among which El Paso is one of the largest. It is not known how long these individuals, who are largely males, may have been in the El Paso/Juarez region, but it is likely that they would have stayed some days to acquire gifts for their relatives or themselves, and for some rest and recreation. It is during this period that they may have engaged in sexual exchanges and may have put the sex worker female population and themselves at risk for contagion with HIV.

Although statistics show that both El Paso and Juarez have a very low incidence of HIV infection, these statistics are only partially reliable. Previous research [1] has demonstrated that the rate is higher than the official U.S. and Mexican estimates. For example, statistics from Mexico report 34 HIV positive cases in 1993 for the entire state of Chihuahua (where Ciudad Juarez is located), while in only one treatment program in Juarez (COMPAÑEROS) the number of HIV positive and AIDS cases for the same year was 64. In addition, a survey by the El Paso City-County Health District and the Southwest AIDS Coalition (SWAC) conducted in 1990 of 25 male sex workers working in El Paso showed that 72 percent had had anal intercourse without a condom in the previous three months, 52 percent had exchanged drugs for sex, and 68 percent had had sex while high on drugs or alcohol [6]. Recent anecdotal evidence from male sex workers showed that since 1990, there have been very little changes in these behaviors.

Seroprevalence Figures and Risk Behaviors
Among Sex Workers in El Paso–Juarez

In the 12 years (1981-1992) since the first HIV epidemiological reports were made available, there have been 258,009 AIDS cases reported in the U.S. and 12,292 cases reported in Mexico. In the U.S., approximately 10 percent of the reported cases have been among women; in Mexico this figure approximates 14 percent [7]. In both the U.S. and Mexico, women tend to become infected with HIV at a younger age than men, and those women who are marginalized (the ethnic and racial minorities in the U.S., and the economically disadvantaged in Mexico) are disproportionately affected by the AIDS epidemic. Epidemiological evidence has also demonstrated that HIV transmission among women in the United States happens primarily through blood exchange; 51 percent of infected women are intravenous drug users. In Mexico, the majority of HIV positive women have been infected through heterosexual activity. The pattern of HIV infection among women in El Paso and Juarez reflect the same pattern [8].

In the El Paso-Juarez metropolitan area, there seems to be a clear separation in the makeup of the female sex workers populations, those who are addicted to injectable drugs and those who are not addicted. This separation is clearly related to which side of the border they work. In the U.S. side of the border, 13 percent of the female sex workers have used an injectable drug at one time in their lives; in Mexico only 0.5 percent had ever used an injectable drug. Alcohol appears to be the drug of choice among female sex workers in the Mexican side of the border [5, 9]. The rate of incidence of HIV among female sex workers in Juarez is only 0.6 percent reflecting their low use of injectable drugs.

The Impact of Migration

As a whole, the U.S.-Mexico border region is becoming one of the fastest growing urban areas in North America. The continued increase in the population in the region has placed additional demands on an already overburdened public health infrastructure in both cities, including the prevention and treatment of infectious and transmittable diseases such as tuberculosis and STDs, including HIV. Since the second World War, there has been a steady increase in the population in the border region and this process has accelerated since the installation of the "maquiladora" industry in the region and with the ratification of the North American Free Trade Agreement (NAFTA). Maquiladoras, also called "twin plants," are assembly and light manufacturing plants belonging to U.S. industries and located in Mexican border towns. The products of these plants are legally exported to the U.S. without paying the usual U.S. customs import duties. The increase in population of the border towns is more noticeable on the Mexican side of the border where cities like Tijuana, Mexicali and Ciudad Juarez have had to cope with the pressures of an enormous internal migration of workers from the interior of Mexico seeking employment opportunities in these cities and in the U.S.

Migrants who legally or illegally cross the U.S. border at El Paso to obtain farm work in the United States are divided into two distinct groups: (a) those who use the region as a transition point to move to other agricultural regions in Texas, or elsewhere for a more extended period of time, and (b) those who are sojourners (i.e., they work for only one day at the time in the U.S. and live in Juarez). In the El Paso-Juarez border, most of these sojourners have a border crossing card ("Pasaporte") that allows them to work in the U.S. for 72 hours at a time. These sojourners fulfill the legal short-term agricultural work niche left vacant when the "bracero" program discontinued some time ago.

Most migrant farmworkers who travel to agricultural areas in the interior of the U.S. return to the interior of Mexico after the harvest season is over. These farmworkers who are in transit from and to the interior of Mexico form a "floating" population who, if infected with HIV, and engaging in recreational sex may place the female sex worker population in El Paso and Juarez at risk for infection. The uninfected workers may also contract HIV if they engage in unprotected sexual encounters in El Paso or Juarez.

Sojourners are also at risk of becoming infected with HIV because they are relatively more affluent than those migrants who are in transit, and may have more opportunities to use the services of a sex worker in either city. This relative affluence is brought about by the smaller expenses they incur for their daily living in comparison to a migrant worker. A migrant who illegally enters the U.S. for an extended period of time has to pay for transportation and bribes to cross the border and incur boarding and lodging costs while looking for a job or working in the U.S.

Methods

Ethnographers conducted systematic interviews of sex workers in El Paso and Juarez. These interviews were framed so as to help answer some questions about the circumstances that placed female sex workers and their clients at risk for HIV contagion, and to help in the development and implementation of HIV prevention and treatment interventions and health education campaigns. Differences in risk taking behavior and in the socio-cultural context of the sex work on either side of the U.S.-Mexico border were particularly explored. These differences were further examined by comparing available data from a second study. The data from the second study was from interviews conducted with Mexican and Mexican-American street sex workers in these "sister cities." Sister cities or "Ciudad Hermanas" refer to those cities which face each other on the U.S.-Mexico border and those that share the same physical, social and cultural environments.

In both studies in-depth, open-ended semi-structured ethnographic interviews were conducted with a total of 22 female sex workers in both El Paso and Ciudad Juarez. Although there were many areas of overlap in information collected in the interviews--which can be viewed as shared characteristics of the border areas and of a communal body of values--it was decided at the outset that the analysis of the interviews would be conducted separately to highlight the comparative significant differences in risk taking behavior of the socio-cultural context of sex work on both sides of the border.

The interviews were transcribed and analyzed using a word processing program to assemble the data in categories. The results are presented in a number of categories relating to family relationships, drug abuse, and issues of sexual relations with clients, specifically migrant workers.

Characteristics of Sex Workers Interviewed
in El Paso and Juarez

The 12 sex workers in the Juarez sample ranged in age from 17 to 45 years and the 10 sex workers in the El Paso sample from 20 to 61 years of age. Excluding this "elder" representative of the profession from the El Paso sample (even though she was occasionally still active), the mean age of the women interviewed was 23.8 years in Juarez and 28.7 years in El Paso. All of the women in the Juarez sample were born in Mexico: seven in the state of Chihuahua, three in Coahuila and two in the southern Mexican state of Morelos. Two of the Juarez women had spent over six months in the United States, one in California and the other in New Mexico. Five women in the El Paso sample were born in Mexico, four were born in western U.S., and one was born in Puerto Rico. This last woman also had a Puerto Rican mother and her interview is not included in this discussion of the results.

In terms of educational attainment and sources of income, from the total sample only two women reported having finished high school, one on each side of the border. However, two of the U.S.-born women working in El Paso were able to obtain a GED later in life. Two women reported having some technical education and job skills. Aside from earning money from sex work or selling drugs, the only legitimate job categories reported by women in the sample were bartenders, working as a waiter, go-go dancing, a brief clerical job, and one "maquila" job at age 14.

Results

Family Histories--Alcohol and Other Drugs in Relationship to Childhood Abuse and Neglect

The women from El Paso and Juarez reported histories of poverty, dislocation, alcoholism and other drug abuse in their families. Alcohol appeared consistently as the most frequently mentioned factor in family disruption and violence. Eighteen of the women reported alcoholic fathers and step-fathers, and three told of their mothers' "heavy drinking". Eleven of the women also told of drug use in their families, one of the eleven had a step-father who used heroin, and many had uncles who were "dope fiends." According to one of the women:

> The only recollection I have of my mom--she was never with us, with me or my sister. She used to work and drink a lot, and some times she would come home at night drunk, this is the only memory I have of my mom.

The womens' histories of alcoholism and other drug abuse are intertwined with childhood abuse and neglect. Six of the Juarez women and four of the El Paso women told of a father, a step-father or other adult male relatives having attempted sexual relations with them; and, when successful, to have maintained a long-term sexual relationship with them. Sexual abuse was the most frequent reason given for leaving home at an early age, although physical abuse was reported more frequently than sexual abuse. In the Juarez sample, 83 percent of the women reported having been in an abusive relationship as children. As one woman recounted:

> My dad drank a lot, he did drink a lot, and he had my mom in
> fear, just like I live with X. Then my dad would come home
> drunk--he was a trucker--all the time. I imagine he also used--
> was a drug addict, because he used to come home really loaded
> all the time, and he would mistreat us. He would shove us out
> into the street, my mom and my other sisters, and he would try to
> beat her.

A similar situation was reported by the women from El Paso. One woman related how she helplessly watched her mother savagely beaten, while protecting her younger sisters and brothers from their father's ire. Another reported that she started "...putting cotton in my ears so I wouldn't hear the screams." Another woman described why she left home: "My life has been very sad. My mother wanted only money, my brother hit me...when my step-father tried to rape me, I ran away."

Verbal abuse was so common that the women almost never reported it unless questioned. It has been our experience that at times when an action is very common it does not get reported and, without prodding the respondent, the interviewer may be able to unveil the actions. A typical example of verbal abuse was, "my mother called us *putas* (whores). I was 8 or 9."

Embarrassment, shame, guilt and fear were common themes. Women spoke of feeling guilty assuming that they were the cause of the family discord: "The problem was with me," one woman reported, "I was the only girl at that time. He (step-father) got mad 'cause my mother gave me more attention 'cause I was a girl. He started going away from her."

Communication with and nurturing by parents appeared largely unknown to these women as children, factors clearly reflected in their self-images and adult lives. When positive relationships were mentioned, grandparents were invariably mentioned as having been their caretakers: "The good times I had with my grandparents, my grand daddy would take me downtown, and even to the bullfights."

Relationship with Non–client Male
Sexual Partners

The adult sexual relationship history of Juarez women was tainted by fear, physical abuse and rape. Two of the women stated that they had been raped or sexually assaulted by a stranger, including clients. More striking was the degree of violence suffered by the women from their steady sexual partners: five women in Juarez had been threatened with physical violence by a steady partner, and four women had been in a physically abusive relationship. Three women mentioned that they were repeatedly forced to have sex with their partners under the threat of being hurt if they did not comply.

All the women from El Paso reported abusive and also drug related relationships with men, even first relationships. "All my boyfriends were drug dealers," said one of the women, "They got a lot of attention, and I was using drugs." All the women from El Paso mentioned drugs as the major compelling force in initiating, shaping, maintaining, as well as destroying their relationships with men. They had a pattern of serial steady sexual partners but the relationships were short-lived.

In discussing their partners, it was clear that these women were not willing or perhaps able to establish relationships with non-alcohol or non-drug using men. The women from El Paso in particular had relationships exclusively with men involved with drugs. One woman reported that "I'm not comfortable around someone who doesn't use dope," another stated that when "...both can get their dope together; there's more communication. Others want you to kick and you don't want to...they don't know what I go through." These unions were maintained despite serious physical abuse and neglect of the women and their children by the woman's male sexual partners.

The women from Juarez, on the other hand, voiced their need and the importance to be in a relationship that was long-standing, in contrast to the short-lived relationship they experienced with clients. As we mentioned before, although these relationships tended to be characterized by physical abuse, the fact that the women stayed on with the abusive partner, tended to reinforce the perception that other forces were at play in the decision to stay on in the relationship. When questioned for the reasons of not moving out of abusive relationships, these women mentioned that the need for economic support by the men was the main reason for staying. Moreover, many family traditional values and ideals operated to keep Juarez sex workers in these relationships:

> I did not want to get married because I did not want to suffer... or I believe that all men are the same...that is why I didn't want to get married...also I was scared of him, since he used all kinds of drugs...(But) during New Year or when we were out celebrat-

ing...I stayed over at his house and next day they told me I had to marry him...my dad...well, he really threw me out of the house.

This need to be in a relationship that was long-standing was also shared by Mexican women who were part of the El Paso sample. As one woman said,

When I was with X, my boyfriend, he used to kick my ass so bad I would wind up in the hospital. He would choke me until I would pass out...an every day thing. ...I was a virgin...my grandma said whoever you go to bed with, you have to stay with...so I thought no one would want me.

Despite all the abuse, however, the dream of a happy family still persisted:

When I feel fine is when all of us are there at home, all together. When we have parties and all of us are happy, I feel very good because I feel that it is a real family...so all of us eat together and when all of us look fine I feel very comfortable.

Drug Use Patterns Among Sex Workers in El Paso and Juarez

The pattern of drug use among sex workers in the two cities was very different. All the women in the El Paso sample were active substance abusers. Although, 59 percent of the women in the Juarez sample reported having used drugs, when alcohol use was removed from the analysis, the prevalence of use of other drugs is even lower.

None of the Juarez sex workers had ever used heroin, speedballs or crack cocaine. One woman had tried cocaine but was not currently using the drug. Prescription drugs, alcohol and marijuana were the drugs of choice in Juarez. While one-half the women in Juarez reported had used amphetamines and alcohol in the past, only one of them was currently using them. The interviews seem to disclose culturally prescribed norms that appear to condone male drug use but put a limit on the substances which were acceptable for women to consume. Among the Juarez sex workers, drugs were an influence in their lives to the extent that their lives were defined by their relations, and that the significant male in their lives was most likely to be a heavy user of alcohol and other drugs.

All but one of the El Paso sex workers were shooting heroin or "speedballing," that is, injecting intravenously a combination of heroin and cocaine. In addition, sex workers in El Paso had started using drugs at a very early age, between 11 and 18 years of age. Except for one woman, all the others reported past use of heroin, cocaine or a combination of both. The one non-heroin user had snorted cocaine until she was 19 years old. In contrast with the Juarez sample where the average age of initiation of drug use was 17 years; in the El Paso sample, the average age of first use was 14 years.

In both El Paso and Juarez, the initiation into the use of substances other that alcohol followed a distinct pattern. Inhalants (chiefly glue and spray paint) and marijuana were used first, followed by gradual use of pills (uppers and downers). Alcohol preceded heroin use by a few years for most of the women. Three of the El Paso women, however, reported that heroin was the first drug they used and that they began by injecting because boyfriends or a family member was a user. Sometimes this initiation into heroin was done voluntarily as an experiment: "My husband and brother were using dope...I used to see them...I felt frustrated until I tried it. I wanted to see what they felt," but sometimes the exposure to the drug was involuntary: "Heroin was my first drug. I started with my kid's dad...I started with him at 13...he was a dealer ...he was putting heroin in my drink."

Although the use of heroin is suspected to exist among Mexican sex workers in Juarez, the interviews did not provide evidence of its use. One possible explanation is that the proximity of the border creates an opportunity for women who inject drugs to migrate into the U.S., to an environment were injection drug use among women is more "acceptable." A Mexican woman who was part of the El Paso sample confided that she began injecting when a Mexican social service institution took her child away because of her "vices" and put the child in her mother-in-law's custody.

There seems to exists a culturally sanctioned use of alcohol. Over one-half of the women interviewed on both sides of the border used al-cohol and accepted its use as the lesser of many evils. One common explanation was:

> I know we all have a past, right?, something that the psychologist feel you need to hide from; that is why he chooses to hide ...lately after he recovered from an illness, he began to work, but he started drinking again. Well at least drinking alcohol isn't using drugs.

Although all of the women who used substances in Juarez and El Paso were poly-drug abusers, their drug-of-choice was different. Among the Juarez women, alcohol and drugs with medical uses (sedatives and amphetamines) were most used; among El Paso women, heroin administered by injection was the drug of choice.

Drug Trafficking as an Economic Strategy for Survival

An important difference between the El Paso and the Juarez samples were the stories of repeated local and federal incarcerations for burglary, parole violation, possession, delivery, credit card and check fraud, forgery and prostitution. One of the women from the El Paso sample reported "somewhere between 23 to 26 misdemeanors and 4 felony arrests," others talked of 8 to 15 arrests, still another explained "Four years on the street, I've been in jail half the time..." All but two of the El Paso women were interviewed while incarcerated in the County Jail, a few blocks from the downtown "stroll." In contrast, in the Juarez sample only two women had ever been in jail; both had been arrested for creating a public disturbance which was the most common excuse for incarceration of a sex worker in the absence of clear laws outlawing prostitution.

In Juarez, trafficking of drugs was common among sex workers with steady sexual partners, sometimes referred as "husbands." As one woman observed:

> ...he was always a hard working man, he started to sell marijuana, that as far as he had gone, then he ran into a friend who had just gotten out of the El Paso (Texas) county jail; he ran into him here in Juarez and he talked him into helping him sell heroin in El Paso, since my husband has a passport, he would smuggle small amounts.

Another woman reported: "it was when my husband met with this *gringo*, he was the one that would sell on his own, he would sell from the house, you know how they talk each other into things, they find someone who will get them drugs or who will help them sell drugs."

Drug Treatment

The drug treatment programs in both El Paso and Juarez do not seem to have been very successful. Typically, the women did not stay for long in the programs, and those who stayed did not stay drug free for very long after the end of treatment. In Juarez there were limited options with only one drug rehabilitation center specializing in treatment for women. The options seem to be more open for alcoholics but again only one program exists in Juarez that specifically targets women. Sex workers in Juarez did not perceive that they had any appropriate or acceptable treatment alternatives to act as a balance to the lure of the alcohol and drugs that always hung over their head. Despite the lack of treatment facilities in Juarez, the jail detoxification self-initiated program mentioned in El Paso (discussed below) was not a viable option to the women.

Sex workers in Juarez worked in an environment that promoted the heavy consumption of alcohol. Having a family history of alcohol abuse, neglect, and without having access to women centered treatment, there seemed to be little hope for the rehabilitation of these women, and their placement into jobs with a lesser risk of HIV infection.

In El Paso, the options that were available to the sex workers were also very limited, jail was seen as the best "treatment" option in El Paso. One woman stated, "we don't care about programs, family, kids-- this (jail) is the only place you're O.K. My mom said, 'it's time for you to get busted.' I'm tired of it...I started too young." In fact, jail was the single most important factor in getting off drugs for these women. "The only time I go straight is in jail" said one "I'm going to ask parole to help me." Another remembered, "I used to ask God to arrest me. I was tired of drugs...no one to help me leave that shit. Little social support is available on the outside." Another women explained, "I like the dope...*me encanta* (I love it)...the crowd, they offer it to you, sell it to you...you see it. *Te van a dar ganas* (you will want it)." The use of incarceration as a non-formal options for detoxification demonstrates the lack of availability of rehabilitation program geared towards sex workers in El Paso.

Sex Work as a Lifestyle

There were marked differences between sex workers in El Paso and Juarez on the reasons given about the circumstances that led them to their present line of work. In the Juarez sample, being a sex worker was seen as a lifestyle imposed on the women due to the lack of opportunities to earn a living in other fields. When questioned, the women in the Juarez sample said surprisingly little about their work; in contrast, they would share in great detail stories about their families of origin, their current families and their sexual partners. The women in the El Paso sample mostly related stories involving drugs and the need to support their drug habit. However, it would be fallacious to stress drug use as the causal factor for their choice of profession. Poverty, abusive families of origin, histories of "spousal" physical and sexual abuse, limited alternatives for supporting themselves and their children with little education and poor job skills were the most likely causative agents. The difference may be due to the self-selection in the sample caused by a greater availability of drugs in El Paso that attracted sex workers who were addicted to heroin or cocaine.

Migration

Most of the women in the El Paso sample had "worked" in other cities away from the border. Some of the cities mentioned included Dallas, Houston, Albuquerque, Denver, Los Angeles, Phoenix, Tucson, Austin and San Antonio. Most of them appeared to have traveled to these cities accompanying boyfriends and husbands, usually for drug trafficking. They reported that the money in Denver was the best. No one wanted to work across the border in Juarez because of the poor pay (in pesos) and the fear to be jailed (fear of jail was related to drug use not to prostitution) under the bad conditions of the Juarez jail.

HIV-related Issues: Condom Use

In both samples, the sex workers had limited information about HIV/AIDS and had received only minimal instruction on condom use. For those who used condoms, fear of STD contagion was a very important motivator. One Juarez woman explained her reasons for using condoms: "I don't use condoms to avoid pregnancy, I have had a tubal ligation, but I take care of myself (use a condom) so I don't get a disease ...because I am scared that some one is going to give me a disease." An El Paso sex worker also mentioned the fear of disease as a reason to wear a condom: "I always use a condom, with blow jobs also. I carry

Kiss-o-Mint. You can still catch things...why don't they want to believe that. If not AIDS, you can catch gonorrhea or syphilis. If a trick refuses, I give him a $15 hand job."

Another stated that she used a condom "always with a trick, except with a blow job" she then added "some tricks want a condom with a blow job..." however, "most tricks don't like to use condoms."

The ethnicity and country of origin of the clients also made a difference in the rate of condom use. As observed by a Juarez sex worker, "The most considerate are the Japanese; they bring their own condoms. The Mexicans never want to use them; and the *gringos* (Americans) do whatever we tell them." An El Paso sex worker noted, "Mexican men don't like using it, it hurts their manhood. They say they can't please a woman with that. Anglo men are smarter to that effect." Still another talked of charging $5 more to have sex without a condom, hoping that they would not want to spend the money and would accept the use of a condom. "But they pay," she said, "man, they're married...they ought to use a rubber. Some men do not care."

Among the women in El Paso, drugs play a role in the risk taking behavior. One of the women explained how she decided whether or not to use a condom, "I use on the street if I see anything weird...I check and make sure he's clear...but you can't tell if he has AIDS." She paused and then added, "I don't have money for condoms...I don't even have money for dope." This woman stated that if she had the money, she would buy drugs before she bought a condom.

All of the above information is consistent with numerous other studies investigating female sex workers and their use of a condom as an HIV prevention strategy. As in this study, most sex workers they did not use condoms with boyfriends or husbands, whether or not they were shooting drugs, just out of jail, or known to have had other sexual relationships [2].

Injection Drug User Sexual Partner

For the Juarez women who have not used drugs other than alcohol before coming to work in a bar, the environment can lead them to use other drugs which may place them at risk for HIV infection. More commonly, however, the Juarez women will be placed at risk by their sexual partner's use of injectable drugs. As one woman noted:

> I worked in a bar and he would be heavy into drugs, he would
> use in the bathrooms, I would see when he would get high, then I
> noticed him , I met him when he was very high, I felt attracted to
> him not because he was handsome, I felt sorry for him; then it
> came time when I took him home, then he continued to use, I
> would not force him to stop using.

HIV Seroprevalence

One statistic that distinguished the Juarez sample from the El Paso
sample was the seroprevalent status of the women. Among the Juarez
women, only one woman had been tested for HIV before participating in
the research and her results had come back negative. Fortunately, none
of the Juarez sex workers who were later tested were positive. The El
Paso sample had a very different serological profile. Of the 10 women
interviewed, four revealed their HIV positive status. These women,
however, attributed their infection with HIV not to their job as sex
workers but through their needle sharing practices. As one El Paso woman observed:

> I got my HIV through them (the transsexuals). In the free world I
> was hanging around with them. I knew something was wrong. I
> didn't want to share their rigs...I didn't share their rigs, but I
> came home and they were shooting up and I shared with some-
> one who shared with them.

Only one woman referred to the sexual transmission of HIV. Her
concern was not about the source of her own infection but instead to the
risk that she might have exposed other people: "I knew something was
wrong with me...a real bad cough. My T-cell count is 600, but all they
give me is vitamins. When I found out I was sick, I didn't want to have
to work no more. I probably did get somebody infected."

Once a sex worker was HIV positive or AIDS symptomatic, there
was a large difference between the level of care provided in El Paso and
Juarez. This observation is based on previous experience by one of the
authors among other HIV infected populations and cannot be collabo-
rated by the sample of this study since none of the women in Juarez
tested positive for HIV. In the El Paso sample, there were clear indica-
tions of the level of care available to these women, at some of the local
institutions: "Me and my uncle talk a lot. He's on AZT...he's my age
...has blotches on his face and high fevers. God made me see I can't live

like this. It's not like I have a choice like other people...I can go into full-blown AIDS."

The experience of another woman in the El Paso sample: "I don't like to come to this doctor (in the jail). He goes 'Oooh, you got AIDS!' I say, 'Man, don't you know the difference!' (She is HIV-positive, asymptomatic.) 'You're *still* infected!' he says."

For the women with unknown HIV status or negative status questions about HIV and AIDS were met with one main response: the word *fear* used over and over again. Most but not all of the women were clearly aware of some of risks for HIV infection inherent in their profession. Among the women in Juarez, there were more reports of risk taking behavior which we believe was based on lack of information. "It is risky", said one, "we all know...but, a lot of girls think that by looking at a guy you can tell if he's sick. I took a lot of chances."

Again, the most salient difference in perceptions of risk factors between the Juarez and El Paso samples was related to the use of injectable drugs with needle sharing. Sharing of needles was an acknowledged risk by El Paso sex workers but, although this knowledge increased the worry and fear of HIV infection among them, it did little to stop the behavior. Although condoms were said not to be used with sexual partners, the perceptions of risk of HIV infection from drug using partners was not very clear among the women sampled.

Discussion

There were marked differences between the HIV risky and protective behaviors among El Paso and Juarez female sex workers. Cultural differences and social roles made the women who worked the El Paso side of the border probably more representative of the "hard-core" sex worker in the region. They had longer drug abuse histories, and criminal behavior and the role that illicit drug use played in their lives was markedly different from the Juarez sex workers. The substances of drug use initiation were also different. Alcohol and pills were use at the onset of adulthood by the Juarez women; while the use of cocaine and heroin, and the adoption of the lifestyle of an addict were seen at an young age among El Paso sex workers.

Most of the El Paso sex workers were Mexican-American. Mexican sex workers who worked in El Paso did so very rarely, and if caught working the streets, were arrested and returned across the border to the Mexican border authorities. Mexican-American sex workers do not work in the Mexican side for fear of being arrested and having to spend time in a Mexican jail.

While most of the Juarez sex workers tended to work to support their families, most of the El Paso women worked to support drug habits. The migration of Mexican female sex workers across the border, to work in the U.S., seems to signify a shift from their use of alcohol to the use of heroin as a drug of choice. In El Paso, although the risk of being incarcerated in greater, there was more money to be made on the streets, money that could be used to acquire drugs.

There were also points of commonalty between the two sub-populations. Most female sex workers in both cities were abused sexually, physically and psychologically, and in the best case neglected while they were children. They seemed to follow the pattern of leaving abusive homes and moving into abusive relationships. Lack of schooling and job skills was present in both samples. In Juarez, the lack of money and support acted as barriers for cessation of drug use and a change in profession; while in El Paso, lack of a nurturing environment made the utilization of existing opportunities a moot point. Among all women, self-concept was very poor and self-esteem was practically non-existent. The almost complete absence of positive role models led these women to look for partners who were similar to their drug using peers, and alcohol and drugs became the controlling factor in sexual partner selection.

Different factors appeared to play a role in the practice of risk-enhancing behaviors among the women from Juarez and El Paso. For the sex workers from Juarez, one fact that became apparent was that the lack of information and cultural barriers and not the need for drugs seemed to play a much more important role for those who did not use a condom with their clients or their IDU sexual partner. For the sex workers from El Paso, while protection against HIV infection was discussed, the need for a "fix" overshadowed all the other considerations. More importantly, sex without protection and the use of shared syringes and needles were accepted by them without much problem.

Even the most "hard core" sex workers asked for a chance to quit their drug habit. As one them enrolled in a detoxification program stated in an anguished voice: "I want so bad to make it this time...my mother is praying for me." Both El Paso and Juarez sex workers asked for detoxification and treatment programs to free them from the lifestyle of a drug using sex worker and for programs that also took into consideration the needs of their children. More resources for drug treatments and job alternatives for sex workers were among the unspoken promises made during the heyday of the North America Free Trade Agreement (NAFTA).

Migrant Farmworkers, Sex Workers and NAFTA

In the eyes of many Mexicans, NAFTA promised to be the solution to most of their economic problems and, through a "trickle-down" effect, the solution to many social problems as well. This promise had implications for the lives of Mexican sex workers because the increased work opportunities would allow many to leave that line of work, since most were selling sex for economic survival reasons and not to support a drug habit. The increase in economic opportunities would have decreased the number of women moving to large urban centers in the border in search of work because economic opportunities would be available in the interior of Mexico.

If there were jobs in Mexico which created the same amount of relative income (measured by the expenses, risks, trouble, loneliness, etc.), Mexicans would not come to the U.S. Although not openly acknowledged, there was a tendency to analyze the migration of Mexicans to the U.S. as a desire to become Americans. The reality, however, was quite the opposite; given a viable economic option, most would stay in Mexico. On the El Paso-Juarez border, this pattern would be the norm if distortions caused by the economic disparities between the two societies were to decrease.

The number of women at risk for HIV infection was expected to decrease as well, since the number of migrants to the border areas would also have decreased. There would been less exposure to STDs, and all the health and social problems associated with sex outside an established relationship. The increase in income in Mexico would have also hopefully eliminated the small number of Mexican women who would cross the border to provide sexual services in El Paso. The economic "boom" brought about by NAFTA would have helped the HIV prevention and treatment efforts in both sides for several reasons. First, there would be a decrease in the migration of already HIV infected farmworkers to the border areas to cross into the U.S. Second, there would be a decrease in the number of farmworkers who returned to Mexico infected with HIV. Third, there would be an increase in the resources to provide treatment for sex workers who used drugs.

The above predictions seemed valid given the knowledge of motivations and behaviors of migrant farmworkers and of sex workers. The economic reality of the currency devaluation in Mexico in 1995, however, have made all these predictions completely wrong. On the contrary, the problem of HIV infection among the migrant farmworkers will become more serious since the exchange rate favors the acquisition of dollars, and income opportunities are more plentiful on the U.S. side. If anything, the migration of farmworkers to the U.S. will increase.

Given the historic disparity in exchange rates between the two countries, which have been aggravated by the latest round of devaluation and the dislocations in the Mexican economy brought about by NAFTA, these agricultural migrant workers will have more disposable income (in Mexican Peso terms) when returning to Mexico, and part of it will be used to purchase sex services while in the border area.

The price for sex in El Paso is higher than in Juarez but, as discussed above, most of the sex workers in El Paso worked to support a drug habit. Furthermore, when the need of a "fix" was great, they "discounted" their services. In addition, there has been a decrease in the price of drugs (heroin, crack, cocaine) and a parallel realignment in the price of sex, since less money was needed to acquire the same quantity of drugs. Although there is no systematic data available to support these assertions, there is anecdotal evidence to support this speculation. Furthermore, the rate of exchange traditionally favored those with U.S. dollars, and this trend will continue, and possibly accelerate, during the readjustments brought about by NAFTA.

We will probably see an increase of the number of legal and illegal migrants crossing the border. Due to the new emphasis on "closing the border" by the Immigration and Naturalization Services (INS), many undocumented sojourners who could commute everyday will stay in the U.S. for longer amounts of time. The longer stay may entice them to procure sex services on the U.S. side of the border, and consequently, increase their chances of becoming infected with HIV. This increase in demand for sexual services will also increase the supply of Mexican sex workers who will cross the border to obtain clients. Furthermore, the Mexican sex workers will be exposed to the drug use pattern of their U.S. counterparts coupled with the increased risk of HIV infection by the use of shared syringes and needles.

In conclusion, there is a real threat for the spread of HIV/AIDS across the U.S.-Mexico border. As indicated in the study, the threat is more of the spread of the infection from the U.S. to Mexico. Given the close cultural, historical, familial and economic bonds that exist bet-

136

ween the sister cities across the U.S.-Mexico border, there is a dire need to address the migration of diseases across the borders.

Acknowledgments

The study was funded by a grant from the U.S. National Institute on Drug Abuse (NIDA) and the Centers for Disease Control and Prevention.

References

1. Ramos R: COMPAÑEROS project: an AIDS outreach program for IV drug abuser and sex workers. *Border Epidemiologic Bull* 1989; Sept/Oct.
2. Abt Associates: *AIDS Outreach to Female Prostitutes and Sexual Partners of Injection Drug Users*. Final Report to the National Institute on Drug Abuse Community Research Branch. Contract N° 271-88-8224, 1992
3. Hyamathi A, Vasquez R: Impact of poverty, homelessness, and drugs on Hispanic women at risk for HIV infection. *Hisp J Beh Sci* 1989; 11(4):299-314.
4. U.S. Conference of Mayors: *The United States Conference of Local Health Officers: AIDS the Second Wave*. United States Conference of Mayors 1992; p. 32.
5. Ortega H, Ramos R: Migratory patterns and HIV disease along the United States-Mexico border. *Border Health* 1991; 4(1):18–24.
6. El Paso City-County Health District. *A Survey of Male Sex Workers in El Paso*. El Paso City-County Health District and the STOP AIDS Project of the Southwest AIDS Committee (SWAC) 1990.
7. Del Rio A, Magis CL, Garcia ML, et al.: Is there a trend to ruralization of AIDS cases in Mexico? VIII International Conference on AIDS 1992; Abstract number POC 4012:C 247.
8. American Public Health Association (APHA): *Women and HIV Disease*. A report of the Special Initiative on AIDS of the APHA 1991; 5.
9. Deren S, Shedlin M, Miller K, et al.: HIV risk behaviors in three groups of Latina prostitutes: Dominican, Mexican and Puerto Rican. IX International Conference on AIDS 1993; Abstract number PO-C14-2902:P701.

7

Risk Factors for HIV and AIDS Among Latino Farmworkers in Pennsylvania

Miguel A. Pérez and Katherine Fennelly

Introduction

The precise number of seasonal and migratory farmworkers in the United States is difficult to ascertain. The General Accounting Office (GAO) estimated that in 1990, there were between 1.5 and 2.5 million farmworkers in this country. Research has found that first generation immigrant Latinos are more likely than non-Latinos to be employed in agriculture [1, 2]. Department of Agriculture figures show that in 1990, 29 percent of hired farmworkers in the U.S. were Latinos [3], however, in the testimony before the Commission on Security and Cooperation in Europe, Kissan estimated that up to 80 percent of farmworkers in the U.S. are Mexican-born [4]. Similarly, results from a Michigan survey indicated that over 75 percent of the farmworkers in that state were of Mexican origin [5].

Discrepancies in the number of farmworkers in this country are easily explained by one of the main problems encountered by researchers in this area, the lack of a uniform definition. For instance, Section 329 of the Public Health Service Act (1962) defines migratory and seasonal agricultural farmworkers as those employed in agriculture and agriculture related industries. The Act excludes the fishing, lumber, dairy, cattle and poultry industries from its definition unless they are connected to a farm. The Department of Agriculture defines a migrant farmworker as "someone who temporarily crosses state or county boundaries and stays overnight to do hired farmwork, or one who has no usual place of residence and does hired work in two or more counties during the year." Moreover, the Department of Education defines a migrant as "anyone who crosses school district lines to be engaged in agriculture or agri-related industry."

A number of researchers have shown poverty and low levels of education as distal correlates of sexually transmissible diseases (STDs). By this measure, migrant farmworkers are likely to have particularly elevated risks, since they are among the most impoverished groups in the U.S. On average, farmworkers complete fewer than eight years of formal schooling and most have incomes well below federal poverty levels [6]. Furthermore, farmworkers are the less likely segment of the population to receive adequate health care services [7]. Farmworkers have been found to live in employer-provided housing, in overcrowded conditions, under poor sanitary conditions, and are exposed to parasitic infections, including viral infections [8].

Several studies have shown that farmworkers are at a high risk for HIV infection and the subsequent development of AIDS relative to other population groups. A national survey of farmworkers attending migrant health clinics reported the seroprevalence rate of 0.5 percent among farmworkers in the Eastern Coast migrant stream [9]. This compares, for example, to a weighted prevalence rate of 10.8 percent among urban African American men [10] and a seroprevalence rate of 2.5 per 1,000 college students [11]. In a study of 554 farmworkers in New Jersey, Lyons [12] found three percent of those tested as HIV positive; however, in a study of 198 farmworkers in South Carolina, Jones et al. [13] found much higher rates; 13 percent of those tested were HIV positive. The authors concluded that, considering the number of those who refused to be tested, the actual seropositive rates may be even higher among this population. Barriers to health care encountered by farmworkers and the fact that many are uninsured and most are ineligible for need-based programs like Medicaid or Medicare may also combine to conceal the higher rates of disease and HIV infection among this population.

In addition to estimates of the prevalence of HIV, there are a number of studies suggesting that migrant farmworkers exhibit *risk factors* that may increase the likelihood of infection. These risk factors include insufficient knowledge concerning transmission modes, prevention means, high rates of STDs and unsafe sexual practices. Fennelly [14] in a survey of social and health care providers in a Pennsylvania county found that 67 percent of the respondents considered AIDS to be a problem among farmworkers. An additional 85 percent believed that STDs were a serious problem among the farmworkers they served.

Lack of information about the modes of HIV/AIDS transmission and appropriate means of prevention are proximal determinants of risk. Farmworkers lack knowledge of female to male transmission modes [15]. Foulk, Lafferty and Ryan [16] found that 69.9 percent of their respondents used douching after sex as a means to prevent against infection with HIV/AIDS and other STDs. Jones et al. [13] found that 16 percent of HIV positive farmworkers claimed not to be involved in high risk behaviors; however, six percent reported engaging in same gender sex, and 39 percent were intravenous drug users. Pérez [17] found that Latino migrant adolescents were not likely to use condoms for reasons ranging from discomfort and awkwardness to do so, and in the case of females, fear of being labeled as being "easy." Furthermore, farmworker adolescents believed it was easier for a woman to "give" AIDS to a male than for a male to transmit the virus to a female.

These lower levels of knowledge among farmworkers in general, and Latino farmworkers in particular, were similar to the lower levels found in the general Latino population. Alcalay, Sniderman, Mitchell and Griffin [18] found that Latinos were more likely than Whites to believe they could get AIDS from blood donations (36 and 15 percent, respectively). The same study found that Latinos were more likely than non-Hispanics to believe that HIV transmission can occur through casual contact. Dawson [19] found that 19 percent of Latinos believed they could catch AIDS from an unclean public toilet, while only eight percent of the White respondents and 10 percent of Blacks believed this to be true. In a telephone survey of Latino and White men, Van Oss-Marin, Gomez and Hearst [20] found that less acculturated Latino men and Latino men living in the Northeast were more likely to report multiple sexual partners.

Knowledge about AIDS seems to vary depending on language preference and among different origin groups, a proxy for acculturation [21]. Spanish-speaking Latinos were more likely than bilingual Latinos to believe AIDS is spread through casual contact [18]. Dawson and Hardy [19] found that Mexican-Americans tend to be less knowledgeable about HIV/AIDS than other Latino groups; only one-half of the Mexican-American respondents in their study indicated it is "definitely true" that "AIDS is an infectious disease caused by a virus," compared with 62 percent of other Latinos. Only 46 percent of Mexican respondents said they knew that blood transfusions are routinely tested for HIV antibodies compared to 55 percent of other Latinos, 72 percent of Whites and 53 percent of Black respondents provided this response.

A few researchers have suggested other potential modes of transmission of HIV among Latinos. These include a possible acceptance of same gender sex which may not be labeled "homosexuality" by the participants [22, 23]. Carrier [24] suggested that same gender sexual encounters are not stigmatized by Mexican culture. Furthermore, some authors suggest that it is not uncommon for men to turn to "effeminate" males to satisfy their sexual needs if no female sexual partner is available, or if they lack the economic resources to visit a sex worker [25].

Carrier [24] reported that unlike their American "gay" counterparts Mexican males engaging in same gender sex prefer anal intercourse over fellatio or other forms of sexual behavior. Furthermore, in contrast to their American counterparts, Latino males are more likely to assume only the "passive" or receptive role during same gender sex. Latino males engaging in these forms of same gender sex may not perceive themselves as "homosexual" or "bisexual" as long as they assume a dominant sexual role [26].

Another possible mode of transmission is self-injection of health and vitamin treatments among persons of Mexican origin. Trotter reported on the self-medication including injectables among Mexicans [27]. It is possible that such self-medication occurs without properly sterilized needles, thus promoting the transmission of infection.

Methods

The purpose of this exploratory study was to validate several hypotheses concerning possible risk factors for HIV and AIDS among Latino farmworkers employed in the mushroom industry in a southeastern Pennsylvania county. Discussions covered knowledge of HIV/AIDS (i.e., transmission modes), attitudes towards sexuality (i.e., "safer sex" communication), and sexual practices present among this population (i.e., same gender sex, condom use, and reliance on sex workers), as well as the use of syringes for self-injection of vitamins and medicines.

The sample comprised of Latino male migrant farmworkers (who comprise up to 98 percent of agricultural workers in the study areas) employed at mushroom farms in a predominantly White southeastern Pennsylvania county. In 1990, 38 percent of the county residents lived in rural areas and the per capita income was higher than that for the state as a whole [28]. The county depends heavily upon the mushroom and horticultural industries for revenues. In 1990, the combined output of this industry exceeded $64 million [29] and more than 1,700 farmworkers were employed to pick crops on more than 35 registered farms.

Sampling farmworkers is complicated by the fact that many are undocumented and are reluctant to be interviewed. In this study, participants were selected following standard sampling procedures. A comprehensive list of registered mushroom camps in the area was obtained from the Pennsylvania Department of Environmental Resources, then camps were randomly selected using a table of random numbers. Following preliminary visits to the camps, the researchers discovered some of the camps had been closed or that it was difficult to be accepted as outsiders. It was then decided that the investigators should be introduced to the groups by a local, well-known and respected minister, and by two social agency case workers who have worked in the area for a number of years. These individuals had visited every camp in the county, met a significant number of the participants, and knew the location of the employer-provided residences. The *confianza* farmworkers had in these individuals allowed the researchers easier access to the population of interest.

A total of 12 focus group interviews were conducted with 117 men in the county in group sizes ranging in size from 6 to 14 participants. Nine focus groups were conducted in April 1993 and, an additional three focus groups were conducted in March 1994. As with many other agricultural products, mushroom workers get paid by the amount of work they perform. So as not to interfere with work, ten focus group interviews were conducted at the participants' residences during the evening hours, and two groups were conducted in a lounge at the worksite during a lunch break. Respondents were provided with refreshments, and at the conclusion of the interviews, received educational materials, condoms, T-shirts and pens as tokens of appreciation.

We followed a rigorous data collection and data analysis protocol. Two focus group moderators were present during each of the interviews, and either one could ask questions not posed by the other. In practice, however, one moderator asked questions while the second took detailed notes, including selected responses, their thoughts on farmworkers reactions to questions and their impressions based on the respondents' body language. Responses were audio-taped, with the farmworkers' permission, by two strategically located tape recorders. At the end of each interview, the researchers debriefed each other and discussed items peculiar to each group. These discussions provided the bases for the field notes kept by each investigator. These discussions allowed for revision of the instrument revision.

The focus group audio tapes were transcribed by an individual not involved in the project until this point. In addition to transcribing the 24 tapes, this person provided some input based on her interpretation of the audio-taped interviews. This input provided yet another level to the investigator triangulation used in this study. Transcript accuracy was verified by the principal investigator. In cases where discrepancies were discovered, they were quickly rectified through the listening of the audio tapes. The transcripts were combined with the field notes to create a master file, which contained not only responses, but thoughts and reactions.

The three investigators conducted an independent data analysis were they searched for emerging themes using the interviewer's guide as a reference. The investigators met with the principal investigator and discussed similarities and differences in their data coding. Based on this input, the principal investigator selected the final themes used in analysis. Consideration was given to areas where the researchers agreed, and, in those areas where there was no agreement, a consensus was reached. Again, the number of emerging themes was kept to under ten, and areas with different names, or closely related domains, were collapsed into one or more themes. The themes were then attached to the master file containing the responses. Data, with its corresponding themes, were entered into the *Ethnograph* computer program. The illustrative quotes presented in this chapter were selected using the *Ethnograph*. Preliminary results were reviewed by the independent panel of experts.

Most participants were unmarried Mexican men in their early twenties, with a mean age of 23.9 (Table 7.1). These proportions resemble estimates of the characteristics of the total population of mushroom workers in the county. All the males interviewed were currently residing with male co-workers in housing rented to them by mushroom farm owners. About one-fourth of the men were married, and many had dependents. Several reported frequent trips (i.e., at least once every two years) to their native towns in Mexico to visit families. Fewer than one percent of the study participants were fluent in English and all respondents indicated a preference for Spanish. Therefore, all of the focus group interviews were conducted in Spanish.

Results

The interviews were designed to provide the respondents the greatest amount of *comodidad*. As a result, interviews were conducted in the evenings, in Spanish, were moderated by bilingual Latino males, and the questions moved from the general to the specific with the most sensitive questions saved for the end of the interviews. Our focus in these interviews was on sexual risk behaviors.

TABLE 7.1. Characteristics of Focus Group Respondents (n = 117) [a]

Characteristics	Number	Percent [b]
Nationality		
Mexican	114	97.4
Puerto Rican	1	0.9
Salvadorian	2	1.7
Total	117	100.0
Age groups, yrs [c]		
14 - 19	67	58.7
20 - 29	15	13.2
30 - 39	12	10.5
40 - 49	20	17.5
Total	114	100.0
Marital Status		
Married	39	33.3
Single	78	66.6
Total	100	100.0

[a] Some percentages are based on fewer than 117 respondents.

[b] Some percentages may not add up to 100 due to rounding error.

[c] Mean age 23.9 years.

Sexually Transmissible Diseases

One important focus of the conversations was a discussion of STDs. As might be expected, the participants' first reaction was one of shyness. After some probing, however, the men candidly discussed STDs and several farmworkers revealed that they, or their friends, had one or more STDs; in one instance, one farmworker offered to show the researchers his symptoms.

The data indicate that in some cases, signs of STDs infection are present even before the men arrived to the U.S. As one farmworker noted, "some men come already sick." Several farmworkers indicated that while STDs were present among them, the diseases did not affect their daily activities "some have the filthy stuff but are not affected." Farmworkers indicated that they dealt with STDs symptoms primarily by resting and added that they sought medical assistance only in extreme circumstances. When asked why they delayed seeking treatment, the farmworkers indicated that the conditions were seldom fatal and that, in some cases, they appeared to accept STDs as a normal by-product of their womanizing: "You know, Mexican men sleep around, but no one dies from it."

The men also reported widespread reluctance to seek treatment for STDs because of embarrassment. This was particularly a problem when they believed that they would have to talk to a female nurse or physician "I know a guy who is sick...and he doesn't want to go because he's embarrassed to be seen by the [female] nurse." Other responses indicated that STDs was not something easily discussed with females: "You can't talk about this with women." Treatment was complicated by the fact that most of the local health care providers depended upon female translators. One farmworker complained that "The time that I went I wanted to talk to the doctor about my 'problem,' but I wasn't about to talk to the woman about it."

A second reason for reluctance to seek treatment was fear of financial loss. Farmworkers who got paid for volume of work done were unwilling to miss a day of work to obtain medical treatment. Some of them indicated: "If I rest for a few days I can keep working without telling the boss I need to go to the doctor." Farmworkers in our groups appeared more concerned with the meaning prescribed to a doctor's visit than with the actual financial loss which resulted even when they took a few days to rest. In order to avoid this problems several respondents indicated that they would welcome a visiting nurse or physician, "If someone came [here] to examine us it would be good for us."

AIDS

The farmworkers joked about AIDS and one mentioned that conversations about the disease were seldom serious, "people say lots of things about AIDS, not important things, but jokes with our friends." They indicated that one reason for not seriously discussing AIDS was the concern that their peers might label them as homosexual: "If I talk about this they will think I am *queer* and I am *macho*." Another reason was the concern that peers might perceive them to already have AIDS, "if I bring it up they might think I have AIDS and then they wouldn't talk to me."

Eighty percent of the groups indicated they had heard about AIDS. The most common form of learning about el SIDA was through word-of-mouth, "you hear about it." When asked where they were more likely to hear about AIDS, they indicated that they were likely to discuss it as they wait to enter the U.S., "at the border before jumping the fence." Other likely places were *las cantinas*, in a few cases grocery stores and the agricultural fields in their native towns in Mexico.

Only one group of respondents claimed they had been exposed to AIDS and HIV education. This training came from a health educator who had made rounds to some of the camps. Although several men gave relatively accurate information about the condition, most men had serious knowledge gaps, "they've discovered you can only get AIDS if you are a homosexual." Others claimed to have little knowledge of AIDS, but indicated they were careful in or during their sexual relationships: "I don't know anything about AIDS--that's for sure, but I always watch whom I get involved with." Most common was an understanding of AIDS-related mortality, or the fear that, "AIDS is a malignant illness that means the end." Fear-based messages, coupled with generally low levels of knowledge and marginal existence, were fertile grounds for the widespread of HIV/AIDS and other STDs.

All the groups indicated an interest in learning about AIDS and in some cases requested information from the interviewers, "You are interviewing us, but you are not telling us anything. We want to learn to avoid infection." In some cases, farmworkers expressed disappointment that they were not included in educational campaigns, "I worked in Washington [state] where the radio has information on AIDS; here they have nothing." These responses indicate Latino farmworkers in our sample were ready and willing to learn more about this potentially fatal condition.

Use of Condoms

All of the farmworkers in the discussion groups were aware of condoms, and many seemed to know that condoms were effective at preventing STDs and HIV; however, many did not know how to use them. In one instance, a farmworker expressed frustration and indicated that he would not use condoms because the instructions were not in Spanish: "What good are condoms if I can't use them, even the instructions are useless." Some farmworkers were unaware that condoms come in a variety of forms and sizes. One farmworker handling one of the condoms distributed during the interview stated: "The condoms I bought did not have this [lubricant] and were big." Farmworkers, as a whole, were willing to handle condoms in the presence of their friends but with some discomfort. Their uneasiness seemed to be based on fear of not using the condoms correctly.

During the conversations, farmworkers talked openly about protecting themselves during sexual activities. When asked to clarify what they meant, several responded: "using condoms and things like that" or "condoms--what else?" This was supported by other respondents who indicated that they sometimes discussed condoms among themselves, "we talk about it all the time. However, the decision to use or not to use condoms was considered a personal affair, and few would consider persuading their friends to using them: "Whoever wants to use them is welcome to, but it's none of my business."

Some indicated condom use would occur only in certain circumstances, "I would only use them with my wife after I had been with a prostitute." Many men expressed a general reluctance to use condoms with long-term female partners, "well, when you know a woman four or five months you don't do it because by then you trust her." When pressed to name an instance when they would absolutely not use condoms, one farmworker stated, "if we know the woman" another noted "if we knew where she lives." There was general reluctance to use condoms with long-term sex partners or with spouses. In the latter case, the men assumed that their spouses or common-law wives were faithful and that the use of condoms was therefore unnecessary: "women are faithful so we are not taking a risk."

Although several of the farmworkers expressed they would not go out of their way to locate condoms, they agreed that they would use them if they were readily available. This opinion was supported by the fact that most of the farmworkers interviewed for this study took some condoms with them at the end of the interview. In sexual contacts with sex workers, the men indicated that condoms were used if the sex worker had them: "The women has them in her house. When you go, the woman knows what to do." Interestingly, the use of prophylactics as contraceptives was never mentioned by the respondents and when questioned about the omission they responded, "The woman takes the pill for that, condoms are used to prevent AIDS."

In conclusion, farmworkers were more likely to use condoms with sex workers, short-term sexual partners and if the condoms were readily available. The data indicates they would not use condoms with a steady sexual partner or spouses. This reluctance was of particular interest considering that some farmworkers develop lasting relationships with their favorite sex workers.

Prostitution

Most farmworkers seemed willing to visit sex workers (*camperas*) to satisfy their sexual needs. In between nervous laughter, one complained about his inability to find them, "I wanted to bring them but haven't found them yet." His friends informed him that he was not looking in the right places. A man acknowledged that when they crave sexual activities they go to *camperas*: "Well, if you feel an urge...of course you have to go to them." These statements, made matter-of-factly, were supported by others either by nodding of their heads, laughter or simply lowering their eyes.

The men in the groups were aware of where sex workers could be found in their areas, "everyone knows where they are" stated a respondent. In response to the question "where could I find a sex worker if I wanted one right now?" most groups were able to provide exact addresses, in some cases provided descriptions of their favorite sex worker, "She's really something" and, in one instance, a name. Additional information provided in response to the above question included ethnicity, age range, price for different sexual acts, and suggestions for negotiating the lowest possible rates. One farmworker even provided a referral to someone he knew, admonishing the researcher to "If she gives you any problems, tell her Chucho sent you and that she should take good care of you!"

The data indicate sex workers are found in the cantinas frequented by farmworkers and in urban areas of the county, "They are easy to find in [city name]." Walking down certain streets known as 'hot spots' was another way of finding sex workers. This data indicated that *camperas* also frequented the camps particularly on payday. When in doubt, the men asked their friends where to find sex workers, and in fact, there appeared to be a fair amount of referrals as indicated above.

There was an awareness that sex workers could transmit disease, with some expressing concern about the risk, and denying their involvement with them: "We are not educated, but we know about it; that's why we don't visit those women." Despite these expressed reservations, most farmworkers perceived decreased risks with sex workers they had known for a length of time, "If you know her, there is no need to be afraid." This extended to practicing unprotected sex as discussed elsewhere in this chapter.

Masturbation

Several farmworkers in the discussion groups frankly admitted masturbating for reasons ranging from temporary sexual relief to total substitution for intercourse. The data indicates masturbation sessions were conducted in solitude, at night, and in the bathroom, "they take a long time in the bathroom," teased some. Fantasies about previous sexual encounters, friends' experiences and pornographic materials were all used to fuel fantasies. The men, however, made it clear that despite some occasional teasing, they never talked about the activities they suspected everyone engaged in.

Some suggested that younger men with less sexual experience were more likely to masturbate than are their older counterparts. Similarly, older farmworkers claimed that although they might have engaged in self-gratification in their days of youth, that was no longer the case: "In this camp, young men masturbate more than the older men." Younger males tended to keep quiet, laugh, and on two occasions to leave the room; however, not one of them challenged these conclusions.

As stated above, masturbation was seen as an alternative to sexual activity at least until the opportunity was present for sexual intimacy with a woman. In only one instance a farmworker stated that he would rather engage in sexual self-gratification than to have sex with a sex worker: "Thanks, but no thanks. I'd rather use my hand than to go with *that* woman)."

Alcohol Use

Research indicates that unprotected (i.e., not using a condom) sexual activity was likely to occur when individuals were under the influence of alcohol or drugs. An earlier survey of social service and health providers working with farmworkers in Pennsylvania [14] found that alcohol was frequently mentioned as a problem. However, in this study the farmworkers themselves did not admit to much drinking: "We only drink water around here." Reasons cited for not getting drunk included the distances between the farms and the cantinas, their lack of transportation, and strict prohibition of on-site drinking by some camp owners, particularly when it came to underage drinking.

In a few cases farmworkers admitted drinking in social settings, but were emphatic in their denial of drunkenness: "We drink at parties but we don't get drunk." It is suspected that farmworkers' denial of excessive drinking may have more to do with cultural definitions of "drinking too much," than with the actual amounts of alcohol consumed.

The data did not support the notion that alcohol use might act as a determinant of risk factors. In response to the question "Do farmworkers have sex while drinking?" almost 70 percent of participants stated a resounding "no." Among the reasons provided for not drinking and engaging in sexual activity were decreasing pleasure and regard for oneself: "Having sex with a woman while intoxicated shows little self-respect." Most men agreed that if an opportunity for sexual activities presented itself, they would take advantage of it regardless of the circumstances or consequences.

Same-Gender Sex

Some authors have suggested that same gender sexual activity may be a high risk factor in the transmission of HIV and AIDS among Latinos. In the groups we interviewed we attempted to find out whether same gender sex was occurring among the farmworkers. Although the men generally acknowledged that it was "likely" that such behavior occurred, "I have heard about it but never seen it" there was universal reluctance to admit to this behavior: "We don't do that."

The respondents indicated that they would not tolerate homosexual behavior among their groups: "I'll beat the s... out of someone who tries to touch me." It was likely that this shared stigma and the group discussion format prevented individuals from disclosing same gender sexual behavior. Nevertheless, once or twice workers mentioned beating up or chasing homosexuals if they were discovered.

Self-Injections

It was hypothesized that self-injection of vitamins could be a risk factor for farmworkers. Focus group participants did not appear to be reluctant to discuss such practices, but were emphatic in their statements that self-injection was not a common practice in their communities. Respondents denied self-medicating, unless they were treating minor health problems, "only for headaches." Others indicated they treated minor work injuries with over-the-counter medications.

Although farmworkers said it was not uncommon for their families to use vitamin supplements in Mexico, they denied using vitamins in the U.S., "no, only those that are in our food." Even when questions were rephrased most groups stated that even though they may have injected vitamins in earlier times, it was not a common practice in this community.

Discussion

This exploratory study was designed to examine several hypothesized risk factors for HIV and AIDS among Latino farmworkers. Our findings indicate that these single adult males living and working away from families engage in high risk behaviors, often without realizing the full impact of their actions.

Although all of the farmworkers in our study admitted that they were sexually active, many did not take precautions to prevent infections with STDs or HIV. Some farmworkers did not consider unprotected sex with a known sexual partner to constitute a risk factor. As a result, they appeared to be less likely to use condoms with partners whom they know (the definition of "knowing" the partner included being referred by a friend), even if this partner was a sex worker. Many farmworkers were reluctant to admit sexual contacts with sex workers but persons familiar with the area report that sex workers frequently visit the camps. In many cases, farmworkers let STDs go untreated until the symptoms forced them to seek medical care.

Despite their willingness to discuss sexual activity during the focus groups, the farmworkers expressed a reluctance to discuss sex-related topics with their female sexual partners. For instance, women were not consulted in the decision concerning whether to use or not use a condom during coitus. This reluctance to approach the topic with partners extends to discussions of sexuality with female medical professionals. Several farmworkers in our study indicated that they would not discuss sexual problems or seek treatment from female health care providers. This is significant since, in many cases, health care providers depend upon female translators to communicate with their patients.

Knowledge of the risks of contracting HIV from sex workers and the prophylactic benefits of condoms were quite high among the men in this study. Despite low levels of schooling and lack of exposure to formal AIDS education efforts, almost all of the men conversed openly and, in some cases, accurately about these topics. The exception was a respondent who indicated that he doubted that AIDS actually existed since he had never seen or met anyone with the disease.

The farmworkers interviewed stated that they seldom discussed sexuality or AIDS among themselves, but most indicated that they would be willing to learn more about HIV and AIDS. This was encouraging since only one of the 12 groups of men interviewed had respondents received any form of AIDS education. Several men asked why educational presentations had not occurred or been publicized. At the conclusion of all the focus groups, farmworkers received a brief presentation on AIDS risk factors and prevention methods by a trained AIDS educator.

One of our hypothesis was generated from reports in the literature and anecdotal evidence suggesting that same gender relationships may be an acceptable form of sexuality for some Latino men. The respondents in this study were openly embarrassed and reluctant to discuss homosexuality. Their discomfort was so marked that we question the validity of the data on this subject. A more appropriate way to collect data on this topic might be through personal interviews where subjects do not have to speak in front of their peers. Almost all the respondents stated that same gender sex did not occur among farmworkers in their area and that a homosexual would not be welcome among them.

A second untested hypothesis from the research literature was that self-injection of vitamins and medicines among Mexicans might lead to infection through shared use of infected needles. Farmworkers in this study indicated that, although some of them had used injectable vitamins in the past, this was no longer a common practice. Several suggested that, rather than using injectable vitamin supplements, they relied on vitamins present in their foods.

The men interviewed in this study sought medical care in only extreme cases. This was not surprising since only a small percentage of employed farmworkers had health insurance. In our sample, just 17 percent of the farmworkers had access to employer provided health insurance. Even in those instances, the employers were unlikely to provide paid leave time for employees to visit their physicians, thereby posing another obstacle to receipt of medical care.

Since few farmworkers visit clinics or physicians regularly, preventive educational messages must be disseminated at places of work or recreation. Such health education/promotion was essential to reduce the propagation of viral infections, including AIDS, among this population. Their expressed interest in learning about AIDS should facilitate the introduction of educational campaigns.

Implications

Farmworkers continue to be a neglected segment of the population;

nation-wide only about 20 percent receive medical treatment at Migrant Health Clinics. This under-utilization may be explained by several factors, including but not limited to migration, low education and legal status. Farmworkers' health and, particularly, AIDS prevention must become a priority for local health care providers and service agencies. Previous assessments by local AIDS networks only mention farmworkers peripherally. Furthermore, political authorities are reluctant to discuss HIV risks to farmworkers, and local social service agencies have been slow to respond. Further delays will lead to the increase of HIV and AIDS in this population with proven risk factors. It is essential to extend health coverage to farmworkers to prevent the spread of STDs and HIV. Farmworkers with access to health care and health education may be less likely to engage in high risk behaviors and more likely to seek preventive medicine and education.

Changes in employer-provided health insurance and the Migrant Health Care Act alone will not furnish coverage to this indigent population. Some farmworkers will continue to be excluded from health care benefits unless Medicaid and Medicare requirements are changed. Currently, residency requirements preclude many farmworkers from receiving services. Partnerships with local health care providers, private insurance companies, and strong networks among agencies working with farmworker populations are needed to begin closing the gaps in the safety net for farmworkers. In addition, employers with five or more workers on the payroll, regardless of the length of employment in a given season, should provide basic health care coverage and paid time for workers to visit their physicians. Additional funds should be allocated for continuous active outreach efforts for farmworkers. This recruitment would not only bring educational materials but would also include visits by medical care professionals to the farms. Care must be taken to insure that any visits to camps are facilitated by bilingual, Latino health professionals.

A number of sites have implemented fragmented AIDS education programs with varying degrees of success. Our study indicates that farmworkers would welcome health education on HIV and AIDS; however, in an era of diminished resources, health education will be neglected unless legislatively mandated. The Migrant Health Care Act does not list health education as a priority area for services to farmworkers. Health care providers and policymakers should propose an amendment to the Act to designate as a priority areas preventive medicine and specifically AIDS education.

As discussed above, farmworkers knew about the benefits of condoms, but expressed a reluctance to use them, especially with familiar partners. They were more likely to use condoms with unfamiliar partners, or when the sexual act would be closely followed by sexual relations with spouses. Condom use should be promoted as a matter of personal responsibility since it appears that some of our respondents placed a higher value on the preservation of their families than they did on personal safety. In some cases, the workers did not know how to use condoms but expressed interest in learning about them.

Health education outreach and worksite AIDS testing are needed because of the difficulty in transporting farmworkers to health care facilities. In the present study, the mushroom farms were clustered near the most populous city in the county; however, there were no reliable forms of public transportation. Paying a taxi or a private party for transportation makes the possibility of visiting a health care center less appealing. Given these transportation and motivational barriers, on-site AIDS testing is warranted. In addition, programs need to be delivered by Spanish-speaking personnel using techniques appropriate for illiterate and low literacy audiences. The use of audio-visual aids (e.g., videos, radio programs, slides) are strongly recommended. Good places to educate this population are ports of entry to the U.S. and sex education in schools or mass media in Mexico and in their home states.

Finally, by improving data collection on AIDS risk and incidence, providing health education, increasing employer provided health insurance, and expanding Medicare and Medicaid coverage we can begin to avert risk factors for HIV/AIDS among farmworkers. Most importantly, education should be used to effect behavior changes (increased condom use and safer sex practices). Such education, in addition to medical services for the treatment of such conditions as TB, STDs and HIV, should serve to lessen the health and social impacts of AIDS.

Acknowledgments

This research was supported in part by a grant from the Pennsylvania Department of Health in cooperation with the Department of Agricultural and Extension Education and the Department of Health Education at the Pennsylvania State University. The opinions expressed are solely those of the authors.

References

1. Dement EF: *Out of Sight, Out of Mind: An Update on Migrant Farmworkers Issues in Today's Agricultural Labor Market*. Washington, DC: National Governor's Association, 1985.

154

2. National Migrant Resource Program, Inc: *Migrant and Seasonal Farmworker HEALTH OBJECTIVES 2000*. Austin, TX: National Migrant Resource Program, Inc., 1990.
3. Oliveira VJ: *A Profile of Hired Farmworkers, 1990 Annual Averages*. US Department of Agriculture. Economic Research Division. Agricultural Economic Report No. 658. Washington, DC: Government Printing Office, 1992.
4. US Congress: *Migrant farmworkers in the United States: Briefings of the Commission on Security and Cooperation in Europe*. Washington, DC: Government Printing Office, 1993.
5. Bletzer KV: Knowledge-Attitude-Belief survey of AIDS/HIV among migrants in Michigan. *Migrant Health Newsline* 1991; 8(1):3.
6. General Accounting Office: *Hired Farmworkers Health and Well-being at Risk*. (GAO/HRD-92-46). Washington, DC: Government Printing Office, 1992.
7. National Migrant Resource Program, Inc.: *Migrant Health Status: Profile of a Population with Complex Health Problems*. Austin, TX: National Migrant Resource Program, Inc, 1992.
8. National Rural Health Care Association: *The Occupational Health of Migrant and Seasonal Farmworkers in the United States*. (2nd edition). Washington, DC: National Rural Health Care Association, 1986.
9. Castro K, Narkumas J: Seroprevalence of HIV infection in seasonal and migrant farmworkers. *Migrant Health Newsline* 1989; 6(4):49-50.
10. Brunswick AF, Aidala A, Dobkin J, Howard J, Titus S, Banaszak-Holl J: HIV-1 seroprevalence and risk behaviors in an urban African-American community cohort. *Am J Public Health* 1993; 83(10):1390-1394.
11. Gayle H, Keeling R, Garcia-Tunon M, Kilbourne B, Narkumas J, Ingram F, Rogers M, Curran JW: Prevalence of the human immunodeficiency virus among university students. *N Engl J Med* 1990; 323 (22):1538-1541.
12. Lyons M: Study yields HIV prevalence for New Jersey farmworkers. *Migrant Health Newsline Clinical Supplement* 1992; 9(2):1-2.
13. Jones JL, Rion P, Hollis S, Longshore S, Leverette WB, Ziff L: HIV-related characteristics of migrant workers in rural South Carolina. *Migrant Health Newsline Clinical Supplement* 1992; 9(2):4.
14. Fennelly K: *Identification of Health and Social Services for Migrant Families in Berks County, PA and an Assessment of Unmet Needs*. Unpublished Report. The Pennsylvania State University, 1991.
15. Valison TM: Knowledge of AIDS among female Hispanic migrant farmworkers in Virginia. *Migrant Health Clinical Supplement* 1992; 9(2):2.
16. Foulk D, Lafferty J, Ryan R, Robertson A: AIDS knowledge and behavior in a migrant farmworker population. *Migration World* 1989; 17(3/4):36-42.
17. Pérez MA: *Migrant Adolescents: Knowledge and Attitudes Regarding HIV/ AIDS*. Unpublished Master Thesis. The Pennsylvania State University, 1993.
18. Alcalay R, Sniderman PM, Mitchell J, Griffin R: Ethnic differences in knowledge of AIDS transmission and attitudes towards gays and people with AIDS. *Int Quart Comm Health Educ* 1990; 10(3):213-222.
19. Dawson DA: AIDS knowledge and attitudes for January-March 1990.

Provisional data from the National Health Interview Survey. Advance Data from Vital and Health Statistics, Number 193. Hyattsville, MD: National Center for Health Statistics, 1990.

20. Van-Oss-Marin B, Gomez CA, Heart N: Multiple heterosexual partners and condom use among Hispanics and non-Hispanic whites. *Fam Plan Perspec* 1993; 25(4):170-174.

21. Hu DJ, Keller R: Communicating AIDS information to Hispanics: the importance of language and media preference. *Am J Preven Med* 1989; 5(4):196-200.

22. de la Vega E: Considerations for reaching the Latino population with sexuality and HIV/AIDS information and education. *SIECUS Report* 1990; 18(3).

23. Coalition of Hispanic Health and Human Services Organizations: *HIV/AIDS the Impact on Hispanics in Selected States.* Washington, DC: Coalition of Hispanic Health and Human Services Organizations, 1991.

24. Carrier JM: Cultural factors affecting urban Mexican male homosexual behavior. *Arch Sex Behav* 1976; 5(2):103-124.

25. Magaña JR, Carrier JM: Mexican and Mexican American male sexual behavior and spread of AIDS in California. *J Sex Res* 1991; 28(3):425-441.

26. Centers for Disease Control and Prevention: Study of non-identifying gay men. *HIV/AIDS Preven Newsletter* 1993; 4(2):6-7.

27. Trotter RT: Remedios caseros: A Mexican American home remedies and community health problems. *Soc Sci Med* 1981; 1513:107-114.

28. Slater CM, Hall GE. (eds): *1992 County and City Extra Annual Metro, City and County Data Book.* Lanham, MD: Bennen Press, 1992.

29. Reid-Mann S: Mushrooms cap a decade of growth. *Agricultural Outlook* 1992; 16-20.

8

Evaluation of an HIV Prevention Program Among Latino Farmworkers

Shiraz I. Mishra and Ross F. Conner

Introduction

The human immunodeficiency virus (HIV) and the acquired immunodeficiency syndrome (AIDS) continue to claim lives around the world. In many places, those with HIV/AIDS remain invisible while living with the virus and even at their deaths. This is especially true for certain sub-groups within the United States including migrant farmworkers. Little research, however, exists on HIV-related knowledge, attitudes and behaviors among this group.

This study evaluated the effectiveness of an HIV prevention educational program created especially for Spanish-speaking, low-literacy, male, Latino farmworkers. The paper has two goals. The first goal is to describe the program which educated farmworkers about HIV transmission, severity, risk factors and prevention. The preventive behavior given primary consideration in the educational program was the use of a condom during sex with a sex worker. The second goal is to provide results that evaluated the program's impact on HIV-related knowledge, attitudes, and behaviors.

Farmworker Population in the United States

The migrant and seasonal farmworker population in the U.S. is estimated between 2.7 and 4 million, with Latinos comprising the largest group [1]. According to the National Agricultural Workers Survey, conducted by the U.S. Department of Labor, the farmworker population is composed primarily of young (median age: 31 years), male, Latino immigrants. The majority are foreign-born (predominantly Mexican); and, contrary to popular belief, 81 percent of the foreign-born farmworkers are legally authorized to work in the United States [2].

Farm work is one of the most dangerous jobs in the U.S. The U.S. Bureau of Labor Statistics has identified agriculture as the nation's most hazardous occupation [3, 4]. Farmworkers are the most vulnerable agricultural workers, exposed to the harsh working conditions. These conditions include employment-related injuries and exposure to pesticides and place farmworkers at risk for skin diseases, chronic back and joint pain, and possibly for certain cancers [4, 5].

Access to health care services for farmworkers is severely restricted; migrant and community health centers provide access to only about 12 percent of the farmworker population. The lack of adequate access to care is compounded by economic and structural constraints such as lack of medical insurance and workers' compensation, limited or no resources to spend on medical care, inconvenient operating hours of the clinics, and language and cultural barriers [6].

Potential HIV-related Risk Factors

There are several factors which increase the likelihood for farmworkers to be exposed to HIV. These factors include sexual practices, condom non-use, use of injectable drugs, and living conditions. First, the probability of farmworkers engaging in high-risk sexual behavior is high. This is especially true for male Latino farmworkers who, although the majority are married, often live without their families at the work-site [2]. Sex workers regularly visit their work and residential sites and provide quick and inexpensive services for the men. Farmworkers find this a convenient sexual outlet, although with drawbacks; many of the sex workers sell sex to support a drug habit [7]. Sex between men also occurs; cultural proscriptions against homosexuality, however, restrict acknowledgment of the behavior [8, 9].

Second, condom use among Latino farmworkers is reportedly very low. Data from one study indicate that Latino farmworkers, compared to non-Latino farmworkers, are more likely to report never having used a condom [10]. Moreover, immigrant compared to non-immigrant farmworkers are more likely to report never having used a condom.

The third factor is the use of injectable drugs. Some farmworkers either inject themselves or have others inject them with therapeutic drugs such as vitamins and antibiotics [11]; in addition, some use illicit drugs. More often than not, needles are reused without proper sterilization. Lack of adequate health access coupled with the fear of losing one's job prompts the farmworkers to utilize any means necessary to safeguard their health on a short-term basis, without realizing the deadly consequences of HIV transmission via infected needles.

Fourth, farmworkers' residential sites (or "camps") in the U.S. often involve extremely difficult living conditions. Farmworkers are generally isolated in their living situations, not only because of limited housing and mobility but also because of language difficulties. Camps range from holes in the ground (called *spider holes*) to enclosures made of old mattresses or cardboard pieces. In some cases, the camps are rooms with several bunk beds. Generally, there is poor nutrition, no sanitation, and inadequate safe drinking water in the camps [12, 13]. These isolated and substandard conditions could endanger farmworkers' health and make them more susceptible to disease.

HIV Prevalence

Data on HIV prevalence among farmworkers are very difficult to obtain. Farmworkers with an undocumented immigration status are resistant to medical studies and reluctant to use health facilities, even when seriously ill, because they fear detection and deportation. Further complicating the situation is the tendency of workers who become sick, whether with HIV/AIDS or any other illness, to return home to Mexico [14]. The few local seroprevalence studies conducted among this population have reported seroprevalence rates as low as 0.5 percent to as high as 13 percent [15, 16].

HIV-related Knowledge and Attitudes

Serious gaps exist in information about farmworkers' knowledge about the HIV epidemic. Most of the information is based on a few local studies and anecdotal research. A significant proportion of farmworkers do not know that HIV can be transmitted sexually and through sharing needles [12], and that a person can be infected but show no signs of the illness [17]. Furthermore, Latino farmworkers were more inclined to attribute illness to diverse non-biomedical etiologies and less likely to seek care [18].

There are, therefore, serious gaps in farmworkers' knowledge about HIV and the epidemic. At the same time, farmworkers are prone to engage in unsafe sexual and injectable drug use behaviors that can provide the opportunity for the spread of HIV. In view of these realities, the circumstances are ripe among farmworkers for the further spread of HIV. Culturally appropriate and sensitive prevention programs are needed, therefore, that especially target low-literacy Spanish-speaking populations such as the farmworkers.

The HIV Prevention Educational Program
for Farmworkers

The HIV prevention educational program created for farmworkers is titled *Tres Hombres sin Fronteras* (Three Men without Borders). Several reasons explain why the use of traditional English-oriented, didactic HIV prevention educational materials were not appropriate for this group. The overwhelming majority of migrant Latino farmworkers are not fluent in English and have low functional literacy in Spanish. Moreover, typical didactic educational materials (in English or Spanish) that prescribe "dos and don'ts" have little effect in this group since the information presented often is not culturally appropriate, sensitive, or comprehensible.

The primary focus of the program was to educate the farmworkers about HIV prevention. Condom use during sex with a sex worker was the prevention method given primary consideration. Behaviors such as needle sharing and sexual abstinence were noted in the educational program but were not a major focus.

The program involved two types of formats, a *fotonovela* (a photo story book) and a *radionovela* (a radio story), which at the time of the study were innovative in the HIV education arena. A novela is a serial story which may appear in several formats, including video, radio, and print. The most common form of novela is a fotonovela which may offer four basic strengths as a health education tool: (1) a low-literacy approach which uses pictures to tell a story; (2) a story line that incorporates lifestyles and health behaviors; (3) a medium that is culturally sensitive and people may read on impulse; and (4) wide dissemination, since one fotonovela may be shared and read by several people. The program materials were developed by the Novela Health Foundation in Seattle, Washington. While unusual for HIV education, these formats were familiar to the farmworkers because of their extensive use in Mexico for many types of educational messages. The picture and audio formats, requiring little or no reading, also are potentially effective ways to teach low-literacy Spanish-speaking farmworkers about HIV and how to prevent it. Prior to the study described in this chapter, we conducted a formative evaluation of the *Tres Hombres* materials to assure their acceptability, appropriateness, cultural sensitivity and clarity as judged by farmworkers themselves [19, 20].

Typically, novelas use a three-model approach to convey issues involved in the decision to adopt a particular health behavior. Of the three models, one consistently demonstrates unhealthy behavior, another demonstrates behavior that is consistently healthy, and a primary model vacillates in behavior between the two poles of "good" and "bad" behavior. The drama shows negative consequences arising out of unhealthy behavior and positive consequences stemming from healthy choices in lifestyle. As the story progresses, the primary model eventually makes a transition towards incorporating healthier behaviors and, as a result, has an improved outcome. The target audience, which generally identifies with the primary model, sees how this character makes a healthy transition in lifestyle relating to the health issue and is encouraged to make changes themselves (Rabinowitz P, personal communication).

The *Tres Hombres* materials included both an 8-page tabloid-sized fotonovela and a 15-segment radionovela (5 minutes per segment). The materials told the same basic story of three farmworking men, Victor, Sergio, and Marco. Victor was portrayed as the character who demonstrated consistently health behavior. He was married and never had sexual relations outside of marriage. Sergio was the character who demonstrated consistently unhealthy behaviors. He was married but had had a history of sexual relations with other women besides his wife, sex workers and other men. In addition, Sergio had used injectable drugs. Marco was portrayed as the primary model. He was single and was open to behavioral experimentation.

As the story continues, these three men leave their families to cross the Mexico-U.S. border and work in the agriculture fields. After work, they meet Karla, a sex worker, who informs them of the risk of HIV and how to prevent it by using condoms. Sergio refuses to heed Karla's suggestion and, in turn, Karla refuses to have sex with him. Marco, on the other hand, listens to Karla's advice on using a condom for the protection against sexually transmitted diseases including HIV/AIDS. As the story progresses, Sergio discovers that his wife and new baby, who had remained in Mexico, were sick and infected with the virus. Marco, who learned to use a condom, and Victor, who abstained from sex, remained healthy. Medical personnel from both folk and modern medical traditions played roles in the story as disseminators of the informa-

162

Marco, Sergio and Victor—three men who leave their town in search of opportunities, they confront danger!

A condom? Why?

Condoms give protection to both of us!

Protection?

FIGURE 8.1. Sample Frames From the Fotonovela, *"Tres Hombres Sin Fronteras"* (Three Men Without Borders), an AIDS Prevention Photo Booklet for Mexican Migrant Farmworkers[1]

tion. Figure 8.1 illustrates a few frames from the fotonovela, featuring Marco and Karla.

The fotonovela included a specially developed mini-fotonovela insert (*Marco Aprende como Protegerse*--Marco Learns How to Protect Himself) containing pictures that explained where to obtain a condom

Yes, protection against diseases like gonorrhea, syphilis, even AIDS!

Because when you get AIDS, there isn't a cure for that.

So then?

OK!

and how to use and dispose of it; the mini-fotonovela also included a couple of condoms for practice and use.

Methods

The implementation and evaluation of the HIV prevention program was conducted in parts of north San Diego County, a semi-rural area of southern California.[2] During the height of the agricultural season, there are about 20,000 predominantly Mexican migrant or seasonal farmworkers in north San Diego County. A local health clinic, with prior experience working with farmworkers, served as our point of entry into the community.

Study Design and Procedures

We used a quasi-experimental design with random assignment of matched and paired study sites into either the Experimental or Control study groups.[3] Furthermore, we used a cohort design and followed the study sample prospectively for six months. During this time period, we conducted an initial screening interview and administered pretest and posttest surveys. Both the Experimental and Control groups were tested at the pretest and posttest on HIV-related knowledge, attitudes and behaviors. The surveys were administered to small groups of respondents by specially trained interviewers using a unique combination of survey administration techniques. The interviewers read aloud the questions and used a flip chart to denote the possible response category corresponding to the question. The respondents independently marked their responses on answer sheets provided to them. This format of survey administration was pilot-tested prior to the study and found to be effective in eliciting responses from respondents who could not read but could comprehend the spoken word and match icons in selecting their responses. The pretest and posttest surveys were separated by about a month during which period the Experimental group received the educational program (discussed above). Each of the pretest and posttest interviews lasted about an hour and the men were paid $5 for each inter view. This type of comparative, prospective evaluation design has been strongly recommended by a number of researchers in the AIDS field to assess the effectiveness of HIV prevention programs in the most rigorous way [21].

After the posttest survey, we conducted focus groups with the Experimental group men to document their suggestions and reactions to the study. The focus group methodology used a carefully planned discussion designed to obtain perceptions on a specific area of interest in a permissive, non-threatening environment [22].

The study sites included 10 farmworker camps which were matched and paired on their size, presence or absence of women, socioeconomic appearance and proximity to each other. In terms of socioeconomic appearance, the study camps were of a temporary nature, that is, camps where the farmworkers lived in *spider holes* and enclosures made of cardboard pieces or old mattresses. The camps were isolated from each other. Movement between camps and work-sites (in instances where the residential camps are not adjacent to the work-sites) was severely limited due to a lack of personal and public transport. Food is brought into the camps by vendors, and farm managers bus farmworkers to their work-sites. This geographical layout of the camp-sites prevented, if not eliminated, the opportunity of intermingling between residents of the various camps, thus reducing the potential for contamination of the different study groups.

Based on the selection criteria, we selected camps that had at least 15 male residents, no women, were comparable in socioeconomic appearance, and were fairly well dispersed from each other. The Experimental and Control groups were comprised of six and four camps, respectively, randomly assigned.

Eligibility criteria for the study included men who were: (1) agricultural workers; (2) from Mexico; (3) aged 18 to 35 years; (4) single or, if married, living separate from their families; (5) primarily Spanish-speaking; (6) intending to stay in the U.S. until the end of the study; and, (7) without prior exposure to an HIV prevention program. The majority of residents at the 10 study sites were eligible for the study.

Based on the eligibility criteria, the study began with 150 eligible men, 90 and 60 in the Experimental and Control groups, respectively. At the end of the study, the cohort with complete data from all three assessments consisted of 89 men: 52 and 37, respectively, in the Experimental and Control groups. The cohort sample size was smaller than the study sample size since some men either lost their jobs and left the study area or were deported by the authorities if found to be undocumented. These factors would be expected to be unrelated to the study.

Measures

The measures were carefully constructed to assess variables thought to be important to attitude and behavior changes in health promotion programs [23-25]. We gave careful consideration to the wording of the questions so that low-literacy Spanish-speakers from rural backgrounds could understand and answer the questions accurately.

The measures included questions about demographic variables, included age, education level, and marital status. There were questions about which language the respondent preferred to use to read, to speak, to think, to talk with friends, and when growing up, scaled from 1 (only Spanish) to 5 (only English) [26].

HIV-related knowledge was measured by 17 items which were scored as either 1 (True) or 0 (False or Unsure). These items were scaled into a knowledge index which comprised of three domains: transmission, severity and external signs. The transmission domain, measured by 12 items, assessed knowledge about transmission routes such as sexual intercourse, pregnancy, casual contact, and blood donation. The severity domain, measured by three items, inquired about the prognosis of the infection. The two-item external signs domain inquired whether HIV could be diagnosed by looking at an infected person. Cronbach's alphas for the scale were identical for the two study groups (alpha = 0.85). Besides these factually-based questions, we inquired whether the men had heard about HIV and how much they knew about it.

HIV-related attitudes measured aspects directly relevant to the information presented in the educational program. These items included attitudes regarding condom use, ability to protect oneself against HIV, and perceptions of severity of the infection. The items were scored as 1 (Agree) or 0 (Disagree or Unsure).

HIV-related behavioral items inquired about past and present sexual activity, and the use of condom and injectable drugs. A series of items inquired whether the men had had ("ever had" and had "during the past month") sex with their spouse (if any), significant other, other men and sex workers. Likewise, items assessed whether the men had used condoms ("ever used" and "used during the past month") during sex with their spouse, significant other, other men and sex workers. Injectable drug use was measured by items that inquired whether the men either had self-injected or had someone else injected them with either vitamins, medicine, or drugs; and, whether the men had shared needles with others during the year prior to the study.

Extent of exposure, comprehension, appropriateness, and cultural sensitivity of the program were measured on the posttest survey for the Experimental group.

Implementation of the HIV Prevention Educational Program

The fotonovela, with insert, was distributed to the Experimental group at the end of the pretest. In addition, the radionovela was broadcast for the benefit of the Experimental group over a three-week period. The Experimental group was given a small radio (along with information about the radio station and air times) to enable them to tune to the broadcast. At the end of the study, following the posttest, we distributed the fotonovela and re-broadcast the radionovela for the benefit of the Control group.

Data Analysis

Analysis of variance and chi-square analyses were conducted to examine pretest differences between the two study groups and the pretest-to-posttest changes within study groups on HIV-related knowledge, attitudes and behaviors. Furthermore, for nominal-scaled dichotomous data, the non-parametric McNemar test (chi-square statistic) was used for significance testing of changes in proportions.

Results

Characteristics of the Experimental and Control Groups

In selecting, matching and randomly assigning camps, our goal was to create comparable study groups. To verify that this had occurred, we compared selected demographic variables such as age, education and language preference and found no significant differences between the two study group cohorts (Table 8.1). In addition, there were no signifi cant differences in marital status between the two study groups cohorts. For instance, 67.3 percent and 59.5 percent, respectively, of the Experimental and Control group cohort were currently single. The two study group cohorts consisted of relatively young men (mean age of about 24 years), with about six years of education, spoke primarily Spanish only and the majority were single.

A few differences were noticed between the cohort and non-cohort samples (participants who either left the study area or did not participate in all the assessments) in each of the two study groups. Men in both the Experimental and Control group non-cohorts compared with those in their respective cohorts tended to be older and married. Mean ages for the Experimental and Control group non-cohorts were 26.7 years ($p = .05$) and 27.8 years ($p < .05$), respectively. Furthermore, 52.6 percent (versus 25 percent of the cohort men, $p < .05$) and 68.2 percent (versus 32.4 percent of the cohort men, $p < .05$), respectively, of the Experimental and Control group non-cohort men were currently married. In addition, the Control group cohort compared with the non-cohort was

TABLE 8.1. Comparison of Selected Demographic Characteristics Between the Experimental and Control Study Group Cohorts (n = 89)

Demographic characteristics	Experimental n = 52		Control n = 37		t-value	p-value
	$\bar{X}$	S.D.	$\bar{X}$	S.D.		
Age, yrs	24.3	(5.8)	24.3	(5.4)	-0.02	0.99
Education level, yrs	6.0	(3.8)	6.9	(4.7)	-0.88	0.38
Language preference	1.1	(0.2)	1.0	(0.2)	0.30	0.76

The comparison of differences between the experimental and control study group cohorts were based on means testing. None of the statistics were significant. Standard deviations are enclosed in parentheses.

slightly more educated (mean education level of the non-cohort men was 4.3 years, p < .01).

Amount of Exposure to the Educational Program

A check of the exposure to the educational program revealed that the large majority of the Experimental group cohort had reviewed the *Tres Hombres* fotonovela and the *Marco Aprende* mini-fotonovela. Out of the 52 Experimental group cohort men, 81 percent and 68 percent reportedly had read the *Tres Hombres* fotonovela and the *Marco Aprende* mini-fotonovela, respectively. Validation of the readability and comprehension of these materials revealed that 68 percent correctly identified the messages contained in three of three frames tested; an additional 26 percent correctly identified the messages contained in two of the three frames tested. Therefore, it appears that the majority of men could read and understand the information presented in the materials.

Regarding the *Tres Hombres* radionovela, most of the Experimental group cohort did not hear many of the broadcasts. Only eight percent heard half or more of the 15 episodes. The average number of episodes heard was about three. From focus group discussions at the end of the study, we learned that the men, despite their interest in the program, found it hard to listen to the radionovela at the same time each day for three weeks. Several men suggested that the 15 short episodes be combined into one or two long episodes that could be heard in one or two sessions. Because of the limited radionovela listening, the study, in effect, became a test of the effectiveness only of the fotonovela and its insert.

HIV-related Knowledge

From pretest-to-posttest, there was a significant, albeit modest, increase in the knowledge index score in the Experimental group (Table 8.2). At the pretest, both Experimental and Control group cohorts knew about half the answers, which was about nine items (median scores for the groups were 10). At the posttest, the Experimental group mean increased significantly with no change in the Control group (median scores were 12 and 9.5, respectively, for the Experimental and Control groups). As seen on the mean scores of the individual knowledge domains, the Experimental group's pretest-to-posttest increase in knowledge was predominantly in the transmission domain. At the pretest, the Experimental and Control group cohorts had nearly similar scores on the three knowledge domains. At the posttest, unlike the Control group cohort, the Experimental group cohort showed significantly higher levels of knowledge about HIV transmission, severity, and external signs.

HIV-related Attitudes

Table 8.3 presents results on attitudinal questions that were a direct extension of the information imparted in the educational program. As reflected by their responses to the question, "Can you protect yourself against HIV--Yes, No or Unsure?", significantly more men in the Experimental group cohort believed at the posttest (76.9 percent; pretest: 53.8 percent, p < .01) that they could protect themselves. The Control group cohort also showed a significant change but in the opposite direction; from pretest-to-posttest, relatively fewer men believed that they could protect themselves.

Positive attitudinal changes were noticed also on issues such as sex with a sex worker and use of condoms, central themes of the educational program. From pretest-to-posttest, significantly more Experimental group cohort men believed that sex workers should ask their clients to use a condom (pretest: 80.8 percent, posttest: 98.1 percent, p < .01) and believed that when a man has sex with a sex worker, he should use a

TABLE 8.2. Comparison of HIV-related Knowledge Scores Within the Study Group Cohorts

Knowledge	Experimental n=52					Control n=37				
	Pretest		Posttest		t-value	Pretest		Posttest		t-value
	X̄	S.D.	X̄	S.D.		X̄	S.D.	X̄	S.D.	
Knowledge Index	9.2	(4.2)	10.9	(4.1)	-4.41 ***	9.4	(4.2)	9.6	(3.1)	-0.49
Knowledge domains										
Transmission	6.4	(2.9)	7.6	(2.8)	-4.40 ***	6.2	(3.1)	6.5	(2.7)	-0.65
Severity	1.9	(0.9)	2.2	(1.0)	-2.39 *	2.0	(1.0)	2.1	(0.8)	-0.75
External signs	0.9	(0.8)	1.1	(0.8)	-2.52 *	1.2	(0.8)	1.0	(0.9)	1.39

The significance testing of differences between the pretest and posttest knowledge index scores and the three knowledge domains was conducted within each study group and was based on means testing. The knowledge index scores ranged from 0 to 17, where 0 = No knowledge and 17 = High knowledge. Scores on the 12-item transmission domain ranged from 0 to 12 and those on the severity domain (three items) and the external signs (two items) ranged from 0 to 3 and 0 to 2, respectively. Standard deviations are enclosed in parentheses.

* p < .05; *** p < .001

TABLE 8.3. Comparison of HIV-related Attitudes Within the Study
Group Cohorts (Percentages)

Attitudes	Experimental n = 52		Control n = 37	
	Pretest	Posttest	Pretest	Posttest
Can you protect yourself against HIV/AIDS?	53.8	76.9 **	67.6	51.4 ***
Should sex workers ask their clients to use a condom?	80.8	98.1 **	73.0	80.6
When a man has sex with a sex worker, should he use a condom?	82.7	96.2 *	91.9	91.9

We asked the respondents to answer "yes," "no" or "do not know" to the questions. Percentages indicate the "yes" responses. The significance testing of the change between pretest and posttest was conducted within each study group and was based on the McNemar test, a non-parametric test of differences in percentages.

$*$ p < .05, $**$ p < .01, $***$ p < .001

condom (pretest: 82.7 percent, posttest: 96.2 percent, p < .05). The Control group cohort, on the other hand, did not show significant changes in their attitudes from pretest to posttest, although there was a very high level of agreement in the belief that when a man has sex with a sex worker, he should use a condom.

HIV-related Behaviors

Knowledge and attitude changes are important outcomes, but unless they result in behavior changes, HIV transmission will not stop. Behavior changes are the most difficult to cause to occur and to measure. In the case of our educational program, the main behavior change message was to use condoms when having sex with a sex worker.

Table 8.4 presents results on self-reported HIV-related lifetime behaviors. Nearly all of the Experimental group cohort (94.2 percent) and all those in the Control group cohort had had ("ever had") sexual relations prior to the study. Furthermore, the vast majority of the men in both the cohorts had had sexual relations with a sex worker (82.4 percent and 86.5 percent, respectively, for the Experimental and Control group cohorts). A few men in both the study group cohorts had had sex with another man; this included one man (1.9 percent) in the Experimental group and four men (10.8 percent) in the Control group. In terms of ever using condoms during sex, 61.5 percent of the Experimental and 89.2 percent of the Control group cohort had used condoms during sex with either their spouse, significant other, sex worker, or other men. In addition, 40.4 percent of the Experimental and 32.4 percent of the Control group cohort reported that they had used injectable drugs in the year prior to the study.

Table 8.5 presents data on self-reported HIV/AIDS-related behaviors during the one-month period immediately preceding the pretest and posttest assessments. During the one-month period prior to the pretest, fewer men in the Experimental than the Control group cohort had had sexual relations (44 percent versus 51.4 percent). More specifically, fewer men in the Experimental than the Control group had had sexual relations with a sex worker (30.4 percent versus 48.1 percent). These initial differences were not significant. In terms of the use of con-

TABLE 8.4. Frequencies of HIV-related Lifetime Behaviors, by Study Group Cohorts (Percentages)

Behaviors	Experimental n = 52	Control n = 37
Had sexual relations	94.2	100.0
Had sexual relations with sex workers	82.4	86.5
Had sexual relations with another man	1.9	10.8
Used a condom during sex	61.5	89.2
Used injectable drugs [a]	40.4	32.4

[a] Data pertains to the use of injectable drugs including vitamins, antibiotics, and other substances during the past year.

TABLE 8.5. Frequencies of HIV-related Behaviors During the Month Prior to the Pretest and Prior to the Posttest, by Study Group Cohorts (Percentages)

Behaviors	Experimental n = 52		Control n = 37	
	Pretest	Posttest	Pretest	Posttest
Had sexual relations	44.0	64.7	51.4	64.9
Had sexual relations with sex workers	30.4	59.1	48.1	37.1
Had sexual relations with another man	0.0	1.9	0.0	5.4
Used a condom during sex	13.7	51.0	13.5	24.3

The pretest reflects behaviors one month prior to the pretest assessment. The posttest reflects behaviors during a one month period between the pretest and posttest.

dom during sex with either their spouse, significant other, sex worker or another man nearly similar proportions of men in the two study group cohorts reported using a condom during sex.

During the one-month period between the pretest and posttest surveys, nearly two-thirds of the men in both the study group cohorts had had sexual relations. Furthermore, 59.1 percent (n = 26) of the Experimental and 37.1 percent (n = 13) of the Control group cohort reported that they had had sex with a sex worker. Very few men in the two study group cohorts (one and two, respectively, in the Experimental and Control groups) had had sex with another man between the pretest and posttest. Regarding condom use during sex with either their spouse, significant other, sex worker or another man, more than one-half the Experimental group cohort (51 percent) compared with about one-fourth (24.3 percent) of the Control group cohort reported using a condom during sex with their spouse, significant other, sex worker or another man.

Table 8.6 presents the pretest and posttest results on the measure of self-reported condom use during sex with a sex worker for men who had the opportunity to do so. During the one-month period *prior* to the pretest, 14 and 13 men, respectively, in the Experimental and Control group

TABLE 8.6. Comparison of Self-reported Condom Use Behavior Within the Study Group Cohorts (Percentages)

Behaviors	Experimental		Control	
	Pretest	Posttest	Pretest	Posttest
	$n = 14$	$n = 26$	$n = 13$	$n = 13$
Reported condom use during				
sex with a sex worker				
Percent Yes	7.1	65.4 ***	0.0	0.0

The pretest reflects behaviors during a one month period prior to the pretest and the posttest reflects behaviors during a one month period between the pretest and posttest. The significance testing of the change between pretest and posttest was conducted within each study group and was based on the McNemar test, a non-parametric test of differences in percentages.

*** p < .001

cohorts had had sex with a sex worker. One man in the Experimental (7.1 percent) and none in the Control group cohort reported that he used a condom during sex with a sex worker.

During the study period, the one-month period *between* the pretest and posttest, significantly more men in the Experimental group cohort reportedly used a condom during sex with a sex worker. At the posttest, 26 men in the Experimental group cohort had the opportunity to use a condom during sex with a sex worker and 17 (65.4 percent) reported that they did so. In the Control group cohort, during the same period, none of the 13 men who had the opportunity to use a condom during sex with a sex worker did so.

To explore further the factors that may explain the change in condom use behavior with a sex worker, we contrasted the Experimental group cohort men who had the opportunity to change their behavior and did so with those who had the opportunity but did not change their behavior. Out of the 17 men who reportedly changed this behavior, 15 men had read the *Tres Hombres* fotonovela. Furthermore, men who changed their behavior were more likely to believe that they could protect themselves against HIV; at the posttest, 100 percent of the men who used a condom compared with 66.7 percent (p = .01) of those who did not use a condom believed they could protect themselves against HIV. Moreover, those who changed their behavior were more likely to live in the same camps, suggesting that changed social norms may have had an influence. There were no differences on age, education, and marital status between those who changed their behavior and those who did not.

Discussion

Summary and Qualifications

The educational program comprising the *Tres Hombres* fotonovela was shown to be an effective way to change HIV-related knowledge, attitudes, and, more importantly, behaviors. The educational program appeared to be appropriate for low-literacy, Spanish-speaking, migrant farmworkers, as indicated by validation of whether the men could read and understand the fotonovela and the focus group discussions at the end of the study. The farmworkers were able to relate to the picture format of the fotonovela, found the story very involving and had no trouble identifying with the characters. Most importantly, the farmworkers understood the ideas about HIV transmission and prevention strategies.

The educational program was shown to be effective in changing HIV-related knowledge and attitudes, particularly if the knowledge and attitude components were specifically contained in the program. Prior to the study, the majority of the farmworkers had heard about HIV and had some knowledge about HIV transmission and prevention. The educational program was able to further increase knowledge. The relatively lower change noticed on the severity and external signs domains could be attributed to the indirect reference made to these domains in the program. In terms of the attitudinal measures, after exposure to the educational program, more men in the Experimental group cohort believed that: they could protect themselves against HIV; sex workers should ask their clients to use condoms; and, when a man has sex with a sex worker, he should use a condom.

On the behavior of primary consideration, condom use during sex with a sex worker, significantly more men in the Experimental group cohort who had the opportunity reported that they used a condom. A caveat must be noted regarding the positive behavioral change. The number of men who had the opportunity to use a condom during sex with a sex worker was small, so the effect, while dramatic in its sharp contrast, occurred for a small number of men.

It is interesting to speculate why the educational program was effective in changing the target behavior. The use of sex workers seems to be a frequent occurrence among the men in the study (more than 80 percent had had sex with a sex worker prior to the study). Consequently, the educational program, with its focus on condom use during sex with sex workers, went to men who were more likely to be familiar with and used the services of sex workers in their camps. The program materials were well targeted to these men and directly relevant to them.

The presence of a new social norm or of a model for the new behavior may have occurred in at least some sites. We noticed that the identification numbers of the men who reportedly used a condom with a sex worker clustered together. This implied that several men in the same camp were using the condoms, perhaps because of the modeling that can occur in the camp setting during the very visible sexual activity with a sex worker. Frequently, the men line up for service and receive it one after the other, sometimes in full view of the other men waiting in line. If the man at the front of the line has his condoms ready for use, the modeling of this new behavior to the other men could be a powerful demonstration and social norm setting event. This issue needs exploration in future research.

Another possible explanation for the clustered observations of behavior changes in certain camps could be unique group dynamics that have been observed in farmworker camps. A typical farmworker camp is comprised of farmworkers from different villages, towns, regions, states of Mexico or other Central American countries. Residents of the camps who have something in common, be it a common village, town, or state in their country of origin, tend to cluster together. Furthermore, within this cluster, there emerges a natural leader who commands the respect of his compatriots and wields his authority to maintain an uniform and stable social structure. The leader could be identified based on a person's age, reputation and experience. The leader tacitly becomes the role model and spokesperson for the group (cluster of residents) under him. Within a camp, there may be more than one group with as many leaders. It is possible that during our study there may have been discussions within a group regarding the use of condoms during sex with a sex worker, or that the leader of a group may have felt it appropriate to use condoms and consequently other men in the group followed suit. If in fact this group dynamic did play itself out, it has important implications for subsequent intervention programs for farmworkers. Further research is needed to explore the dynamics within groups and between groups existent in farmworker camps.

The issue of men having sex with other men, which was only tentatively explored in the current study, also needs fuller exploration in future work. Interviews in small group settings, while useful for many of the issues of interest, were not the appropriate vehicle to explore this fairly common but rarely discussed behavior among Mexican men. From our formative research that preceded this study [19, 20], we know that this sexual behavior occurs and that men, in the right context, will discuss it. What is needed is a more conversational format over a longer period of time. Men having unprotected sex with other men could be a means of HIV transmission that cannot be ignored. Special materials probably would have to be developed which go beyond the brief reference to male-to-male sex in the fotonovela. The content of these materials can best come from suggestions from the men themselves, followed by careful development and testing of the materials prior to use. The research reported here confirms the need to target HIV prevention and education interventions very carefully and precisely.

Limitations of the study are those inherent in cohort studies and studies that research sensitive issues such as those addressed here. There is the potential bias due to attrition of men in a cohort study. Since the attrition was primarily due to factors beyond the control of the study (job loss and deportation), there is no reason to believe that men who lost their jobs or were deported would differ from those in the cohort on the behaviors under study. The relatively small sample sizes of the study groups may call into question the robustness of the study findings. This would, however, be more of an issue in correlational, one-group, study designs. The stringent sampling criteria and the two-group, quasi-experimental cohort design with randomization argue for the cause-effect findings presented here. The primary outcome variable was self-reported condom use instead of direct observation of condom use. There may have been a response bias, with men providing socially desirable responses, although this type of bias probably would not explain the large difference between the Experimental and Control group self-reports. Direct observation of condom use, although theoretically preferable, would be realistically impossible. There was some evidence, through informal discussions with sex workers working near the study sites, that there was indeed an increase in condom use behavior by some men in some camp-sites. Lastly, it could be argued that the availability of condoms in the fotonovela materials may have led to the behavior change. This is unlikely since outreach efforts by the local health clinic, operating in the research setting both before and after this study, have included free distribution of condoms among the farmworkers but have not resulted in a change in the level of condom use (Sañudo F, personal communication).

Implications

This project and research have several implications for health promotion and disease prevention programs. The first implication relates to behavior change theories that guide program development. The educational program and evaluation have suggested the importance of social networks as a critical variable in the behavior change process. As mentioned earlier, men who reported increased use of condoms with a sex worker were predominantly concentrated in a few camps. We speculate that it was something about the social context that catalyzed the change. There might have been discussion among the men about the educational program or perhaps the powerful model provided by one man who used his condoms.

The second implication relates to the implementation of health promotion programs. Following extensive formative work to target materials to specific sub-populations, HIV prevention service providers must make access to the program as easy as possible. The fotonovela was easy for the men to obtain; the radionovela component of the educational program, in contrast, simply was not accessible to the majority of men. Even with an enjoyable, interesting radio program on the air and with new radios in hand to receive the program, the men could not control their schedules enough to tune regularly every day for three weeks.

The third implication relates to the study methodology. Our prospective comparative design was the key to our discovery of program-caused effects as well as of the differential effects between the study groups. Prospective designs are always a challenge, particularly when the population is in the field and migratory. Nonetheless, the careful planning, long hours, and persistence necessary to follow up with the participants have yielded data that provide evidence of effectiveness and insights about more or less effective program components.

Finally, this research has demonstrated that the best experts to help us understand the reasons why certain health promotion programs generally, and HIV programs specifically, are or are not effective, are the participants themselves. They not only have the answers but they also are anxious to contribute them. One anecdote from the study captures this well. A man in one of the study groups lost his job in the fields and had no choice but to return to Mexico. Prior to the next surveying, however, he illegally crossed the border and returned to the camp just to participate in the survey. The $5 we were paying him was far less than the cost of his return trip; nonetheless, he felt that the study was important and that we wanted his opinions, so he returned.

We are grateful for the efforts of this man and many others in helping to develop even more effective HIV prevention programs.

Acknowledgments

This study was supported by grants from the California Community Foundation and the American Foundation for AIDS Research. The contents of the manuscript are solely the responsibility of the authors and do not necessarily represent the views of the funding agencies.

Notes

1. These materials were developed by the Novela Health Foundation, supported by a grant from the California Community Foundation; used with permission. The study of the materials' effectiveness was also supported in part by the California Community Foundation, along with support of the American Foundation for AIDS Research.

2. The implementation and evaluation of the HIV prevention program was conducted in two sites, in parts of Riverside and San Diego Counties. This chapter reports on the findings from the study conducted in parts of San Diego County.

3. The University of California, Irvine's Human Subjects Review Committee reviewed and approved the study protocol.

References

1. U.S. Department of Agriculture: *Agricultural statistics*. Washington, DC. Government Printing Office 1986; 370-382.
2. U.S. Department of Labor: *Findings from the national agricultural workers survey (NAWS), 1990: a demographic and employment profile of perishable crop farmworkers*. Washington, DC: U.S. Department of Labor 1990; 89:97-98.
3. U.S. Department of Labor: Occupational injury and illness incidence rates by industry (Table 48). *Monthly Labor Rev* 1988; 118-119.
4. Mobed K, Gold EB, Schenker MB: Occupational health problems among migrant and seasonal farm workers. *West J Med* 1992; 157:367-373.
5. Meister JS: The health of migrant farm workers. *In:* Cordes DH, Rea DF, (eds): Health Hazards of Farming. *Occ Med* 1991; 6:503-518.
6. Migrant Health Program: *Outreach Health Services to Migrants: The Reality, the Dream*. Rockville, Maryland: U.S. Department of Health and Human Services, 1990.
7. Magaña JR: Sex, drugs, and HIV: an ethnographic approach. *Soc Sci Med* 1991; 33:5-9.

8. Carrier JM: Sexual behavior and spread of AIDS in Mexico. *Med Anthropol* 1989; 10:129-142.

9. Bronfman M, Minello N: Sexual habits of temporary Mexican-migrants to the United States: risk practices for HIV infection. Presented at the International Conference on AIDS, Netherlands, July 19-24, 1992; 8(2):D423.

10. Foulk D, Lafferty J: AIDS knowledge and risk behaviors of migrant and seasonal farmworkers in Georgia. The Migrant Health Newsline. Austin, Texas: National Migrant Resource Program, Inc., July/August 1989.

11. Lafferty J, Foulk D, Ryan P: Needle sharing for the use of therapeutic drugs as a potential AIDS risk behavior among migrant Hispanic farmworkers in the eastern stream. *Int'l Quart Comm Health Educ* 1991; 11:135-143.

12. Mishra SI, Conner RF, Lewis MA: AIDS prevention among Latino migrant workers: evaluation of an intervention program. Presented at the Plenary Sessions of the 16th annual meeting of the Society of General Internal Medicine, Arlington, VA, April 28-30. Reprinted in *Clin Res* 1993; 41:589A.

13. Commission on Security and Cooperation in Europe. Implementation of the Helsinki Accords: Migrant farmworkers in the United States. Briefings of the Commission on Security and Cooperation in Europe, Washington, D.C., U.S. Government Printing Office, May, 1993.

14. Magaña R, Greenwood R, Carrier J: Seroprevalence and behavioral study of farmworkers in the state of California. Ist International Symposium on Education and Information about AIDS, Ixtapa, Mexico, 1988.

15. Centers for Disease Control: HIV seroprevalence in migrant and seasonal farmworkers. *MMWR* 1988; 37:517-519.

16. Castro K, Narkunas J: Preliminary results: seroprevalence of HIV infection in seasonal and migrant farmworkers. The Migrant Health Newsline. Austin Texas: National Migrant Resource Program, Inc., July/August, 1989.

17. Bletzer KV: Knowledge-Attitudes-Belief Survey on AIDS/HIV among migrants in Michigan. Migrant Clinicians Network Clinical Supplement. Austin, Texas: National Migrant Resource Program, Inc., Jan/Feb 1991.

18. Smith LS: Ethnic differences in knowledge of sexually transmitted diseases in North American Black and Mexican-American migrant farmworkers. *Res Nursing Health* 1988; 11:51-58.

19. Magaña R, Conner RF, Mishra SI, Lewis MA: An AIDS prevention program for Hispanic/Latino farmworkers. Presented at the annual meeting of the American Public Health Association, New York, Sept 30-Oct 4, 1990.

20. Conner RF: *AIDS prevention with Hispanic farmworkers: a formative evaluation.* Report to the California Community Foundation, Los Angeles, CA, 1990.

21. Coyle SL, Boruch RF, Turner CF (eds): *Evaluating AIDS Prevention Programs.* Panel on the Evaluation of AIDS Intervention, Committee on AIDS Research and the Behavioral, Social and Statistical Sciences, National Research Council, National Academy of Sciences. Washington, DC: National Academy Press, 1991.

22. Krueger RA: *Focus Groups: A Practical Guide for Applied Research.* Newbury Park, CA: Sage, 1988.

23. Wallston BS, Wallston KA: Social psychological models of health behavior: an examination and integration. *In:* Baum A, Taylor SE, Singer JE, (eds):

Handbook of Psychology and Health (vol. 4) Hillsdale, NJ: Erlbaum, 1984.

24. Fishbein M, Ajzen I: *Beliefs, Attitudes, Intention and Behavior: an Introduction to Theory and Research.* Reading, MA: Addison-Wesley, 1975.

25. Farquhar JW: The community-based model of lifestyle intervention trials. *Am J Epidemiol* 1978; 108:103-111.

26. Marin BV, Otero-Sabogal R, Perez-Stable EJ: Development of a short acculturation scale for Hispanics. *Hispanic J Behav Sci* 1987; 9(2):183-205.

PART THREE

Conclusions

9

HIV Prevention Policies and Programs: Perspectives from Researchers, Migrant Workers and Policymakers

Ross F. Conner, Shiraz I. Mishra
and J. Raul Magaña

Introduction

The goal of science is knowledge discovery and creation. There is an additional goal for those scientists who work with groups like migrant Latinos and on pressing social topics like HIV prevention: The generalization of research findings to develop recommendations for changes in policies and programs affecting the groups under study. The seven sets of researchers whose work has been presented in the previous chapters created knowledge about HIV prevention which has potential utility to those in policymaking or program administration positions. The researchers' findings can be used to change policies to foster HIV/ AIDS prevention for migrant Latinos in the United States and to improve HIV prevention programs for this population. By decreasing the spread of HIV among this population, just as with any other population group in the U.S., we will be able to stem the spread of HIV and AIDS and to reduce the social and financial costs to all.

This chapter brings together the conclusions and recommendations from the seven sets of researchers. Next, it presents the views of migrant Latinos themselves about the utility of the researchers' recommendations. These judgments were collected during a small series of focus groups with Latino migrant workers, during which the participants shared their ideas about the recommendations of the researchers that were relevant to migrant workers. The chapter then presents the feasibility assessments of the researchers' recommendations made by a set of state- and federal-level policymakers and administrators involved in HIV and AIDS policy and programs. Finally, the chapter ends with some concluding thoughts for researchers, migrant workers and policymakers about HIV prevention for migrant Latinos.

Researchers' Perspectives

Based on their work with different segments of the migrant Latino community, the seven sets of researchers developed different ideas about the best HIV prevention policies and programs for this community. Depending on the particular characteristics of the subgroup with whom they worked (for example, migrant female mothers or single migrant men; members of the West Coast stream or of the East Coast stream), the researchers focused their recommendations in different ways. There were, however, enough similarities among the recommendations that they could be combined and grouped into four areas. These areas reflect the group of individuals to whom the recommendations are directed: HIV service providers, policymakers, researchers or migrant workers themselves. Below, the four groups of recommendations are presented and discussed.

HIV Service Providers

a. Recommendations. The recommendations for providers of HIV-related services to migrant workers are organized into three areas: general strategies and issues, specific methods and approaches, and the content of HIV messages for this population.

1. General strategies:
   - use and build upon the current health infrastructure for HIV education programs; this will give prestige to the AIDS message via the respected health staff (doctors and teachers) and foster the spread of the message.

- recognize that behavior change related to sexual behaviors do not change easily or quickly; therefore, take a long-term time frame.
- recognize the social ecology of the situation; participants are embedded in multiple social systems and effective HIV prevention programs must address as many parts of the systems as possible.
- understand that, although individual behaviors are targeted for change, the means of achieving and maintaining this are more likely through changes in group and peer norms; this is particularly true in Latino cultures, where the family and the group are more important than individuals in determining individual's attitudes and behaviors.
- understand that, for low-income migrant workers, HIV is low on the hierarchy of daily, pressing concerns.
- develop partnerships with private insurance companies, health care providers, health clinics and agencies working with migrant workers.
- in Mexico, instruct public health workers in Mexico about the interrelationship of HIV and TB.
- in the U.S., increase the number of bilingual Latino health professionals.

2. Methods and approaches:
   - use outreach programs to overcome barriers such as lack of transportation.
   - use Spanish-speaking personnel.
   - use techniques appropriate for preliterate audiences.
   - use audio-visual aids.
   - provide community-based outreach in places familiar to the target group.
   - "piggy-back" HIV education with other activities (e.g., English classes).
   - use indigenous staff and models who know the language, community and culture.
   - use a holistic approach; HIV prevention is embedded in the complex problems of drug addiction, alcoholism, violence, racial discrimination, and poverty.
   - for the subpopulation of women, address women's economic development and empowerment and reinforce their sense of self and independence.

- use mobile clinics for screening.
- provide transportation to clinics.
- use leaders in the community as lay health advisors and HIV educators.
- use home visitation using lay and professional workers.
- provide HIV education at recreational sites used by farmworkers.
- have late night clinic hours for farmworker clients.
- be sensitive to cultural realities of the participants.
- develop different programs for different populations, sensitive to the particular dynamics and realities of their lives.
- use television campaigns for general education, focusing on personal testimonials from those with HIV.
- use models/teachers appropriate to the audience (e.g., the teacher for students, the priest for religious groups) who have the trust of the audience and who can build upon positive relationships to foster changes.
- for the subpopulation of men, put HIV education information (especially condom use) in pornographic magazines and videos produced for these men.

3. Message content:
   - address misconceptions such as:
     - HIV and STDs among U.S. sex workers are controlled by the Health Department,
     - the signs and symptoms of HIV and STDs are similar to those seen when exposed to other environmental and biological threats, such as pesticides,
     - HIV and STDs can be cured by the application of pungent substances on open sores, and
     - the natural history of symptoms of HIV and STDs (i.e., symptoms appear then disappear) imply a successful cure.
   - include discussions of sexual behaviors in general and different, specific sexual behaviors in particular with participants, to remove the taboo on these discussions.
   - adapt language to the literacy level of the target audience.
   - provide more detailed information to less educated target audiences (e.g., do not simply recommend condom use but also explain how to use a lubricant, how to put on a condom, how to dispose of a condom, where to obtain a condom).

- be as explicit as possible with terms (e.g., "sexual relations" may mean only vaginal sex for some clients).
- for Mexican subpopulations, dissociate HIV/AIDS with
certain groups (e.g., "gringos," homosexuals) and emphasize
general susceptibility of everyone.
- emphasize that an individual's own behaviors affect
susceptibility to HIV, not factors outside the individual's
control or "mystical" factors.
- promote condom use as a matter of personal responsibility.
- educate that lack of external, visible symptoms does not
mean someone is HIV negative.
- have different messages for different genders and ages.
- for men, include reference to men-with-men sexual relations
as a possible mode of HIV transmission.
- for women, instruct that condom use does not mean infidelity or does not contradict feelings of love and affection.

b. Discussion. The researchers' recommendations in this area
highlight the need to understand a number of realities in migrant workers' situations if HIV prevention programs are to be effectively designed and implemented. First, several recommendations emphasize
the importance of an individual's social system in determining his or
her attitudes and practices related to sexual behavior and HIV. As one
recommendation states, the family and the group are more important
than individuals in determining a person's attitudes and behaviors.
Effective HIV prevention programs, then, will need to target more than
individual knowledge, attitudes and behaviors related to HIV and
AIDS.

Second, HIV education should be conducted in a language and format familiar to migrant Latinos. For this group, materials should be in
Spanish and use words which are familiar to particular subgroups of
migrant workers. Formats such as fotonovelas (photo picture books) are
better for this population than are didactic lists of "dos and don'ts," for
example.

Third, HIV education should be nested within accepted settings
and come from respected individuals. HIV prevention programs, therefore, should relate to clinics and settings which are already familiar to
migrant workers. These, however, are not the only settings in which
HIV education can usefully occur. Consequently, fourth, unusual sites
(for example, recreation settings and English language classes) and
unusual modes of information (for example, pornographic movies or

"high class" prostitutes, for the subpopulation of males) should be considered to reach the greatest number of individuals.

Fifth, HIV message content may have to deal with new information (for instance, modes of transmission) as well as with misconceptions (for example, that only someone who looks sick could have HIV or AIDS).

Finally, those of us working in the HIV prevention arena need to remember that migrant Latinos have daily concerns which are more pressing, in their minds, than the risk of contracting AIDS. Shelter, food, money, sleep and other basic needs confront migrant workers daily; HIV can seem a distant threat.

Policymakers

a. Recommendations. The recommendations for policymakers working on HIV issues related to migrant workers are organized into four areas for changes, those in (1) laws or regulation, (2) organizational policies, (3) organizational activities, and (4) funding.

1. Changes in laws or regulations:
    - amend the Migrant Health Care Act to list health education as a priority for services to farmworkers.
    - mandate collaboration among individual organizations/providers in federal guidelines for HIV-related acts/programs such as the Ryan White CARE Act, the Maternal and Child Health Block Grants and the Community and Migrant Health Center Programs.
    - change Medicaid and Medicare eligibility requirements so residency requirements do not preclude migrants from receiving services.
    - mandate employers with five or more employees, regardless of length of time of employment, to provide basic health care coverage.
    - mandate employers to provide paid time off (sick leave) to visit health providers.
    - require that outpatient and residential treatment facilities include provisions for women and children.
    - allocate monies for migrant worker-specific data collection and research, through the Health Resources and Services

Administration and the Centers for Disease Control and Prevention.
- expand National Institute of Health guidelines regarding recruitment of under-represented populations in community clinical trials to explicitly include migrant workers.

2. Changes in organizational policies:
   - at local level, use inclusive community-based planning methods, with wide representation, to develop HIV education priorities (pattern after the CDC's state-level community planning groups).
   - at the local and state levels, require individual HIV service organizations to plan together as part of the community-based planning efforts.
   - at the national level:
     - health care reforms are instituted that maintain or strengthen current migrant-focused public health programs, such as migrant health centers;
     - DHHS specifies that migrant worker service agencies, including Migrant and Community Health Centers, be priority entities for receiving grant money, including special set-asides for HIV testing and drug treatment programs;
     - the Maternal and Child Health Block grant program encourages states to develop HIV prevention programs and materials;
     - the Ryan White CARE Act (all Titles) includes guidance that migrant worker service organizations be part of HIV/AIDS planning and service provision; and
     - the Department of Education and the Department of Health and Human Services coordinate efforts and target HIV/AIDS education for women within the Migrant Education and Migrant Head Start programs.

3. Changes in organizational activities:
   - National Migrant Clinicians Network and the Division of Migrant Health at DHHS should sponsor symposia to develop uniform health education curriculum for farmworkers.
   - U.S. DHHS should develop HIV/AIDS materials for people from a variety of ethnic and racial backgrounds, then aggressively disseminate the materials through the Na-

tional Maternal and Child Health Clearinghouse and the National Migrant Resource Program.
- U.S. Immigration Service should provide HIV general prevention materials at ports of entry.
- consulates and other passport-visa issuing agencies should provide HIV educational materials.
- correctional facilities should provide HIV educational materials.
- industries and businesses employing migrants should provide HIV educational materials.
- collect demographic data which will identify migrant workers in data sets.
- collect data nationally on HIV/AIDS incidence among migrant farmworkers (pattern after the U.S. DOE's migrant school data transfer system).
- provide ID cards to migrant workers to allow visits to health care centers and blood tests (but be sure safeguards are in place to protect human rights and maintain confidentiality).
- provide HIV testing at worksites.
- institute long-term programs and projects (as contrasted with short-term, one-shot projects) to cause and sustain behavior change.
- require organizations and agencies receiving CDC or Ryan White CARE Act funds to document if and how their services address HIV needs of migrant workers.

4. Changes in funding:
- increase funds for HIV prevention outreach to migrant populations.
- ensure continuous funding for long-term outreach programs.
- increase funds for general health care for migrant workers.

b. Discussion. The researchers' recommendations for policymakers involve a variety of issues. First, changes can be made in specific laws and regulations to facilitate HIV education and AIDS service provision to migrant Latinos. Some of these changes are quite difficult, such as the recommendation to require employers to provide basic health care coverage. Second, changes can also be made in organizational policies to increase the consideration given to HIV education and services for migrant workers. For example, the Migrant Head Start Program could include women's HIV education in the array of information given to mothers. Third, there are a number of organizational practices which could be changed or added to foster HIV education. Fourth, new and unusual settings should be considered for HIV education. These include ports of entry into the U.S., immigration offices, and correctional facilities. Finally, more funds are needed to support HIV-related outreach and health services for migrant workers.

Researchers

a. Recommendations. The recommendations for researchers working with HIV prevention issues related to migrant workers are organized in two areas: collaboration and research methods.

1. Collaboration:
   - form collaborative partnerships with community-based organizations to
     - gain entry to migrant populations, and
     - develop sensitive, valid and reliable research designs and measures.
   - work closely with policymakers to
     - inform them about conditions, issues and realities, and
     - stay informed about developing policy considerations and realities.

2. Research methods:
   - use a variety of research techniques and measures, both quantitative and qualitative, including pretest-posttest measures, comparison groups, participant observation and in-depth interviews.

b. Discussion. The number of recommendations related to researchers was smaller than those for service providers and policymakers, probably because we did not specifically highlight this aspect to the researchers. The few recommendations which were made, however, highlight two important aspects of conducting research relevant to social programs and policies: the need to form partnerships with service organizations and with policymakers, and the need to use a variety of research techniques and measures.

Migrant Workers

a. Recommendations. The recommendations for migrant workers stress the importance of including them in all aspects of HIV prevention planning:

- involve migrant workers in all stages of HIV prevention programs--planning, implementation, evaluation and dissemination.
- include HIV/AIDS within the realm of issues addressed by migrants themselves, in social conversation at such non-threatening venues as community centers or self-created "social centers" within migrant camps (such as impromptu cantinas or restaurants).

b. Discussion. As with the set of recommendations directed at researchers, the set of recommendations directed at migrant workers is small but includes important issues. The main idea is that migrant workers themselves should be full participants in all aspects of HIV prevention programs, not simply "clients" about whom decisions are made and to whom things are done.

Migrant Latinos' Perspectives

All of the researchers who contributed recommendations had worked closely with migrant workers in their research, treating them more as "full participants" than simply "research subjects." Because of this, we expected that the researchers' recommendations would be acceptable to migrant workers. Nonetheless, we believed it was important to share the recommendations with different groups of migrant workers to confirm this assumption and to obtain their perspectives on the recommendations. Consequently, we arranged two focus groups of Latino migrant workers, one with Western Stream migrants (in California) and one with Eastern Stream migrants (in Florida). The format for both focus groups was similar. Approximately 10 men were recruited by a community-based clinic with a long history of working with Latino migrant workers. Lead by a trained Latino facilitator, the men met for approximately two hours to discuss the recommendations that had most relevance to them (see listings in the previous section). The discussions were wide-ranging, frank, humorous at time, and dead serious at other times.

Below, we list the comments from the two focus group discussions, cast in the form of specific recommendations, like those of the researchers. We should note that the men only occasionally stated their comments in this explicit way; Mexican culture requires a more polite public statement of ideas. For example, in regard to researchers, the men's recommendation is listed below as "use individual interviews...do not group interviews." In reality, the men's statements were more like "we might suggest that.." or "we would favor..." or "you might consider..."-- all more polite and respectful than the simple declarative statement we listed.

A. Recommendations

The recommendations made by the migrant workers are grouped in five areas which reflect the group of individuals to whom they are directed: HIV service providers, policymakers, researchers, migrant workers, and farm owners.

HIV Service Providers. The recommendations related to HIV service providers are organized into six groups: general health beliefs, access to health care, strategies to improve access to health care, the content of HIV messages, the format of HIV education programs, and the appropriate source of HIV education.

1. Regarding general health beliefs, be aware that:
   - we are concerned more with medical treatment rather than with preventive education services.
   - our providers need to be sensitive and culturally appropriate.
   - we believe our greatest likelihood of exposure to HIV and other sexually transmitted diseases is through interactions with sex workers.

2. Regarding access to health care services, our access is limited due to:
   - a lack of public and private transportation.
   - inconvenient operating hours of clinics.
   - the high cost of health care.
   - the refusal of care by providers due to issues of eligibility.

3. Regarding barriers to health care access:

- to overcome the access problems due to lack of transportation:
  - use mobile clinics that come to our work-sites and camp-sites,
  - have regular outreach visits by providers to our camp-sites,
  - provide medical services directly at our camp-sites,
  - conduct HIV/AIDS-related education at camp-sites, and
  - conduct HIV testing at our work-sites and camp-sites.
- to overcome the inconvenient operating hours of clinics:
  - have extended operating hours of the clinics to make them accessible during times when we do not have to work, and
  - select and train one of our peers to administer medications, especially during an emergency.

4. Regarding message content of HIV prevention programs, the programs should include information about:
   - the proper use of condoms.
   - modes of HIV transmission, signs and symptoms, risk factors such as needle use and unsafe sexual practices, the availability of treatment, and testing services.
   - issues around morality and HIV-related risk factors such as sexual intercourse with sex workers.
   - how one can access services.

5. Regarding appropriate educational formats for HIV prevention programs:
   - use educational fotonovelas.
   - use group education rather than one-on-one education format.
   - use role play in education.
   - do not use educational brochures.
   - provide information in *Castellano* (Spanish) and in selected dialects.

6. Regarding providers of HIV/AIDS information and services:
   - it is important for us to have credible and trustworthy educators. Trust and credibility of educators can be enhanced if they:
     - visit our camp-sites on a regular basis,
     - are Hispanic,

- have bilingual skills, and
- can translate information for us in medical settings.
- appropriate, competent and credible providers of HIV/
  AIDS information and services include:
  - doctors (specialists in HIV),
  - health educators,
  - peers educators who can to teach us about HIV/AIDS,
  STDs and TB, and
  - sex workers for selected educational topics such as use of
  condoms.

Policymakers. The recommendations for policymakers are in three areas, those directed towards: the governments of Mexico and the United States, and policymakers in general:

1. The Mexican government should:
   - prohibit prostitution.
   - provide more education and social services.
   - mandate HIV testing.
   - make medicines cheaper.
   - use the electronic media (radio and television) to educate the populous.
   - create community (free clinics).

2. The United States government should:
   - have laws against unsafe behavior.
   - have laws that prohibit prostitution.
   - provide more assistance for HIV positive persons in the farmworking community.
   - provide more prevention education for the migrant workers.
   - address the drug problem.

3. Policymakers should involve us in regular dialogue to discuss issues such as our needs for:
   - more on-site health care services.
   - adequate and improved housing.
   - local health clinics.

Researchers. For researchers, the migrant workers recommended that they:

1. Use individual interviews for evaluation research.
2. Do not use group interviews.

Migrant Workers. Their recommendations for other migrant workers was to get involved in the planning of programs.

Farm Owners. Recommendations directed towards the farm owners primarily focused at better living and working conditions. The farm owners should:

1. Develop a centrally located, multi-purpose community center or a gathering room for us to use for educational and recreational activities.
2. At this center, the farm owners should:
   - provide appropriate amenities at the center such as electricity, sanitation, a recreational area, and cooking facilities, and
   - invite providers (doctors, educators) for educational presentations and delivery of services.
3. Support the farmworkers and cooperate with them.
4. Increase the hourly pay rates.
5. Provide better job conditions (i.e., better equipment).
6. Provide better housing.
7. Educate themselves on the harmful effects and symptoms of pesticides.

B. Discussion

In general, the men agreed with and supported the researchers' recommendations. Their comments, however, were focused less on agreement with general conceptual issues and more on specific implementation details. For example, they provided a detailed list of the information to include in HIV prevention messages, including some topics (e.g., morality) which HIV educators and researchers ignore. They also provided new ideas on settings, educational formats and education providers for HIV prevention. They had some strong suggestions for both U.S. and Mexican policymakers (for instance, prohibit prostitution), some of which might not be possible. The migrant workers strongly supported the idea of including them in planning HIV education programs, and their interest and energy for doing this were evident at both focus group meetings. Finally, the migrant workers had suggestions for a group which the researchers did not mention: the farm owners. Better pay, better housing, and better equipment were among their recommendations related to maintaining their health.

Policymakers' Perspectives

A major part of the researchers' recommendations focused on actions which policymakers could take to improve the availability and provision of HIV prevention and AIDS services for migrant workers. What did policymakers' themselves think about these recommendations? In particular, did they believe, based on their experience and the political realities in late 1995, that these recommendations were feasible?

Policymaker Interviews: Methodology and Results

We conducted interviews with 12 individuals who either were senior-level policymakers and program administrators in AIDS-related agencies at the federal or state level (n = 9) or who worked closely and regularly with these senior officials (n = 3). Four of those interviewed were California policymakers, four were Florida policymakers, and four were federal policymakers. Each person rated each of the 30 policymaker-focus recommendations made by the researchers on a four-point feasibility scale: "definitely feasible," "possibly feasible," "not feasible," and "don't know." They were explicitly directed to focus on feasibility of implementation, not on desirability. That is, while many of the recommendations were desirable from their standpoint, not all could be feasibly implemented. We instructed them to consider the political situation and other contextual realities in their sphere of influence when they made their judgments. Consequently, the assessments presented next are time-bound, especially for a topic as politically volatile as migrant workers. (Indeed, this topic was so volatile at one point in our work on this project that we temporarily suspended our activities, in order that the strong anti-immigrant sentiments coming from certain prominent political figures would not overwhelm policymakers' judgments.) These judgments were made in late 1995, following a period of strong anti-immigrant rhetoric from California Governor (and short-time presidential candidate) Pete Wilson and prior to the Republican Presidential Primary campaigning in 1996.

The summary results are presented below. It is important to keep in mind that these judgments are based on a small number of policymakers and therefore may not reflect the opinions of all policymakers. The people we interviewed were not selected randomly but instead with attention to their centrality to AIDS-related policy making within their sphere of influence. For the California and Florida cases in particular, we interviewed people who are at or near the center of AIDS policy making and programming for their states. Consequently, in spite of the small numbers, we are confident that we obtained feasibility ratings from the individuals best positioned to make these assessment. In the U.S. case, the AIDS arena is so large that many more interviewees would have been required to do a comprehensive feasibility assessment. Nonetheless, our interviewees have broad and deep experience with U.S.-level AIDS programs and policies which qualifies them to provide useful judgments. The degree of representativeness of the U.S.-level feasibility assessments, however, is the most questionable, and the reader should keep this in mind when interpreting the results presented below.

Tables 9.1, 9.2 and 9.3 each focus on just one group of policymaker interviewees: California, Florida or U.S. Consequently, the judgments of four people are summarized in each table. Within each table, the individual recommendations are in four general groups (changes in laws or regulations, changes in organizational policies, changes in organizational activities, and changes in funding). Within these four general categories, the recommendations have been listed in subgroups in order of decreasing feasibility, as judged by the interviewees.[1]

Discussion

The large majority of the recommendations are judged by policymakers at all levels to be "definitely or probably feasible". Policymakers, however, did discriminate among the recommendations and judged some to be "probably not feasible or unfeasible." Among the recommendations for changes in funding, for example, no interviewee in any of the three groups considered any to be "definitely feasible." There were only three recommendations, across the three groups, which were judged by a majority of the interviewees within a group to be "not feasible."

TABLE 9.1. Summary of California Policymakers' Feasibility Ratings for Actions Suggested by Researchers: Ordered from Most to Least Feasible Within Four General Categories

Changes in Laws or Regulations
Definitely Feasible:
- expand National Institute of Health guidelines regarding recruitment of under-re-presented populations in community clinical trials to explicitly include migrant workers.
- allocate monies for migrant worker-specific data collection and research, through the Health Resources and Services Administration and the Centers for Disease Control and Prevention.

Probably Feasible:
- require that outpatient and residential treatment facilities include provisions for women and children.
- amend the Migrant Health Care Act to list health education as a priority for services to farmworkers.
- mandate collaboration among individual organizations/providers in federal guidelines for HIV-related acts/programs such as the Ryan White CARE Act, the Maternal and Child Health Block Grants and the Community and Migrant Health Center Programs.

Probably Not Feasible:
- mandate employers to provide paid time off (sick leave) to visit health providers.
- mandate employers with five or more employees, regardless of length of time of employment, to provide basic health care coverage.
- change Medicaid and Medicare eligibility requirements so residency requirements do not preclude migrants from receiving services.

Changes in Organizational Policies
Definitely Feasible:
- at the local and state levels, require individual HIV service organizations to plan together as part of the community-based planning efforts.
- at the national level, health care reforms are instituted that maintain or strengthen current migrant-focused public health programs, such as migrant health centers.

Probably Feasible:
- at local level, use inclusive community-based planning methods, with wide representation, to develop HIV education priorities (patterned after the CDC's state-level community planning groups).
- at the national level, the Maternal and Child Health Block grant program encourages states to develop HIV prevention programs and materials.
- at the national level, the Ryan White CARE Act (all Titles) includes guidance that migrant worker service organizations be part of HIV/AIDS planning and service provision.
- at the national level, the Department of Health and Human Services and the Department of Education coordinate efforts and target HIV/AIDS education for

(continues)

Table 9.1 *(continued)*

women within the Migrant Education and Migrant Head Start programs.
* at the national level, DHHS specifies that migrant worker service agencies, including Migrant and Community Health Centers, be priority entities for receiving grant money, including special set-asides for HIV testing and drug treatment programs.

Changes in Organizational Activities
Definitely Feasible:
* National Migrant Clinicians Network and the Division of Migrant Health at DHHS sponsor symposia to develop uniform health education curriculum for farmworkers.
* DHHS develops HIV/AIDS materials for people from a variety of ethnic and racial backgrounds, then aggressively disseminates the materials through the National Maternal and Child Health Clearinghouse and the National Migrant Resource Program.
* collect demographic data which will identify migrant workers in data sets.

Probably Feasible:
* Immigration Service provides HIV general prevention materials at ports of entry.
* consulates and other passport-visa issuing agencies provide HIV educational materials.
* industries and businesses employing migrants provide HIV educational materials.
* require organizations and agencies receiving CDC or Ryan White CARE Act funds to document if and how their services address HIV needs of migrant workers.
* correctional facilities provide HIV educational materials.
  collect data nationally on HIV/AIDS incidence among migrant farmworkers (pattern after the U.S. DOE's migrant school data transfer system).
* institute long-term programs (as contrasted with short-term, one-shot projects) to cause and sustain behavior change.

Probably Not Feasible:
* provide HIV testing at worksites.

Not Feasible:
* provide ID cards to migrant workers to allow visits to health care centers and blood tests (but be sure safeguards are in place to maintain confidentiality and protect human rights).

Changes in Funding
Probably Feasible:
* ensure continuous funding for long-term outreach programs.
* increase funds for HIV prevention outreach to migrant populations.
* increase funds for general health care for migrant workers.

TABLE 9.2. Summary of Florida Policymakers' Feasibility Ratings for Actions Suggested by Researchers: Ordered from Most to Least Feasible Within Four General Categories

---

Changes in Laws or Regulations
Definitely Feasible:
- mandate collaboration among individual organizations/providers in federal guidelines for HIV-related acts/programs such as the Ryan White CARE Act, the Maternal and Child Health Block Grants and the Community and Migrant Health Center Programs.
- expand National Institute of Health guidelines regarding recruitment of under-represented populations in community clinical trials to explicitly include migrant workers.
- allocate monies for migrant worker-specific data collection and research, through the Health Resources and Services Administration and the Centers for Disease Control and Prevention.
- require that outpatient and residential treatment facilities include provisions for women and children.

Probably Feasible:
- amend the Migrant Health Care Act to list health education as a priority for services to farmworkers.
- mandate employers with five or more employees, regardless of length of time of employment, to provide basic health care coverage.

Probably Not Feasible:
- mandate employers to provide paid time off (sick leave) to visit health providers.
- change Medicaid and Medicare eligibility requirements so residency requirements do not preclude migrants from receiving services.

Changes in Organizational Policies
Definitely Feasible:
- at the local and state levels, require individual HIV service organizations to plan together as part of the community-based planning efforts.
- at local level, use inclusive community-based planning methods, with wide representation, to develop HIV education priorities (patterned after the CDC's state-level community planning groups).

Probably Feasible:
- at the national level, health care reforms are instituted that maintain or strengthen current migrant-focused public health programs, such as migrant health centers.
- at the national level, the Maternal and Child Health Block grant program encourages states to develop HIV prevention programs and materials.
- at the national level, the Ryan White CARE Act (all Titles) includes guidance that migrant worker service organizations be part of HIV/AIDS planning and service provision.
- at the national level, the Department of Health and Human Services and the Department of Education coordinate efforts and target HIV/AIDS education for

(continues)

204

Table 9.2 *(continued)*

women within the Migrant Education and Migrant Head Start programs.

Feasibility Uncertain:
- at the national level, DHHS specifies that migrant worker service agencies, including Migrant and Community Health Centers, be priority entities for receiving grant money, including special set-asides for HIV testing and drug treatment programs.

Changes in Organizational Activities
Definitely Feasible:
- require organizations and agencies receiving CDC or Ryan White CARE Act funds to document if and how their services address HIV needs of migrant workers.
- correctional facilities provide HIV educational materials.
- provide HIV testing at worksites.
- collect data nationally on HIV/AIDS incidence among migrant farmworkers (pattern after the U.S. DOE's migrant school data transfer system).
- collect demographic data which will identify migrant workers in data sets.
- industries and businesses employing migrants provide HIV educational materials.
- DHHS develops HIV/AIDS materials for people from a variety of ethnic and racial backgrounds, then aggressively disseminates the materials through the National Maternal and Child Health Clearinghouse and the National Migrant Resource Program.

Probably Feasible:
- Immigration Service provides HIV general prevention materials at ports of entry. consulates and other passport-visa issuing agencies provide HIV educational materials.
- institute long-term programs (as contrasted with short-term, one-shot projects) to cause and sustain behavior change.
- National Migrant Clinicians Network and the Division of Migrant Health at DHHS sponsor symposia to develop uniform health education curriculum for farmworkers.

Feasibility Unclear:
- provide ID cards to migrant workers to allow visits to health care centers and blood tests (but be sure safeguards are in place to maintain confidentiality and protect human rights).

Changes in Funding
Probably Feasible:
- ensure continuous funding for long-term outreach programs.
- increase funds for HIV prevention outreach to migrant populations.

Feasibility Unclear:
- increase funds for general health care for migrant workers.

TABLE 9.3. Summary of U.S. Policymakers' Feasibility Ratings for Actions Suggested by Researchers: Ordered from Most to Least Feasible Within Four General Categories

Changes in Laws or Regulations
Probably Feasible:
- amend the Migrant Health Care Act to list health education as a priority for services to farmworkers.
- mandate collaboration among individual organizations/providers in federal guidelines for HIV-related acts/programs such as the Ryan White CARE Act, the Maternal and Child Health Block Grants and the Community and Migrant Health Center Programs.
- require that outpatient and residential treatment facilities include provisions for women and children.
- expand National Institute of Health guidelines regarding recruitment of underrepresented populations in community clinical trials to explicitly include migrant workers.
- allocate monies for migrant worker-specific data collection and research, through the Health Resources and Services Administration and the Centers for Disease Control and Prevention.

Probably Not Feasible:
- mandate employers with five or more employees, regardless of length of time of employment, to provide basic health care coverage.

Not Feasible:
- mandate employers to provide paid time off (sick leave) to visit health providers.
- change Medicaid and Medicare eligibility requirements so residency requirements do not preclude migrants from receiving services.

Changes in Organizational Policies
Definitely Feasible:
- at the local and state levels, require individual HIV service organizations to plan together as part of the community-based planning efforts.
- at the national level, the Maternal and Child Health Block grant program encourages states to develop HIV prevention programs and materials.
- at the national level, the Ryan White CARE Act (all Titles) includes guidance that migrant worker service organizations be part of HIV/AIDS planning and service provision.
- at the national level, the Department of Education and the Department of Health and Human Services coordinate efforts and target HIV/AIDS education for women within the Migrant Education and Migrant Head Start programs.

Probably Feasible:
- at local level, use inclusive community-based planning methods, with wide representation, to develop HIV education priorities (patterned after the CDC's state-level community planning groups).
- at the national level, health care reforms are instituted that maintain or strengthen

(continues)

206

Table 9.3 *(continued)*

current migrant-focused public health programs, such as migrant health centers.

Feasibility Unclear:
- at the national level, DHHS specifies that migrant worker service agencies, including Migrant and Community Health Centers, be priority entities for receiving grant money, including special set-asides for HIV testing and drug treatment programs.

Changes in Organizational Activities
Definitely Feasible:
- Immigration Service provides HIV general prevention materials at ports of entry.
- consulates and other passport-visa issuing agencies provide HIV educational materials.
- correctional facilities provide HIV educational materials.

Probably Feasible:
- DHHS develops HIV/AIDS materials for people from a variety of ethnic and racial backgrounds, then aggressively disseminates the materials through the National Maternal and Child Health Clearinghouse and the National Migrant Resource Program.
- require organizations and agencies receiving CDC or Ryan White CARE Act funds to document if and how their services address HIV needs of migrant workers.
- National Migrant Clinicians Network and the Division of Migrant Health at DHHS sponsor symposia to develop uniform health education curriculum for farmworkers.
- industries and businesses employing migrants provide HIV educational materials.
- collect demographic data which will identify migrant workers in data sets.
- collect data nationally on HIV/AIDS incidence among migrant farmworkers (pattern after the U.S. DOE's migrant school data transfer system).
- institute long-term programs (as contrasted with short-term, one-shot projects) to cause and sustain behavior change.
- provide HIV testing at worksites.

Feasibility Unclear:
- provide ID cards to migrant workers to allow visits to health care centers and blood tests (but be sure safeguards are in place to maintain confidentiality and protect human rights).

Changes in Funding
Probably Feasible:
- increase funds for general health care for migrant workers.

Probably Not Feasible:
- increase funds for HIV prevention outreach to migrant populations.
- ensure continuous funding for long-term outreach programs.

TABLE 9.4. Recommendations Policymakers Judge to Be Definitely Feasible, by General Category of Recommendation (with Policymaker Level in Parentheses: CA, FL, U.S.)

Changes in Laws or Regulations
- expand National Institute of Health guidelines regarding recruitment of under-represented populations in community clinical trials to explicitly include migrant workers. (CA, FL)
- allocate monies for migrant worker-specific data collection and research, through the Health Resources and Services Administration and the Centers for Disease Control and Prevention. (CA, FL)
- mandate collaboration among individual organizations/providers in federal guidelines for HIV-related acts/programs such as the Ryan White CARE Act, the Maternal and Child Health Block Grants and the Community and Migrant Health Center Programs. (FL)
- require that outpatient and residential treatment facilities include provisions for women and children. (FL)

Changes in Organizational Policies
- at the local and state levels, require individual HIV service organizations to plan together as part of the community-based planning efforts. (CA, FL, U.S.)
- at the national level, health care reforms are instituted that maintain or strengthen current migrant-focused public health programs, such as migrant health centers. (CA)
- at local level, use inclusive community-based planning methods, with wide representation, to develop HIV education priorities (pattern after the CDC's state-level community planning groups). (FL)
- at the national level, the Maternal and Child Health Block grant program encourages states to develop HIV prevention programs and materials. (U.S.)
- at the national level, the Ryan White CARE Act (all Titles) includes guidance that migrant worker service organizations be part of HIV/AIDS planning and service provision. (U.S.)
- at the national level, the Department of Education and the Department of Health and Human Services coordinate efforts and target HIV/AIDS education for women within the Migrant Education and Migrant Head Start programs. (U.S.)

Changes in Organizational Activities
- National Migrant Clinicians Network and the Division of Migrant Health at DHHS sponsor symposia to develop uniform health education curriculum for farmworkers. (CA)
- DHHS develops HIV/AIDS materials for people from a variety of ethnic and racial backgrounds, then aggressively disseminates the materials through the National Maternal and Child Health Clearinghouse and the National Migrant Resource Program. (CA, FL)
- collect demographic data which will identify migrant workers in data sets. (CA, FL)
- require organizations and agencies receiving CDC or Ryan White CARE Act funds to document if and how their services address HIV needs of migrant workers. (FL)
- correctional facilities provide HIV educational materials. (FL, U.S.)

(continues)

208

Table 9.4 *(continued)*

- provide HIV testing at worksites. (FL)
- collect data nationally on HIV/AIDS incidence among migrant farmworkers (pattern after the U.S. DOE's migrant school data transfer system). (FL)
- industries and businesses employing migrants provide HIV educational materials. (FL)
- Immigration Service provides HIV general prevention materials at ports of entry. (U.S.)
- consulates and other passport-visa issuing agencies provide HIV educational materials. (U.S.)

Considering only those recommendation judged by a majority of the interviewees within a group to be "definitely feasible," there were 7 of these among the California policymakers, 13 among the Florida policymakers, and 7 among the U.S. policymakers. Table 9.4 lists these top-rated recommendations, organized by general category.

A minority of the 20 recommendations in the "Definitely Feasible" set is selected by two or more groups of policymakers. Only one recommendation, related to local HIV service organization cooperative planning for HIV prevention, was selected by policymakers at all three levels among their top-ranked choices. This particular top-ranked choice provides a degree of validation of the rankings, in that this activity is currently being conducted and financially supported by the Centers for Disease Control and Prevention within every state in the U.S., as part of its program for community planning for HIV prevention. Consequently, the policymakers could confidently state that this was definitely feasible.

The majority of the top-ranked choices were specific to state or level. Florida policymakers, in contrast to California policymakers, tended to judge local actions as definitely feasible. For example, the Florida policymakers thought it was definitely feasible to provide HIV testing at worksites, to have businesses and industries provide HIV educational materials, and to require that outpatient and residential treatment facilities include provisions for women and children. California policymakers tended to focus on national-level changes as being most feasible (such things as instituting health care reforms that strengthen migrant-focused public health, and having national organizations (National Migrant Clinicians Network and DHHS Division of Migrant Health) undertake activities to improve migrant health and HIV prevention). Also, in contrast to Florida policymakers, California policymakers judged certain local activities, such as providing HIV testing at worksites, to be probably not feasible. The U.S. level policymakers tended to focus their top-ranked recommendations on federal-level activities, such as having the U.S. Immigration Service provide HIV prevention materials at ports of entry. It is clear from the diversity of these judgments at different levels that there are few recommendations which could be advocated at any and all levels; the context and realities change from state to state and from local to federal levels.

These are many recommendations in the "probably feasible" category. These are presented in Table 9.5. Considering the "definitely" and "probably feasible" rankings together (those in Table 9.4 and Table 9.5), the state-level policymakers tend to view more of the recommendations as "definitely" feasible than do the U.S. policymakers. In two of the general categories (changes in laws and regulations and changes in funding), U.S.-level policymakers judged none of the recommendations to be definitely feasible. Of the 30 total recommendations in all categories, 21 were judged by policymakers at all three levels (California, Florida and United States) to be feasible, either definitely or probably.

At the state level, Florida policymakers are more likely to judge recommendations to be feasible than their California counterparts. Florida policymakers, for example, believe that it is feasible to mandate small employers to provide basic health care coverage; California policymakers viewed this same recommendation as probably not feasible.

Tables 9.6 and 9.7 present those recommendations which policymakers viewed as least feasible to implement. In general, policymakers at all levels were pessimistic about recommendations related to changes in funding. They also tended to think employer mandates for changes in organizational policies were not feasible (although Florida policymakers were occasionally the exception). None of the policymakers believed that providing ID cards to migrants to allow health care visits was feasible, nor that Medicaid or Medicare eligibility requirements could be changed to allow migrant workers, regardless of residency status, to receive services.

In sum, policymakers at all levels (California, Florida and U.S.) tended to view most of the recommended changes in laws and regulations and the changes in organizational policies and activities as feasible, with the exception of those related to employer mandates and

TABLE 9.5. Recommendations Policymakers Judge to Be Probably Feasible, by General Category of Recommendation (with Policymaker Level in Parentheses: CA, FL, U.S.)

Changes in Laws or Regulations
- require that outpatient and residential treatment facilities include provisions for women and children. (CA, U.S.)
- amend the Migrant Health Care Act to list health education as a priority for services to farmworkers. (CA, FL, U.S.)
- mandate collaboration among individual organizations/providers in federal guidelines for HIV-related acts/programs such as the Ryan White CARE Act, the Maternal and Child Health Block Grants and the Community and Migrant Health Center Programs. (CA, U.S.)
- mandate employers with five or more employees, regardless of length of time of employment, to provide basic health care coverage. (FL)
- expand National Institute of Health guidelines regarding recruitment of under-represented populations in community clinical trials to explicitly include migrant workers. (U.S.)
- allocate monies for migrant worker-specific data collection and research, through the Health Resources and Services Administration and the Centers for Disease Control and Prevention. (U.S.)

Changes in Organizational Policies
- at local level, use inclusive community-based planning methods, with wide representation, to develop HIV education priorities (patterned after the CDC's state-level community planning groups). (CA, U.S.)
- at the national level, the Maternal and Child Health Block grant program encourages states to develop HIV prevention programs and materials. (CA, FL)
- at the national level, the Ryan White CARE Act (all Titles) includes guidance that migrant worker service organizations be part of HIV/AIDS planning and service provision. (CA, FL)
- at the national level, the Department of Education and the Department of Health and Human Services coordinate efforts and target HIV/AIDS education for women within the Migrant Education and Migrant Head Start programs. (CA, FL)
- at the national level, DHHS specifies that migrant worker service agencies, including Migrant and Community Health Centers, be priority entities for receiving grant money, including special set-asides for HIV testing and drug treatment programs. (CA)
- at the national level, health care reforms are instituted that maintain or strengthen current migrant-focused public health programs, such as migrant health centers. (FL, U.S.)

Changes in Organizational Activities
- Immigration Service provides HIV general prevention materials at ports of entry. (CA, FL)
- consulates and other passport-visa issuing agencies provide HIV educational materials. (CA, FL)
- industries and businesses employing migrants provide HIV educational materials. (CA, U.S.)

(continues)

Table 9.5 *(continued)*

- require organizations and agencies receiving CDC or Ryan White CARE Act funds to document if and how their services address HIV needs of migrant workers. (CA, U.S.)
- correctional facilities provide HIV educational materials. (CA)
- collect data nationally on HIV/AIDS incidence among migrant farmworkers (pattern after the U.S. DOE's migrant school data transfer system). (CA, U.S.)
- institute long-term programs (as contrasted with short-term, one-shot projects) to cause and sustain behavior change. (CA, FL, U.S.)
- National Migrant Clinicians Network and the Division of Migrant Health at DHHS sponsor symposia to develop uniform health education curriculum for farmworkers. (FL, U.S.)
- DHHS develops HIV/AIDS materials for people from a variety of ethnic and racial backgrounds, then aggressively disseminates the materials through the National Maternal and Child Health Clearinghouse and the National Migrant Resource Program. (U.S.)
- collect demographic data which will identify migrant workers in data sets. (U.S.)
- provide HIV testing at worksites. (U.S.)

Changes in Funding
- ensure continuous funding for long-term outreach programs. (CA, FL)
- increase funds for HIV prevention outreach to migrant populations. (CA, FL)
- increase funds for general health care for migrant workers. (CA, U.S.)

Medicaid and Medicare changes. They judged the recommendations related to changes in funding as least feasible.

Conclusion

The picture of migrant worker HIV prevention which emerges from the perspectives of the researchers, the migrant farmworkers and the policymakers is a complementary one. The researchers, who have worked with many different segments of the migrant worker population, present a picture of individuals at risk for HIV but also of individuals who are increasingly aware of HIV and AIDS prevention measures. The researchers provide examples of individuals who have changed their attitudes and behaviors to protect themselves from HIV providing data to document these effects. The researchers also identified impediments to behavior changes. These include the same

TABLE 9.6. Recommendations Policymakers Judge to Be Probably Not Feasible or for Which Feasibility Is Uncertain, by General Category of Recommendation (with Policymaker Level in Parentheses: CA, FL, U.S.)

Changes in Laws or Regulations
- mandate employers to provide paid time off (sick leave) to visit health providers. (CA, FL)
- mandate employers with five or more employees, regardless of length of time of employment, to provide basic health care coverage. (CA, U.S.)
- change Medicaid and Medicare eligibility requirements so residency requirements do not preclude migrants from receiving services. (CA, FL)

Changes in Organizational Policies
- at the national level, DHHS specifies that migrant worker service agencies, including Migrant and Community Health Centers, be priority entities for receiving grant money, including special set-asides for HIV testing and drug treatment programs. (FL, U.S.)

Changes in Organizational Activities
- provide HIV testing at worksites. (CA)
- provide ID cards to migrant workers to allow visits to health care centers and blood tests (but be sure safeguards are in place to maintain confidentiality and protect human rights). (FL, U.S.)

Changes in Funding
- increase funds for general health care for migrant workers. (FL)
- increase funds for HIV prevention outreach to migrant populations. (U.S.)
- ensure continuous funding for long-term outreach programs. (U.S.)

TABLE 9.7. Recommendations Policymakers Judge to Be Not Feasible, by General Category of Recommendation (with Policymaker Level in Parentheses: CA, FL, U.S.)

Changes in Laws or Regulations
- mandate employers to provide paid time off (sick leave) to visit health providers. (U.S.)
- change Medicaid and Medicare eligibility requirements so residency requirements do not preclude migrants from receiving services. (U.S.)

Changes in Organizational Activities
- provide ID cards to migrant workers to allow visits to health care centers and blood tests (but be sure safeguards are in place to maintain confidentiality and protect human rights). (CA)

---

challenges all of us face in changing well-entrenched behaviors (established habits, lack of skills), but, in addition, they involve special challenges resulting from being part of several cultural systems and from the migratory lifestyle. From their work, the researcher developed recommendations for changes in laws and regulations, changes in organizational policies and activities and changes in funding to facilitate migrant HIV prevention.

The migrant workers reviewed these recommendation and supported them. They provided suggestions on actions and activities that exemplify and extend the researchers' recommendations. They also proposed other arenas for action, such as work with farm owners. The policymakers reviewed the feasibility of the researchers' recommendations and, in large measure, believed them to be feasible to implement in today's political climate.

This complementary picture presented by researchers, migrant workers and policymakers is also a complex picture. As the data in the first chapter demonstrated, the migrant community is diverse and ever-changing. In developing and implementing effective HIV prevention programs for this community, there are a number of challenges that all the participants face.

First, migrant workers themselves must become more centrally involved in all aspects of these programs. There are positive signs that this can happen, based on the experience of the researchers whose work is reported here and the comments from the migrant workers who participated in the focus groups. In planning, implementing and evaluating HIV prevention programs, we need migrant workers' advise and suggestions. Only they have the first-hand knowledge required to develop individually- and culturally-sensitive programs to educate and change attitudes and behaviors related to sexual practices and drug use behavior. Equally important, migrant farmworkers must be part of the implementation strategies and methods, so that they are working with each other to change attitudes, behaviors and social norms related to HIV and AIDS.

Second, policymakers must continue to strive to understand the diversity, the strength and the realities of the migrant worker community so they can work to educate legislators and administrators about this important segment of many U.S. communities. Farm workers have little voice in the halls of government, although they play a critical role in the success of U.S. agriculture and contribute more to society in taxes than they receive in services. Policymakers can serve as liaisons to those with power and authority, providing information to inform decision making.

Finally, researchers working in the HIV arena face the challenge of continuing and improving their scientific study of HIV prevention with migrant populations. This book brings together the largest and most diverse set of research studies on HIV-related issues focused on migrant Latino workers to date. As the long list of recommendations showed, these studies generated many ideas for improvements in HIV prevention. Additional studies using even more rigorous methods will generate even more beneficial insights and recommendations for action.

Notes

1.   The "Definitely Feasible" subgroup consists of those recommendations judged "definitely feasible" by 3 or 4 policymaker interviewees. The "Probably Feasible" subgroup contains the recommendations judged "definitely" or "possibly feasible" by 3 or 4 interviewees, excluding the recommendations which would fit into the "Definitely Feasible" category. (That is, these subgroups, along with the other two, are mutually exclusive and exhaustive.) The "Probably Not Feasible" subgroup consists of those recommendations judged "possibly" or "not feasible" by 3 or 4 interviewees, excluding the recommendations which would fit into the "Not Feasible" category. The "Not Feasible" subgroup is made up of the recommendations judged "not feasible" by 3 or 4 interviewees. In six instances out of the 90 total sets of judgments, the four individual judgments were widely split, precluding easy categorization. In these instances, a new subgroup is listed: "Feasibility Uncertain." There were relatively few "don't know" judgments or missing judgments (25 out of 360 total judgments; 6.9 percent).